SO-AXM-306

"This book works well on two levels—as an account of learning a new language with an unfamiliar alphabet and multiple dialects, and as an account of traveling through nations where that language is dominant. Zora O'Neill is a keen observer of cultures fresh to her and a fine writing stylist. The tragic timeliness of . . . Syria gives O'Neill's account unplanned urgency for readers in 2016–17."—**Society of American Travel Writers Lowell Thomas Award citation for Best Travel Book 2016–17**

"In her engaging, colloquial account, freelance and travel writer O'Neill recounts how, at the age of 39, just after the events of the Arab Spring, she decided to return to Egypt and take up a more vernacular approach to studying Arabic rather than approaching it 'as if it were a dead language' . . . A valiant chronicle of the author's 'Year of Speaking Arabic Badly.'"—***Kirkus Reviews***

"[O'Neill] engages in Arabic with anyone she can, studies colloquial expressions, and chronicles vocabulary, usage, and contradictions. People she interacts with while picnicking, hitchhiking, even at the aftermath of a car accident are opportunities for an exchange. What emerges is the idea of language as a connection, passion, and a reflection of the lives and history of diverse Arab peoples, a view which is lacking in the general news coverage of Middle Eastern conflict. Glimpses of daily life, particularly of Arab women, are intriguing and sometimes unexpected, including the rich assortment of Lebanese cursing while driving. A useful complement to Middle Eastern study and essential for Arabic learners as well as an enjoyable peek into contemporary lives in the region."—***Library Journal***

"O'Neill's prose is affable and chatty . . . and her approach to her travels is almost recklessly upbeat. . . . Her tale of her 'Year of Speaking Arabic Badly' is a genial and revealing pleasure."—***Seattle Times***

"Along with exploring fascinating local cultures and customs, [Zora O'Neill] ties in her unique experiences attempting to master Arabic. Like her journey, her memoir is colorful, comical, and compelling."—**Bustle, "16 Must-Read Nonfiction Books Due Out In June 2016"**

"As [Zora O'Neill] explores local Arabic cultures, she also highlights the often humorous trials and tribulations of learning the difficult language. Along the way, her writing brings to life dynamic settings and captivating people."—**Romper, "New Summer Books to Enjoy on Your Warm Weather Adventures"**

"O'Neill doesn't teach readers to be fluent in Arabic, but she imparts a more valuable lesson on how (and how not) to learn a language, and the journey is more fascinating than the result."—*Publishers Weekly*

"This charming memoir . . . is sure to bring a nod of recognition to any student of Arabic, however uncomfortably he or she ever sat in that classroom, as well as to enthrall those never-students curious about the world's fifth-most-spoken language."—**Louis Werner,** *AramcoWorld*

"Zora O'Neill is a wonderful writer, a *hakawati* who can spin a tale with the best of them."—**Rabih Alameddine,** author of *The Hakawati* and *An Unnecessary Woman*

"O'Neill masterfully weaves together vignettes, linguistic musings, and a colorful cast of thousands into an always-thoughtful, often hysterically funny paean to a part of the world about which most Americans remain woefully ignorant."—**Suketu Mehta, author of** *Maximum City: Bombay Lost and Found*

"Wry, witty, and charmingly erudite, this lovely book goes through the looking glass of the Arabic language and emerges with a radiant image of the Arab world."—**Diana Abu-Jaber, author of** *Life Without a Recipe, Crescent, The Language of Baklava,* **and others**

"You will travel through countries and across centuries, meeting professors and poets, revolutionaries, nomads, and nerds. O'Neill's generous storytelling makes the intricacies of Arabic grammar seem fascinating and inexplicably glamorous. And the most unforgettable character you encounter may be the Arabic language itself, which will feel like an old friend by the time you finish this warm and hilarious book."—**Annia Ciezadlo, author of** *Day of Honey*

"In a witty memoir, [O'Neill] chronicles her attempt to learn Arabic in the Middle East. The tome is on Seth Meyers' shelf."—*Us Weekly*

All
Strangers
Are Kin

Adventures in Arabic
and the Arab World

Zora O'Neill

The American University in Cairo Press
Cairo   New York

This paperback edition first published in 2018 by
The American University in Cairo Press
113 Sharia Kasr el Aini, Cairo, Egypt
420 Fifth Avenue, New York, NY 10018
www.aucpress.com

Copyright © 2016, 2018 by Zora O'Neill

An earlier version of this book was published in hardback in 2016 by
Houghton Mifflin Harcourt.

All rights reserved. No part of this publication may be reproduced, stored
in a retrieval system, or transmitted in any form or by any means, electron-
ic, mechanical, photocopying, recording, or otherwise, without the prior
permission of the publisher.

Exclusive distribution outside Egypt and North America by I.B. Tauris & Co
Ltd., 6 Salem Road, London, W2 4BU

Dar el Kutub No. 13705/17
ISBN 978 977 416 865 9

Dar el Kutub Cataloging-in-Publication Data

O'Neill, Zora
    All Strangers Are Kin: Adventures in Arabic and the Arab World /
Zora O'Neill.—Cairo: The American University in Cairo Press, 2018.
    p.   cm.
    ISBN 978 977 416 865 9
    1.   Arabic Language
    492.7

1 2 3 4 5   22 21 20 19 18

Designed by Chrissy Kurpeski
Printed in the United States of America

For my family

and in memory of James Conlon

Everything in its time is sweet.

— ARABIC PROVERB

Contents

Lebanon

Morocco

Preface to the Paperback Edition

Hello, and thank you for considering the new paperback edition of my book. I would like to make two small suggestions:

1) Read it, please—it's urgent; and

2) don't read anything you don't want to.

Regarding the first point, I'm sure you understand that the stakes are higher than they have ever been. When I first started thinking about this book almost a decade ago, my aim was a pie-in-the-sky wish. Wouldn't it be nice, I mused, if people knew more about the Arab world?

Now, though, especially just in the short time since the book was first published, this wish has ratcheted up to something more like panic. For the sake of world peace and general happiness, I feel like screaming, *please* learn more about the Arab world!

Unfortunately, this state of screaming panic has somewhat dampened my sense of humor. I find it difficult to write a jaunty new invitation to read, here in America in 2017, when I see daily reminders of the harm that can be done when people consider a place and a people as dangerously foreign—or don't even consider them at all. Blanket travel bans. Barrier walls. "Road rage" incidents that end in murder.

In the face of all that, this book is a tiny thing. But fortunately for you, dear reader, it was written before the nerve-racking era of President Trump, and so maintains a lighter tone (it even references al-Qaeda on the first page—how quaint, compared with the current activities of ISIS). Its three hundred or so pages tell many stories contrary to what you probably see in the news. The media, with their focus on tragedy, war, and the bad actions of a relatively tiny number of people, inevitably build a sense of difference and fear. This book heads in the opposite direction, toward common ground. It, too, focuses on a small number of people—but they are far more representative of Arabs as a whole, of hundreds of millions of people. The personal stories in this book, though less dramatic, are nonetheless as true and valid as anything in a news story.

As for point no. 2, *don't read anything you don't want to*: this is for those of you who haven't studied Arabic and may be thinking you don't need to read a whole book about this immensely complicated language. Not to worry—Arabic is only a cover story. It gave me a reason to travel and a framework for writing about the Arab world without getting (too) mired in politics or war. But there will not be a quiz at the end. You have my blessing to skip right through, for instance, the second chapter, all about that mind-blowing morphological system of Semitic languages. Of course I'd be gratified if your mind is blown, too, but absolutely nothing later in the book rides on this. If your eyes glaze over, or test anxiety sets in when you see a foreign word in italics, just skip it.

Reserve your energy and attention for the people. They are the real reason I wrote the book, and I want everyone to meet them. No one in this book is famous or a noted expert on foreign policy or terrorism or whatever other credential gets you noticed by the media these days, and that is precisely the point. As a writer, I would be far more gratified to hear that you read this book and went on to tell a friend about Medo, Houria, or Amgad, or one of the two women named Rana. My aim in this book is to bring average people in the Arab world to your attention. I want you to imagine what their lives might be like.

None of us spares enough imagination for people in other places, as I realized at one stage in my countless manuscript revisions. An early reader commented on a scene at a four-year-old's birthday party at a hotel in Egypt. When the family gathered around the cake, the reader wrote in the margin, "Interesting that this is the same tradition as in the U.S."

I was taken aback. I knew that potential readers weren't very familiar with the Arab world—that was why I was writing the book, after all. But I hadn't realized that I'd have to start with birthday cake. All at once, my task felt overwhelming.

After a few weeks of despair, it finally dawned on me: I had never spared a minute to imagine a kids' party in countries I had never visited—Madagascar, say, or Ukraine. And then I had to laugh at myself, because I had set out to write a book precisely about such mundane things in the Arab world, and I had panicked when someone expressed interest. In fact, my project was right on track.

So you may be a reader who has eaten her share of birthday cake in Egypt, or you may be a reader who is pondering the phrase "birthday cake in Egypt" for the very first time. You may be a reader who can identify the root of a past-tense second-person hollow verb and flip to the correct page in Hans Wehr in less than three seconds, or you may cheerfully know nothing about Arabic at all. I believe there is something for all of you in this book.

But, you may still be thinking, time and attention are finite. Birthday cakes and grammar sound pretty trivial. Shouldn't we be focusing on important things, such as the latest news of unstable leaders and grinding wars? I would counter that when the headlines are at their grimmest is precisely when we should think about the regular people who live closest to those headlines.

Please give the people in this book a little of your time, a little of your imagination. They are the point, the heart of it, far more than any facts about the Arabic language. And what is language, after all, other than a way to learn people's stories?

I hope some of the people surprise you. I hope you enjoy your time with them as much as I did.

Prologue

In America, in the era of the War on Terror, Arabic has taken on a certain air of menace and danger. There's a jihad, a holy war, going on, the newspapers report. In clips from the front lines of conflict, insurgents bellow *"Allahu akbar!"* from behind grenade launchers. Hijabs are symbols of extremism or tools of misogynist oppression, depending on which television pundit is talking. Fatwas are synonymous with death sentences. Al-Qaeda has become a generic term for Islamic terrorists of any kind.

But from daily life in Egypt, where I first studied Arabic, I gleaned entirely different meanings for these same words. A jihad is that extra effort you put in to achieve a personal goal. People exclaim *"Allahu akbar!"* in the same way I say "Oh. My. God!" Women wear hijabs as cute accessories that pull an outfit together. Fatwas are doled out by radio and TV personalities, combining entertainment and advice much as Judge Judy and Oprah do in America.

Al-Qaeda, though? Fair enough. That word has always struck terror in me, not for its literal meaning, "the foundation," but because its plural is the term for grammar.

This is a book about the Middle East, but it is not about holy wars or death sentences or oppression. Instead, it is about the Arabic language and how it's used every day: to tell stories, sing songs, and discuss personal troubles, aspirations, friendships, and fashion choices. It is about Arabic for its own beautiful sake, and as a key to culture and the three hundred million people who speak the language.

Few Americans have a clear image of daily life in the Arab world, which means they have no baseline against which to compare the latest shocking newspaper headlines. Without a sense of what's normal (the news is, by definition, the abnormal), all the riots, car bombs, and civil wars easily expand to fill the imagination. This book attempts to show what's not normally covered in the media, the familiar settings — shoe shops, parking lots, chicken restaurants, living rooms — that exist in even the most foreign-seeming countries.

This is also a book about how I learned Arabic, or tried to, in my travels around the Arab world. At age thirty-nine, in pursuit of some kind of fluency, I embarked on a series of trips to Egypt, Lebanon, Morocco, and the United Arab Emirates. If this were a story about French or Italian, I wouldn't have to explain further. European languages frequently inspire lifelong romances, and people decamp to Tuscany or Provence without a second thought. With Arabic, it's not so simple.

In fact, you could say that with Arabic and me, it's complicated. We go way back, to the early 1990s, when the language was an obscure field in America, considered about as useful as Old Norse. (An acquaintance assumed she had misheard, and that I studied *aerobics,* because that made more sense.) I took it up as a college freshman, bent on reinvention. Arabic was interesting, I reasoned, and would make me seem interesting too.

Arabic wasn't my first foreign language — I had high school French and a bit of Spanish — but it was the first I used in a foreign land. When I went to Egypt to study for the summer, at age twenty, I marveled at how I could utter a seemingly random collection of sounds to a waiter, and presto, there appeared a glass of fresh strawberry juice, garnished with a sprig of mint. I felt like a magician. In the classroom, Arabic had been hypothetical; in Cairo, it *worked*.

The marvel of that summer drove me for years of classes in America. But by the time I returned to Cairo, for a full year of advanced Arabic, I was burned out. I don't think it's making excuses to mention that Arabic is hard. As a professor once told me, Arabic takes seven years to learn and a lifetime to master. Arabic grammar is a complex web of if-then statements. The vocabulary is deep enough to drown in — the word for dictionary originally meant sea.

Most confounding of all is that there is not one Arabic, but many. Written Arabic is relatively consistent across five million square miles, from the Indian Ocean to the Atlantic. Spoken Arabic, by contrast, takes dozens of forms, in twenty-five countries in Africa and Asia. For seven years, I studied primarily the written language. I could parse a poem composed in the sixth century, but barely chit-chat with my landlord in Cairo. When I left school, I had a master's degree, yet I had felt fluent only a few times.

After school, I moved to New York City. At first, I maintained a little connection to my studies — as a tourist, I visited Lebanon, Syria, and Morocco. But soon I built a career as a travel writer to other destinations; I got married and bought a house. Those years of Arabic, I thought, were an unfortunate diversion, a false start on adulthood.

Yet the language continued to rattle around in my brain. I noticed it everywhere my work took me. In New Mexico, the irrigation ditches are called acequias, from *as-saqiyah*, the waterwheel. At a flamenco show in Spain, the audience cries *"Ojalá!"* (*Allah!*) I lectured my friends on the Arabic etymology of English words: "'Algebra,' sure, everyone knows that — but did you know 'sugar,' and 'coffee,' and 'alcohol'?"

In 2007, after nine years away from Egypt, I went back, to update a guidebook. I was surprised to find my Arabic not as rusty as I'd expected, despite so much neglect. I enjoyed speaking Arabic. I even missed it a little.

Here is where I should mention that I am sometimes overly optimistic, or a bit greedy, or just delusional. My father, at age seventy-seven, often jokes that he's still looking for a musical instrument that he can play without having to practice. I have the same hopeful attitude toward languages. I have tried a bit of Persian, a year of Dutch, a week of Thai; I dip into Spanish every few years. I imagine that if I could find the one language that clicks in every way—the right teacher, the right culture, the right mix of fascinating quirks and charming yet logical idioms—I might finally be fluent in something.

Yes, Arabic is monumentally difficult, but my return to Egypt reminded me that the language is full of the quirks and idioms I loved. I wanted to plunge back into Arabic, to rekindle the thrill I'd felt on my first trip to Cairo at the age of twenty. The key was to find the right circumstances.

When I started investigating classes in the Middle East, my husband, who had known me in graduate school, was skeptical. "Are you sure you want to study Arabic again?" he said. "You were so miserable then."

Things would be different this time, I told him. I would focus on spoken Arabic, not on the written version and all its grammatical complications. I would interact with people, not books. Classes had improved since the 1990s, when only about five thousand students were studying Arabic in the United States. Some of my professors in those years had taught Arabic as if it were a dead language, reading the text aloud, line by line, then translating to English and analyzing the grammar. Now thirty-five thousand students were enrolled in Arabic classes, and they had more dynamic teachers, jazzier textbooks, and colorful flashcards to help.

I had changed too, in ways that would make me a better, happier student of Arabic. Approaching middle age, I was less insecure than

I had been in my twenties, better traveled, and—key for language learning—more comfortable making a complete idiot of myself.

I also wanted to spend a while in the Arab world, to reassure myself that the places and, more important, the people were as I remembered them. I wanted to step behind the curtain of news and talk about everything else that was happening: this movie, that new job, this old friend. In search of regular life, I embarked on four trips over the course of a year. Each was five or six weeks, studying and traveling. In between, I returned to New York, to reassure my husband; a couple of times, he visited me. But for the most part, I was alone—the better to meet new people and push myself to practice Arabic at every turn.

I departed on the first trip in the fall of 2011, just as the hopes inspired by recent popular uprisings—the so-called Arab Spring—had begun to dim. My itinerary was a sort of linguistic Grand Tour: I visited four countries that represent the main dialects in the Arab world, as well as a wide variation in Arab culture. I began in Egypt, to reconnect with friends and to freshly appreciate the country's distinct sense of humor. Then I went to the Persian Gulf—mainly the United Arab Emirates, but also Oman and Qatar—to fill a large gap in my education: I had never visited the peninsula where Arabic first flourished and where the poetry I studied in graduate school was composed. With somewhat lower intellectual aspirations, I continued to Lebanon, where I hoped to absorb a bit of Beirut's glamour, starting with the lovely-sounding Levantine dialect.

Last, I traveled to Morocco. In addition to being the far-western fringe of the Arab world—with an accompanying far-out dialect—Morocco was also my oldest personal connection to Arabic. Off and on in the late 1960s, before I was born, my parents lived there. I grew up with their stories and souvenirs; even my name came from a woman my mother once knew in Tangier. My trip started as others had, with classes in the local dialect. Then my parents, on their first time back in Morocco in more than forty years, joined me, and together we relived some of their travels — the ones that had, in large part, set me on my own path.

It was an awkward, funny, and gratifying year. I rediscovered words I had long since forgotten and learned new ones that changed what I thought I knew. I was reminded of what I'm not particularly good at, but I also developed skills I had never been taught in the classroom. And I confirmed the adage I had heard early in my studies. Seven years was a drop in the bucket; Arabic could indeed consume a life.

A few notes before we begin: Many names have been changed to protect those who shared their intimate stories with me, not knowing they would become characters in this book. In a few spots, I have altered the chronology of my trip slightly, to spare the reader some of my U-turns and false starts. Arabic words have been transliterated in a relatively loose way, spelled so as to best suggest their pronunciation to non-Arabists. On the one hand, this goes against my perfectionist urges and my schooling; on the other, it relieves us of pages cluttered with scholarly-looking ḍiʿācrīṭics like ḍis (a tiny joke for those in the know; there are more, along with the more arcane grammar details, in the endnotes). Likewise, I have used some common English terminology and naming conventions: Nasser, not Abdel Nasser, for instance, and "medieval," reserved in its strictest sense for Europe's Dark Ages, to refer to the same centuries in the Middle East, which were a shining era, the golden age of the Islamic empire. It will make academics twitch, but my aim in this book is — as it was in my travels — to make the Arab world a more familiar place, not a stranger one.

Yalla. Let's go.

MASR

Egypt

September–November 2011

ضِحِك ب

(*dahika bi*) To laugh at

◆

ضاحك

(*dahaka*) To laugh with

◆

استضحك

(*istadhaka*) To make someone laugh

Empty Talk

CAIRO'S TRAFFIC WAS worse than ever. My taxi ride from the airport, well after midnight, was stop-and-go. The smell of burning fields, marking the end of the growing season, lent a faintly apocalyptic air to our halting progress. An accident blocked two lanes, and volunteers in sports jackets and ragged T-shirts directed us around the wreckage, lit by sputtering flares.

How was Cairo doing now, eight months after the January 25 revolution? I asked my driver. (We spoke English, as the only foreign words that had popped into my head on arrival were, perversely, Spanish ones.) Did he feel safe? American newspapers had been reporting a "crime wave" of muggings and black-market gun sales. This had worried my friends and family as I planned my trip, but I knew this was statistically nothing compared with America's crime rates. Besides, I simply couldn't imagine Cairo turning dangerous—the crowds left little room for criminal behavior. Whereas New Yorkers, I had found in my life there, coped with crowding by ignoring everyone around them, Cairenes took the opposite tack: Get involved in your neighbors' business, or that of your fellow metro passengers, fellow shoppers, fellow walkers-wading-into-traffic. Pull people close and bind them to you.

The city was still safe, my driver said as we sailed down an exit ramp into Ramses Square, though he didn't take his family out too late anymore, just in case. They usually came home by midnight or one. Now it was past two in the morning, and we plunged into the square in front of the train station as if into breaking waves. People bustled, dashed, or simply stood nibbling sunflower seeds. Vendors' carts lit by dangling fluorescent bulbs displayed packages of socks and bootleg CDs.

I rolled down my window. Horns blared and tinny synthesizer music snaked from distant speakers. Everywhere — in greetings, imprecations, opinions — was the hum and snap of Arabic.

"Ya gamoosa!" the taxi driver yelled affectionately at a slow-crossing pedestrian. Move it, you water buffalo!

I sat back, letting the sound-surf wash over me, and laughed.

In September 1990, on my first day of Arabic class, the professor, tall and stern, marched in and picked up a piece of chalk. Her straight hair, parted in the middle, swung as she wrote:

باب

"Bab," she enunciated. She pointed to the door. "Bab," she repeated, almost as a challenge. There was the door — we could use it right now, if any of us wanted.

The Arabic I studied for the next two years was the very serious kind, what most American teachers refer to as Modern Standard Arabic (MSA), a slightly streamlined version of the medieval language. Arabs call it al-'arabiya al-fusha, literally "eloquent Arabic." Fusha (pronounced FUS-ha, with a heavy s and a whispery h) struck my ear as lovely but formal — the language of beseeching bureaucrats, or at its liveliest, florid poets. The only jokes I heard were based on grammar.

"How are you?" goes one.

4

"Accusative!"

I suppose it does lose something in the translation.

When I went to Cairo to study in the summer of 1992, I encountered an entirely different kind of Arabic, a more flexible one that lent itself far better to jokes and gibes. Across the Arab world, Egyptians were known for their good humor, their wit, and their skill in *kalam farigh* — empty talk, but with a positive spin, the back-and-forth of an aimless afternoon.

Not that I could tell at first. The city was an undifferentiated din. Nothing, not even "Hi" and "How are you?," sounded anything like what I'd been taught. My stern professor had failed to mention that no one speaks Fusha aloud except newscasters and particularly cliquish Islamic fundamentalists. The former are reading from scripts, and the latter are inspired by God.

What Egyptians speak is *al-'ammiya al-masriya* — literally "Egyptian dialect," but it struck me almost as a new language. The basic vocabulary of Ammiya, as Egyptians call it, differs from Fusha, as does its pronunciation and word order, and most of Fusha's more intricate grammar rules are chucked right out the window.

That summer, I started Arabic again from scratch, in a beginner Ammiya class. Day by day, I learned to pick out words amid the street noise. First was the rhyming salutation I heard each morning from the newspaper seller: "*Ahlan wa-sahlan!*" Then I recognized song refrains as they trailed out of taxis and from cassette sellers' kiosks; it was the summer of heartthrob pop star Amr Diab pleading, *Habeebi* (my darling), *khudni ma'ak* (take me with you), over handclaps and a synthesized beat. Before long, I could recognize the sentence "You speak Arabic very well" — which every Egyptian was kind enough to tell me, though it wasn't true.

Speaking my limited and old-fashioned Fusha, I sounded as if I had arrived from the tenth century — or, really, a tenth-century home for not-very-bright children. Egyptians often laughed when I talked, though not unkindly. Even after I had learned a bit of Ammiya, shopkeepers and taxi drivers still grinned whenever I opened my mouth. This, I eventually understood, was because I was American, and foreigners studying Arabic, especially colloquial Arabic, were so rare that people could not quite believe their ears.

Ammiya struck me as a bit funny-sounding too. Egyptians spoke in the present participle, always going and wanting and waiting, and like overwrought heroines clutching their bosoms in shock, they tacked their question words on at the end: "The bus stops *where?*"

The melodramatic effect was heightened by the influence of one of my teachers, a plump matron in her sixties. Her chief pedagogical tool was video clips from Egyptian soap operas. From her, I learned to purse my lips and say, *"Azzzzdak eih bizzzzzabt?"* —You mean *what,* exaaaaactly?—in imitation of the neighborhood busybody, the one whose gossip invariably provokes a television hour of dramatic misunderstandings. My teacher encouraged us to mimic the actress's moves too, shaking shoulders and slapping hand over hand at the waist, the gesture for "Tell me everything." Reenacting this on the street, I was a one-two punchline: a twenty-year-old American squawking like an Egyptian lady of a certain age.

Eventually I learned to work with the aging-soap-queen diction, hamming it up for maximum effect. When it was clear I was intentionally contributing to the comedy, Egyptians began to let me in on their jokes. *"Gibna gibna wa-hatinaha fi-gibna . . . ,"* a shopkeeper once chanted to me while I was fishing for cash. He had to explain, in pantomime, the series of homonyms, a tongue twister: "We brought cheese and put it in our pocket . . ." It made no literal sense, but the flash of understanding between us—the I-get-it moment, which really means "I get *you*"—was gratifying enough to fuel me for a week.

Now, as I arrived in September 2011, Egypt was still basking in the afterglow of a brief period of exceptionally good humor, the January 25 revolution that deposed President Hosni Mubarak. With clever signs, absurdist tableaux, and running gags, the demonstrators had worked together to maintain a largely positive and peaceful atmosphere during an eighteen-day sit-in on Tahrir Square. The uprising had inspired Americans too. Labor organizers in Wisconsin had marched to protest the governor, bearing signs that read *Walk Like an Egyptian* and *Egypt = 18 Days, Wisconsin = ??* Occupy Wall Street, another movement with a sense of humor, was gathering momentum every week.

More than a decade had passed since I had used a textbook. My vocabulary was primitive; grammar, only a ghost. So much had been lost, and I couldn't retrieve it all. I needed to focus. My goal, I decided that night, as my taxi driver parted the crowds to deliver me into the noisy heart of Cairo, would be to interact with Egyptians in the way they treasured: to laugh with them, to understand their jokes, and to tell some myself.

Some days later, I presented myself at the school where I would be taking classes for a month. My oral placement exam started easily enough. What was my name, asked the teacher, where was I from, and how had I learned Arabic?

These answers I knew cold. I had been repeating them for two decades. Zora O'Nile — I applied the twangy Ammiya diphthong — was my name. I came from the state of New Mexico, and I had learned Arabic in college in America and here in Egypt. But that was *min zamaaaaan* — a very long time ago — I added, and I had forgotten a lot.

From there, we moved on to the typical Egyptian conversation.

How did I like this country?

The only right answer was to love it.

And how did I find Cairo?

This question gave more room for nuance, though even here, I found myself digging for some of the first words I had learned, almost twenty years earlier. That first summer in Cairo, I had learned to greet people with "morning of light" (*sabah an-noor*) or "morning of jasmine" (*sabah al-full*). I had learned the word for officer: *zabit,* with a heavy, menacing *z*. There had been one on nearly every corner, though not so menacing, just bored in a kiosk, leaning on a machine gun. I had learned to complain about the *zahma*—crowds, of both people and traffic. This new vocabulary shaped my image of the city: here was a metropolis that could crush me, perhaps arrest me, but also fill my morning with light or fragrant white flowers.

To the teacher evaluating me, I declared my sincere love of Cairo—people were so kind, and greeted me in such lovely ways. Although, I mentioned delicately, there was of course the problem of the *zahma*, the traffic.

"*Aywa, bi-gedd,*" the teacher concurred. And it was worse now, she said, after the revolution. Now there was not a single *zabit* to be seen—all the police officers had disappeared from the streets, leaving no one to enforce the rules of the road.

There was another matter I wanted to mention, but the word eluded me. "*Izzay bit'ooli* 'pollution'?" I asked.

"*Talawwus!*" she answered with quick, enthusiastic recognition of where this conversation was headed.

"*Aywa, at-talawwus,*" I parroted back. Now I remembered it, also from that first summer in Cairo. The pollution had hung over the Nile in the mornings and made my snot run black by nightfall. "*At-talawwus, ya'ani—hua magnoooon!*" Here I stretched out the word for crazy, to buy myself time. I rolled my eyes and threw my hands up in theatrical despair.

The teacher nodded in immediate affirmation. "Do you drive in Cairo?" she asked. Her smile suggested this too was truly *magnoon*, for a hapless foreigner like me to attempt driving.

I hesitated, not because I didn't understand, but because I was shaky on negating verbs. In Ammiya, it requires making a little sandwich, squishing the verb between a *ma*– and a *–sh*, and often changing the rhythm of the whole construct in the process. So I dodged it with a wordless, definitive no: a brusque *tsk* and dramatically raised eyebrows.

8

In the past few days, my Arabic had just started kicking into gear. The last time I had spoken Arabic like this — broken, brazen, filling in gaps with body language — had been at the end of that first Cairo summer. My girlfriends and I had gone to the archaeological site of Saqqara, and the guard had found some problem with our tickets. I stepped forward to advocate on our behalf. Under the white glare of the sun, I mustered the key vocabulary I had learned. "Morning of goodness, Mister Officer," I said. "We paid. We good. The tickets good." I placed my hand over my heart to emphasize my sincerity. "We wanting to enter. If we not entered, the situation not good."

The guard looked me over. A thin black dog watched from the shade cast by a tour bus, long legs in front and ears straight up, as if it had stepped out of an ancient wall painting.

"Morning of jasmine, my lady," the guard said, his face suddenly radiant with a glittering smile. "You speak Arabic very well. You are good. Please, enter."

I had been nervous about this exam, in part because I had decided not to take classes in Fusha, the Arabic I knew best. I was relieved to turn my back on Fusha's crushing rules, but that left me only with shaky Ammiya. Now, though, I remembered how satisfying it could be to communicate in this dialect, even in the most basic way. I would ace this. Buoyed by memory, I leaned forward and made the "crazy" gesture — like turning a doorknob at my temple — and said, "*Ya salaaaam!*" This all-purpose expression could be deployed with a variety of intonations, to mean anything from "So lovely!" to "I am *shocked.*" I was aiming for something like, "Driving in Cairo is the most ridiculous idea I've ever heard."

This produced the desired result: the teacher burst out in a full-throated laugh.

Inside the Word Factory

"OH, A B-MINUS!" my mother trilled down the phone line from New Mexico. It was the spring of 1991, most of the way through my freshman year, and midterm exam grades were in. "Honey, that's great for you!"

She was always telling me things like this. Both my parents were hippies, and I was not, or not exactly. I had always been careful and focused. I did not babble, and I spoke, first at age four, in full phrases. Shortly thereafter, I announced I would call my parents by their first names, Beverly and Patrick. This annoyed my mother, but what utterly maddened her was my habit of telling long-winded imaginary stories, and restarting them fresh from the top every time I made the smallest mistake: "And then Mr. Fox fell in the river — no, the lake!" *Stamp foot, breathe deep.* "Once upon a time . . ."

At least this thoroughness served me well later on. By age seventeen, it got me to college, as I requested brochures, filled out financial-aid forms, edited my essays. Now Beverly called frequently, to make sure I wasn't taking my fancy East Coast education too seriously.

"Follow your bliss, honey!" she said. "Remember, the best thing is just to wing it!"

Arabic is not conducive to winging it, I retorted. It has rules, systems, a right answer and a wrong answer, every time. It's like math, and I liked it for that reason.

Especially in those early years, Arabic both attracted me and fueled my worst perfectionist tendencies. Yes, it was *hard,* but I loved its efficiency. The Arabic alphabet, for instance, has twenty-eight letters, only two more than the English alphabet, but it is a completely phonetic representation of all the sounds native to the language. Some of those sounds are familiar — *alif* (ا) and *ba* (ب) at the beginning of the alphabet, and a little string closer to the end that goes *kaf* (ك), *lam* (ل), *meem* (م), *noon* (ن).

In between, though, many of the letters represent sounds I had never heard before, much less made myself: a whispery *h* (*ha,* ح), a throaty *kh* (*kha,* خ), and the *qaf* (ق), which sounds like an English *q* without a *u* after it, a delicate cough from the back of the throat. I particularly liked the drama of what our professor called the "heavy" letters, the portentous *sod* (ص), for instance, and the *dod* (ض), a *d* as dramatic and ponderous as the voice of God in a black-and-white Bible epic.

The *'ayn* (ع), however, briefly untethered me from certainty. The first time I heard it, I stared, bewildered, as our professor repeated the letter. Her lips barely parted, yet a tremendous, odd sound emanated from her, half foghorn, half heartsick wail. It had a hint of an *r,* a bit of an *n,* and something not consonant-like at all, more like a vowel, as its round hum had neither beginning nor end. Trying it myself, I contracted my larynx as our professor directed, hand on my throat to feel the muscles, then swallowed, simultaneously pushing sound up and out. My eyes bulged with effort.

Of the twenty-eight letters, only three are vowels, all long: *alif* (ا), a long *a; waw* (و), like *oo;* and *ya* (ي), a simple *ee.* The *waw* and *ya* do double duty as consonants, a *w* and a *y,* respectively. In my textbook, a man in a long robe was frozen midstride: يمشي (*yamshee,* he walks), with a *ya* beginning the word as a consonant and ending it as a vowel.

The short vowels — *a, i,* and *u* — are indicated only with little hashes and curls above and below the letters. A tiny circle called a *sukoon* perches above a letter to indicate an absence of a vowel, and a *shadda,* a mark that resembles a miniature English *w,* signals that a consonant should be pronounced twice. The *shadda* is the key difference between a pigeon (*hamam,* حمام) and a bathroom (*hammam,* حمّام). Be careful, our professor advised, in the first moment of outright humor in class, that you don't ask a waiter, "Excuse me, where is the pigeon?" — or, conversely, order a roasted toilet.

But the marks were only training wheels, she warned us. Texts for anyone over the age of ten or so didn't show them — th qvlnt f wrtng lk ths n nglsh. The one special case for grown-up readers was the Quran, always printed with full vowel marks, to dispel misreadings. Our professor showed us a verse, the letters of which, to my untrained eye, appeared to be surrounded by a cloud of midges:

اقْرَأْ وَرَبُّكَ الْأَكْرَمُ * الَّذِي عَلَّمَ بِالْقَلَمِ * عَلَّمَ الْإِنسَانَ مَا لَمْ يَعْلَمْ

"Read: Your Lord is the most generous, who has taught by means of the pen, has taught man what he did not know."

Sentences were efficient too. True, they were flipped around — verb first, then subject, then object — but if the subject was a personal pronoun, there was no need to say it. The verb *fahima,* all on its own, is a complete sentence: he understood. I recognized this concision from Spanish: *entiendo* is the same as *fahimtu,* I understand.

Arabic has a verb, *laysa,* that means "not to be." *Lastu talibatan mutamayyizatan* — I am not an exceptional student.

The opposite verb, *kana,* "to be," is often unnecessary. It is grammatically correct to say *ana batee'a* — I slow.

Then there's the dual. In Arabic, you can specify two of anything, or two people doing anything. I appreciated the precision, and how the verb and noun endings matched, like a miniature poem. *Madha yaf'alu at-talibani? Yadrusani.* What are the two students doing? They are studying.

Plurals sowed a moment of doubt. "Sound" plurals, so called because the noun stays intact, seemed sensible enough — they are formed by tacking a syllable on the end. *Imtihan* (exam) becomes *imtihanat* (exams); *mudarris* (teacher) becomes *mudarrisoon* (teachers). Most plurals, however, are "broken," or rearranged internally, by some inconsistent process. The result is that the singular noun appears to have been tossed in the air and left to fall in a jumbled heap. *Kitab* (book) rumples up to become *kutub* (books). *Shubbak* (window) cracks into *shababeek*. *Mushkila* (problem) splinters into *mashakil* (problems).

I knew about problems; hence my mother's pep talks over the phone. I was accustomed to coasting through school on educated guesses. Arabic, though, was so unfamiliar that I had no instinct, and I could not expand my vocabulary by guessing, because there were no cognates.

Case endings restored some of my faith, though our professor had to stop the class to explain to me, the only student without a background in Latin, that cases indicate the function of a word in a sentence. Arabic nouns have three cases, indicated with vowel marks — those little hashes and curls — over the last letter of the word. In class, we were required to pronounce the cases clearly.

I loved this concept the same way I had loved diagramming sentences in seventh grade. Case endings were like a diagram that was written onto the sentence. The drawback was that penciling in the case endings made my homework take twice as long, and even when I had the marks correct on the page, I consistently failed to say the right thing out loud.

The most beautiful efficiency in Arabic is its root system, a characteristic of all Semitic languages, and after I learned about it, I never doubted Arabic again. Our stern professor scratched three letters on the board:

ك ت ب

"*Kaf-ta-ba.* This is a root. Three consonants," she said. "Think of it like the roots of a tree."

Next, she wrote the same three letters, joined in a single word:

كَتَبَ

"*Kataba,*" she said. "You know this verb: to write, or, technically, he wrote, the simple past-tense verb. This verb is the trunk of the tree."

From this trunk, she wrote in related words, perched on lines like branches — *kitab* (كِتاب), book; *maktab* (مَكْتَب), desk or office — and proceeded to explain how these branch words followed set patterns. In the word *maktab,* for instance, the letter *meem* and the short vowels — these together indicate that it is a so-called noun of place, in this case, the place-where-you-write.

"This way, the word's very shape and rhythm give you a clue to its meaning," our professor said. "If you know the root verb and you recognize the pattern in the word, you can guess what it means."

She prodded us for other nouns of place from our limited vocabulary. A *matbakh* is a kitchen, we deduced, from the verb *tabakha,* to cook; a *majlis,* a living room, from *jalasa,* to sit; a *masjid,* mosque, from *sajada,* to bow down in worship. Then one of the two graduate students, a glum pair who always sat in the back row, arms folded, spoke up: "Oh! *Mabal.* Like for hermaphrodites."

"That's right," our professor said. "From the root *ba-waw-lam,* which gives the verb *bala,* to urinate." She was normally not one for digressions or jokes, but she paused to explain: a *mabal* was an important term in medieval Islamic law, a field deeply concerned with gender. Whether you were a man or a woman determined what you inherited, where you prayed, how your corpse was washed before burial. The occasional hermaphrodite presented a quandary, and the *mabal* — the place-where-the-pee-comes-out — was the answer, jurists decided. If the *mabal* resembled a man's, then the subject would be treated like a man; if a woman's, a woman. Our professor turned back to the board, as though we had not briefly dipped into something utterly bizarre.

Next she wrote, continuing with the verb *kataba:*

كاتِب

"*Katib,* with the long vowel *alif,* and then a short *i,* is the pattern for the active participle: 'I am writing.' Grammatically, it's an adjective, so it can be feminine or masculine," she explained, "but it can often take the meaning of a noun. So, not just is-doing, but one-who-is-doing — in this case, one-who-is-writing. By which I mean a writer."

Tik-tik-tik went our professor's chalk, and there was another word:

مَكْتوب

"*Maktoob,* the past participle, with a long vowel *oo.* 'Written,' an adjective. You also know, for instance, *matbookh,* cooked." She paused for a moment. "But, again, you can also look at *maktoob* as a noun, the written-thing, by which I mean fate." Here she allowed herself a small, wry smile.

I wrote the word *maktoob* and circled it. With three consonants and a few chalk marks, our professor had taken a series of leaps, each one farther than the last — from a simple, tangible book all the way to the abstract notion of destiny.

Next, our professor passed around copies of a table with rows numbered I to XV. These were the verb forms in Arabic, fifteen ways that three-letter roots could be transformed into new, even more complex meanings. Form I was what we had learned so far: *tabakha* (to cook, طَبَخَ), say, and trusty *kataba* (to write, كَتَبَ), with a short vowel on each of the three root consonants. Form II had the doubling mark in the middle and granted transitive or causative properties: *kattaba* (كَتَّبَ), to make someone write something.

On we went through the chart, tweaking the vowels and consonants and producing meanings intensive, reflexive, passive, and more. "Although," our professor granted, "not every three-letter root produces every form — not even close. And Form IX is only for defects and colors. Oh, and XI to XV are pretty antiquated, so you won't see them very often." I appreciated her candor so early on; in my fourth-year French class a few weeks earlier, I had been blindsided by a bunch of rare literary subjunctives, long after I thought my verb work was done.

The chart was proof of Arabic's uniquely elegant productivity. German builds ungainly compound words, and English tacks on Latin and Greek suffixes, such as "inter–" and "–ology." Arabic has two verb forms where the "inter–" is built right in. *Takataba* (تَكاتَبَ), Form VI, we had just learned, means to write to each other.

Walking out of class that day, I clutched the verb chart to my chest. An image bloomed in my head: *kataba* in the center and its related words clustered close or far, tethered with a strong silken thread. No, that metaphor was too easily tangled. It was a tree, as our professor had said. Or a chugging word factory, reshaping raw materials into widgets both concrete and abstract. Or perhaps it was a solar system, each root a sun, orbited by planets and their moons — which made Arabic a whole universe, really.

That idea was overwhelming, so I pushed it away and looked again at the verb chart, with its orderly rows. It was a lot to memorize, but it was a key to the door I had been shown on the first day of class.

The root system opened up the world of Arabic dictionaries, whole storehouses of words that are alphabetized not by first letter necessarily, but by the root of a word. Don't look for *maktab* (desk) under the letter *meem*, but under *kaf-ta-ba*, where you'll find it listed with all the other products of that root: *kataba* (to write), *katib* (writer), and so on. My first was Hans Wehr's *Dictionary of Modern Written Arabic*. Hans (we were quickly on a first-name basis) accompanied me everywhere. Its grass-green cover rapidly creased, and the edges of the Bible-thin pages turned gray from flipping.

Hans lends itself to idle browsing. Looking up, say, *ra-seen-lam,* a common root, I could discover that the main verb, *rasila,* means "to be long and flowing (hair)," yet branches out into such words as *rasool* (messenger or apostle), *risala* (letter), *tarassul* (a verbal noun from the Form V verb, to mean the art of letter writing), and *mustarsil* (an active participle from the Form VIII verb, meaning flowing; also, affable). Faced with such a web of meanings, I would make a game of linking them all in a story: one day, a lush-locked apostle began a friendly letter to his pen pal . . .

Hans seemed to contain everything strange and wonderful about Arabic. I was thrilled to discover that there is a verb, *qarfasa,* "to squat on the ground (with thighs against the stomach and arms enfolding the legs)," and that *fallaka,* "to have round breasts," is related to *falak,* "celestial sphere." But the sheer profusion of delightful words became a deterrent to actually learning them. Every time I considered making a flashcard, I would think, Is this word more important than any other? Each one seemed both essential and hopelessly weird.

In graduate school, I made the acquaintance of another, even more distracting dictionary, the one everyone called Lane. This is the eight-volume *Arabic-English Lexicon,* written in the late nineteenth century by one Edward William Lane, a British Orientalist who gadded about Cairo dressed as a Turk. His compendium and translation of more than a hundred medieval dictionaries is an admirable piece of scholarship, but it trails off two-thirds of the way through the alphabet, in the letter *qaf.* A fitting end, as that delicate cough of a letter was, in this case, the point where Lane himself coughed his last and died, after thirty-four years of labor.

A library date with Lane could start with a simple question: why does *beit* mean both a house and a verse of poetry? Lane's sources would ramble over a page and a half, bickering across the centuries. A *beit* is a goat-hair tent, one source attested. Not at all, retorted the next — the desert Arabs did not have goats with hair long enough to weave. A *beit* is a tent with at least two poles, some agreed. A *buyeit* is a miniature tent; only "the vulgar" use *buweit* as the diminutive.

A *beit* is a house of worship, sometimes, and a *beit al-ma'* (house of water) is a privy. Just when I thought I had made sense of all of those images, I would go to the next column: a *beit* is a grave, a family, even a wife. Only after a page or so would Lane offer anything approaching an answer to my question. As a line of poetry, a *beit* is part of a larger metaphor: a good verse has a strong internal structure, as a tent does.

I treasured a third dictionary too, one I bought after my formative first summer in Cairo. This book's full title was *A Dictionary of Modern Egyptian Arabic,* but I came to think of it as my Badawi, after one of the authors. As my Arabic education progressed and I delved into ever older Fusha texts, I would often take a break with Badawi to remind myself of the living language, the bantering Ammiya I had encountered in Cairo.

The lexicon bursts with such color and life that I imagined this Dr. Badawi had collected each and every example in person. In a tiny living room, a woman lamented, *"'Umru goozi ma-warraani f-yoom riiq hilw"* — My husband has never spoken to me kindly in his life — and Dr. Badawi cocked his head with empathy. On the banks of the Nile, Dr. Badawi scribbled in his notebook as a dripping-wet man complained, *"Ghiri't wa-ma-hadd-ish ghasni"* — I was drowning and no one came to my aid. Tell me about it, I would think as I returned the book to the shelf and dove back into my Fusha homework.

In the spring of my second year in graduate school, I consulted Badawi more and more frequently, because I had finally been accepted to an intensive, high-level Arabic program in Cairo. And whereas Hans Wehr and Edward William Lane were both long dead, Dr. Badawi was very much alive, and I would meet him soon, because he was the Cairo program's director.

When he welcomed us students on a 90-degree day in June, he looked as poised and thoughtful as I had always imagined, white hair brushed back, in a crisp oxford shirt and a camel-brown jacket.

He had once been in our shoes, he assured us. At graduate school in London, he had studied for months with no progress; then, one day on a bus, the conversation across the aisle had rung through his mind as clear as a bell. "The penny dropped," he said, switching into English to savor the idiom. Decades later, his face still glowed as he recalled this first flash of enlightenment.

Dr. Badawi concluded his speech with a few language-learning tips. The most important thing, he told us, was not to be discouraged if we didn't understand something. We shouldn't immediately run for our dictionaries; we should maintain forward momentum. "Just make something up!" he said, his eyes sparkling.

I had spent the previous two years of graduate school poking around in ever dustier corners of the Arabic word factory, in long-disused word warehouses. The language I had initially thought so elegant and efficient had piled up to form unstable stacks of grammatical arcana, around which I could only tiptoe. In light of this, Dr. Badawi's freewheeling advice sounded impossible to implement. Still, I tucked it away for future use.

A Prophecy

MAKING THE EVALUATOR laugh during my placement exam worked better than I could have dreamed. When I checked the class rolls, I found I had been placed in the highest level. The teacher was a tall, thin man with sad eyes who stooped by the whiteboard. He welcomed us and said dolefully, "I would like to discuss the social problems of the youth of Egypt in this new revolutionary era." He passed out a sheet of vocabulary words that my fellow students — a Belgian woman with architectural eyeglasses and a redheaded American college student — lunged at eagerly.

I perused the list with less enthusiasm: *tafahum* (consensus), *tamarrud* (rebellion), *ghawgha'iyah* (demagoguery). These dreary, abstract words made my heart sink. The teacher pressed play on a video clip, an excerpt from a policy-oriented talk show. My stomach began to hurt.

In Cairo in late 1997, about halfway through my yearlong advanced Arabic program with Dr. Badawi, I came to two grim conclusions. Together they made it clear that I had taken a wrong turn in graduate school, and I needed out. The first moment of understanding came from my writing teacher. Early in the semester, she told me, "You have such a big vocabulary!" I had been larding my compositions with juicy finds from the pages of Hans Wehr, and it felt good to have my hard work recognized. I redoubled my efforts. Near the end of the term, she asked, her eyes clouded with concern, "Why are you still using all these strange words?"

Oh. My big vocabulary was a *bad* thing? It was obvious in hindsight: dictionary-mad, I had made a simple What I Did This Weekend essay into one in which I "strode forth" from my apartment, to "orate" to my friends while we "imbibed" strong black tea.

The second epiphany came during my spoken Fusha class. This oxymoronic exercise, talking the way no one ever talked, was my least favorite class. But I did like listening to one fellow student who had a talent — rare among us, and even among native Arabic speakers — to declaim fluidly in the classical Fusha language. One morning, he sat up straight and gestured grandly: "Verily, I ascended to the bus this day, and it was chaos with respect to people . . ." It was his standard joke, but it killed every time: a mundane, modern story in the most antique words. He spoke with full case endings, and his speech sounded beautifully *complete.* I could almost see the words falling into their assigned grammatical slots, like linguistic Tetris blocks.

Our teacher called us to order. "Let us now address the matter of the article of yesterday," he said. The reading was yet another editorial about how the Arabs had given the world algebra, then fallen into their current state of misery. "What, in your respected opinions, is the problem with the Arab world in this modern era?"

Everyone else clamored to answer. I sat back and stared out the window. My head hurt and my stomach churned; I had spent much of the semester sick, swamped with work, and lonely. The problem wasn't Arabic — I still loved its eccentricities and intricacies and all its lovely words. But at this advanced level, no one was using it to say anything I cared about. I should be outside, I thought, with the traffic, the crowds, the arguments and gossip, the greetings and jokes.

The tall, thin teacher stooped to press the pause button on the video clip. He turned to the class for comments on the policy talk show, and the Belgian woman raised her hand. Her research, she said as she pushed her architectural glasses up her nose, was in child development in the Arab world, and she agreed with the talk show's guest. The cause of the social problems of Egypt, so prevalent among the youth of today, was the education system.

This Belgian woman had an impressive ability to repeat back whole sentences from what we had watched. My listening comprehension had never been strong — all those years sitting alone reading dictionaries hadn't helped — and it had been the first skill to go when I gave up my studies.

Perhaps a lack of creative thinking, the Belgian woman concluded, could lead to *ghawgha'iyah,* demagoguery. She didn't even have to look down at her vocabulary list as she said it.

After I knew I would leave graduate school, the rest of my time in Cairo was easier. To get outside more, to use Arabic in the street rather than in my dismal spoken Fusha class, I accepted any and every social invitation. Happy hour at the Australian consulate. French fries and chicken livers at the twenty-four-hour rooftop bar. An accidental date with an earnest Egyptian writer, who took me to the British pub at the Marriott and told me that his fiancée was a lesbian, then read me a short erotic poem.

I met other, less lascivious Egyptians too. They were part of the larger American University circle, and we usually spoke English. But after my isolated first semester, talking to any Egyptian in any language was an education — and a reminder of why I'd wanted to come back to this city. People loved to talk. My landlord, a sad-eyed hydrologist, dropped by periodically to scare my roommates and me with Nile pollution statistics. Hassan, a cheerful, round-faced man with a wheezy laugh, had studied dentistry in the Soviet Union but switched to archaeology. He was a guide for Russian tourists and regaled us with stories of their strange behavior, such as their propensity for wearing hot pants when touring ancient ruins. Hassan's friend Saad, with his slightly crossed eyes and wicked grin, provided an endless stream of jokes.

In mid-May, a few weeks before the end of the school year, Hassan had a party at his apartment. After dinner, we guests settled outside on the terrace to watch the sunset; the call to prayer drifted across the rooftops, signaling the ease of evening. As the sky darkened and the neighbor's pigeons whirled back home to roost, the conversation shifted into Arabic. At first I was tense, worried I would miss a detail. I took a swig of my beer and a few sips from the joint that was making its way around. (In Ammiya, one doesn't "smoke" a cigarette, a joint, or a *sheesha* pipe; one "drinks" it.)

Saad, reclining like a pasha on a cushion-strewn bench, played the role of social director. As a desert guide, he was an expert in building a good *haflit samar*, a party around a campfire, and he goaded others into telling stories and jokes. In the run-up to the punchlines, I remembered Dr. Badawi's advice: just make something up. If I missed something, I could always spin a joke in my own head.

My anxiety dissipated, and some door in my brain opened. Through it, words passed easily without my having to analyze each and every one. After about fifteen minutes, I realized I wasn't actually making anything up. Saad's face glowed above a flared match, and I perfectly understood his joke about Egyptians stealing Hosni Mubarak's watch. The rest of the night went by in a pleasant blur — I even threw in a few witticisms of my own. In that balmy night, high above the roaring city, I felt, for the first time, completely at ease in Arabic and in Cairo. Not only was I finally using the language as intended, as a social connector, but we were, I grandly mused, carrying on the long and noble rhetorical tradition Arabic had cultivated since it was born in the desert so many centuries before. Only in our case, instead of trading poems, we were swapping yo' mama jokes and wisecracks about Egyptian rednecks.

A week before my departure, some fellow students threw a party in their sprawling colonial-era apartment, fueled by the miscellaneous liqueurs we had collected from the duty-free shop. The Egyptian poet who'd taken me to the British pub attended, and at a hazy point late in the evening, after we had to turn down the music but before the cops came, he stripped off all his clothes except his socks and danced alone under the chandeliers.

In the taxi on the way to the airport, a wave of nostalgia—for the life I had only just begun to live here—welled up in me so fast and hard that it prickled in my nose. The looming apartment buildings we passed shone with the lights of countless other lives, and for a moment, I loved every person in the vast, dusty metropolis.

The redheaded American student raised his hand and offered his take on the tall, thin teacher's video clip. Rebellion was a natural phase, he surmised, both in human development and in the development of a nation. Consensus was a sign of further maturity. As he spoke, he spun his pen around his thumb like a debater.

The teacher then turned to me. What was my opinion on the social problems of the youth of Egypt?

The redheaded American tapped his pen on the table expectantly. All I could think of were barbed comments about spoiled kids. "If everything the teenagers they ask for it, they get it, then this is bad," I offered. "It means they do not have something . . . strong inside?"

The Belgian girl winced, but the teacher gave a surprised smile and a nod of recognition.

After class, I went to the office to request a transfer to a lower level. Abstract principles, hypothetical proposals, social problems—I didn't want to talk about any of this. The one time I had felt fluent was that dreamy evening on Hassan's roof way back in 1998. It was a good scale on which to grade myself. If my performance on Hassan's roof was an A-minus in bantering fluency, I was at a C-plus now. I wasn't going to improve that score by discussing consensus and demagoguery.

"I don't want to talk about politics," I told the administrator, a woman named Madame Zuzu. This wasn't exactly right, but it seemed like a more concise way of explaining my dislike of abstraction. "I don't really have friends here" — not any I spoke Arabic with, anyway — "so I need practice talking to people I don't know, about regular, daily things."

Madame Zuzu raised one eyebrow. "Don't be so sure," she replied. Her head was swaddled in a blue nylon turban, which made her look like a storefront psychic and her pronouncement sound like prophecy.

One minute into our conversation, I regretted calling Medo. He was insisting I spend the whole day with him, despite my repeated assertion that I didn't *have* an entire day to spend with him. Nothing resolved, I hung up, feeling unreasonably angry at all Egyptians — that same street-corner chattiness that I loved, that urge to pull people close, could be exhausting as well.

I was also angry with myself. What had I expected, calling up a total stranger just because he'd left a nice comment on my blog? "i hope its not rude if i ask u to let me know when u come . . . ," Medo had written.

And something he had said on the phone had made me nervous.

"Do you know how old I am?" he had asked.

"Er . . . no . . . twenty-five?" I guessed, generously.

Medo laughed self-consciously. "I'm, well, no, I'm twenty."

That put him squarely in the realm of *shabab,* a word we had just been using in class: a period of golden youth afforded by the precision of Arabic vocabulary, the stage of life after adolescence and

25

before full adulthood. Back in my own golden youth, my relationship with Egyptian *shabab* (it was a plural noun too) had been a bit troubled. There were the downtown idlers who hissed, and the ones who called me names. One day I happened to learn the word *sharmoota* — whore — from an Egyptian friend; the very next day, strolling down the street, I passed a man who barked the word at me, out of the blue. (At first I had been gratified to understand; only two blocks later did it occur to me to be angry.) Then there were the sweet but unnervingly persistent *shabab,* such as the slim man with big eyes who had followed me on a thirty-minute walk home, then stood outside my building for hours, staring up at my window. In my private lexicon, *shabab* had taken on a distinctly negative connotation.

Now, though, the word rang out in songs and was heralded in newspaper stories, for it was the *shabab,* those brave young men (and women), who had led the demonstrations during the January 25 revolution. The energy of youth had toppled the grizzled old pharaoh Mubarak.

After I got off the phone with Medo the *shabb,* it seemed prudent to email him and mention that I was married.

"lol, but seriously hadn't any intentions lol," he wrote back. "just want to get to know u and show u parts of my country too."

Over a few more calls, I bargained him down to a coffee date, in the suburb of Heliopolis, noted for its historic cafés where British soldiers caroused during World War II.

"You know where the Starbucks is?" Medo asked.

I arrived late, frazzled and sweating; he was looking cool in sunglasses, with artfully gelled sandy-brown hair. He shook my hand and smiled, revealing braces. He was so tall he barely fit in his chair.

He had brought his sister, sixteen-year-old Sara, who also wore braces. Perched shyly next to her brother, she looked trim and sensible in jeans and a simple, powder-pink headscarf. "She doesn't speak much English," Medo said in apology. "I will translate." I knew Medo wanted to practice his English, so I let him go.

Our conversation was as awkward as a job interview and a first date combined. I was acutely aware of our age gap. He was in college, studying journalism, he told me, but his school — staff and students — was on strike at the moment. This was slowing him down. "I want to leave Egypt as soon as I can," he declared. "This country is a disaster. This is why I practice English."

I glanced at Sara. Did she know her brother wanted to move away? I hadn't expected this. In his comments on my blog and in his email, he had sounded proud of his country.

"Yes, I want to show people what is good about Egypt," Medo explained. "So they are not afraid." Medo had one foot in the country, one foot out — an ambivalent ambassador.

As we slurped the last of our drinks, Medo said, "Sara has a dentist appointment. It's a couple of blocks from here. *Yalla.*"

It was 9:30 p.m., which was not unusual — doctors kept late hours to accommodate working families and the heat. As a social outing, though, visiting a dentist was new to me. A few blocks down, we turned into a seemingly abandoned mini-mall where stray cats nosed through trash on the stair landings. The dentist's lobby was spotless. The three of us sat on an old turquoise vinyl sofa in the waiting room.

A wall-mounted TV showed a classic black-and-white Egyptian movie, from that golden era in the mid-twentieth century when Cairo was the center of cultural production in the Arab world. The heroine, her hair sculpted in dramatic black waves, fought passionately — and wittily — with the be-fezzed hero. "The dresses then were amazing," Medo sighed.

The dentist called us all in, and Medo and I sat to one side while Sara's braces were tightened. When the dentist was done, he sat down to chat. He had been following the Occupy Wall Street movement, he told me in English, and he saw parallels between it and Egypt's situation, which was growing tense as the parliamentary elections crept closer.

For decades, Egypt had been so stagnant that political machinations had no bearing on daily survival, except to change the price of bread. Regular people rarely bothered to discuss politics in any detail; instead, they cracked a joke or two and carried on. Now, though, every political shift was felt immediately in daily life, and everyone had an opinion. I found myself wishing I could participate and reply to the dentist in Arabic.

Oh, Madame Zuzu, I thought, looking over at Medo and Sara. Of course you were right, with your blue turban and your prophecy. Of course you looked skeptical when I said I didn't have any friends and didn't want to talk about politics.

Two Tongues

THE TEXTBOOK I used in my first year of Arabic class, in 1990, had none of the elements that were common in my French curriculum from the same time—no cultural sidebars, no recurring college-age characters who meet frequently at a café to chat. Instead, its stilted design matched the basic, formal Fusha it taught. The glossy pages were entirely in Arabic, not typeset but handwritten, in simple calligraphy. Watercolor illustrations of objects—cats, desks, pencils, disembodied limbs—floated in space. In one image, a boy's head tilted over a small bowl, a delicate stream of liquid pouring from his mouth. An existential red question mark hovered over him—what could be the matter? *'Andi qay'*, read his answer: I have vomit.

The textbook shaped my image of Arabic, and not in an entirely positive way. Not only did the phrase *'andi qay'* still pop to mind every time I felt queasy, but from the start I had the impression of a language that was cryptic, intimidating, and not quite rooted in place. I kept the book for more than twenty years, as a relic from an earlier time, and it sat on my shelf, undisturbed, until I was packing for my return to Cairo. I reached for my beloved Badawi dictionary, that lively catalog of life in Egypt, and my glance happened to fall on the spine of the adjacent volume, my old textbook. All this time I had never bothered to read the author's name, written in Arabic.

Dr. Elsaid Badawi.

This confounded me. All this time I had pegged Dr. Badawi, with his just-make-something-up ethos, as a freewheeling colloquial guy. How could the same man have written my stodgy Fusha textbook too? They were opposite poles of the Arabic language!

As soon as I arrived in Cairo, I made an appointment to meet Dr. Badawi. He was officially retired, and I doubted he remembered me, as I had not distinguished myself as a particularly good student. Now I was making fresh efforts, though, and I wanted to ask him about the best language-learning strategies. I also wanted to ask him a thornier question: Fusha or Ammiya, the language of books or the language of the street? Where did his true loyalties lie?

Dr. Badawi still kept an office at the American University in Cairo, but in the time since I had last studied there, the institution had ceased to be technically in Cairo. The prestigious school had pulled up stakes from its small, nearly century-old campus on Tahrir Square, with its tree-shaded courtyards, to a massive new lot in a satellite city to the east. The bus hurtled past the city I knew, onto a desert highway edged with billboards for new communities — AUC's partners in exile, or escape. Riviera Heights, La Rêve, Smart Village, and a place called, unfortunately, Rehab (it means open space, from the verb *rahiba,* with a whispery *h,* to be roomy).

In the years since I had first run up against the stark difference between written and spoken Arabic, between Fusha and dialects like Ammiya, I had learned the proper linguistic term for the phenomenon: diglossia, literally "two tongues." Communities that exhibit diglossia typically use a "high" version of a language for formal situations and a "low" one in casual contexts. In Arabic-speaking countries, that meant fancy Fusha for reading and writing and general impressing, and the local dialect for everyday conversations.

Many communities once characterized as diglossic — Haiti, for instance, split between French and Creole — had since closed the gap through official policy. But for Arabic, spoken in more than two dozen countries, there has never been a single regulating body to push changes, and more important, Fusha has been too closely linked to heritage, history, and religion to be phased out. In fact, according to some linguists, the situation has split into triglossia. Most students in the Arab world learn three registers of Arabic: the language of the Quran (even if the students are not Muslim), a somewhat more modern style of Fusha found in newspapers and contemporary books, and their own spoken dialect. In any case, no Arab learns Fusha as a mother tongue. Children grow up hearing and speaking a dialect; elementary school brings Fusha, essentially as a second language.

Foreigners typically learn Arabic the other way around. Fusha is taught as the base, the scaffolding, and after some years, a dialect is laid over it like a tent. I had built up so much Fusha infrastructure that when it came time to lay on the dialect, it didn't fit right — my Fusha kept poking through. Functionally this was fine, as Egyptians could understand me, and this was how teachers had always justified a Fusha-first approach. But for fluency, it didn't help. Spoken Fusha, with its archaic grammar and vocabulary, always sounds unnatural, like speaking in Shakespearean forsooths and whithers and thous, with some biblical begats for good measure. Plus, I was forever analyzing everything in terms of my trusty Roman-numeral verb chart, which slowed down my speech.

Over the years, as I contemplated the problems I had encountered learning Arabic, I wondered whether I had gone about it wrong. Learning Fusha first didn't mimic how Arabs learned their own language. Then again, maybe that wasn't the right model either, as many Arabs I'd met positively loathed their Fusha educations, rarely felt comfortable writing, and seldom read Arabic for pleasure. Even worse, I had found that many Arabs were barely aware of the magnificent root system, the engine that drove their own language — and I couldn't very well give up thinking about that, could I?

Dr. Badawi was an expert in the field of Arabic education, so surely he could advise me. And to have written two such utterly divergent books, he must have resolved diglossia in his own life, as Arabs must do if they want to move between formal and informal situations.

The bus sighed past one last fantastical compound — *Future,* read the sign on the faux Roman coliseum — and dropped me on the edge of the new campus. I wandered lost among vast plazas edged with sleek, geometric buildings in striped earth tones, their walls cut through with dramatic arches. On the stairs by a food court, I phoned Dr. Badawi for guidance. "I just passed the Cinnabon?"

A few minutes later, Dr. Badawi strode across the courtyard, looking relaxed and cheerful, in a camel-brown blazer and striped shirt, his white hair brushed back — just as I remembered him. He led me to his office, fetched me tea, and settled in behind a desk strewn with papers.

When I told him how I'd noticed two seemingly contradictory books on my shelf, both by him, he laughed. "I recently wrote a dictionary of the Quran. Now *that's* the exact opposite of Ammiya!" The book had taken him five years to write, and it garnered the annual Islamic book prize from the government of Iran, he was proud to report. He went to Tehran to accept the award, and shook President Ahmedinejad's hand.

But how did Dr. Badawi reconcile these two — or three — sides of Arabic? How should it be taught?

"The sensible thing, the most efficient thing — though we don't always do that, do we? — is to start with the written language," Dr. Badawi said. This was not the answer I had been hoping for. "Because if you focus on speaking," he continued, "the only person you have to speak to is your teacher. With a book, you have it with you always."

Dr. Badawi seemed to be conjuring a vision of scholarship from the past, the kind in which students sat alone in the library and communed with the ancients. Generations of Arabists in the West had learned this way. One of my most erudite professors had never learned a dialect; he cheerfully spoke Fusha to taxi drivers when he traveled to Jordan for research. According to Dr. Badawi, professors of Arabic at Oxford were notorious for beginning the semester by saying, "Here's the alphabet and a text to read. Go home and start working, and we'll discuss next week." Class enrollment would then drop to three freakishly dedicated students, enough to justify the professors' existence and "give them money for the wine at their dinners," as Dr. Badawi put it.

Although I loved the quirks of the classical language, Fusha always felt a bit theoretical when I read it, more like solving a calculus problem than anything else. When I read the colloquial phrases in Badawi's dictionary, I could hear a voice in my head saying the words, an amalgam of all the teachers and taxi drivers I'd ever had. It never happened when I read Fusha; all I heard was my own faltering voice. To internalize the flow of classical Arabic, I would have had to listen to thousands of hours of dull news broadcasts. Speeches by politicians worked too—perhaps Hassan Nasrallah, the fiery, eloquent leader of Hezbollah, or less controversially, Gamal Abdel Nasser, the Egyptian president who led the 1952 revolution and who was still admired for his moving Fusha oratory.

So I wondered if I had gone wrong in progressing too far along the path of reading Fusha. "It was only after I came to Cairo and learned some Ammiya, and really spoke to people," I told Dr. Badawi, "that I started to believe in Arabic as a real language, attached to a real culture." After all, even Nasser spoke Fusha only for effect, setting up a grand idea in the loftiest possible tones, then underscoring it with an

Ammiya punchline. The people listening weren't native Fusha speakers; no one was.

"It's true," Dr. Badawi acknowledged. "Without colloquial, you don't really know the language."

He reconciled the gap between writing and speaking by emphasizing what he called *'ammiyat al-muthaqqafeen*, or cultured-people's colloquial, the type of Arabic an educated person uses to discuss serious or abstract subjects. It's characterized by colloquial word order (subject, then verb) and other simplified grammar, but most of the vocabulary comes from the classical language or is borrowed, where necessary, from foreign languages. Dr. Badawi considered this the best approach for his foreign university students, because "your target is your counterpart in the society — not a carpenter, not a janitor. You want to know *my* language. So that's what I do — I teach *my* language."

If your goal was to be a scholar, this was great. In the long run, you would be hobnobbing with other professors from all over the Arab world, and you would be able to express yourself eloquently. But it wasn't my goal to be a scholar, as I had realized while staring out the window in my spoken Fusha class in 1997. Speaking educated Arabic about educated things was not something I had ever found particularly fun. And if there was one thing I was determined to do in Cairo this time, it was to have fun.

I confessed my ambivalence to Dr. Badawi. Yes, I loved the morphology of Arabic, its mechanical way of producing vocabulary for every situation. I had swooned over the rhythmic grace of old poetry. And I did admire Dr. Badawi's eloquence, and how much he enjoyed his job.

But now, in my late thirties, I had come to terms with what my brain craved. I was a dilettante, an amateur, a lowbrow. All I wanted to do in Arabic was talk to people, to gossip and make jokes.

Unfortunately, my subconscious wasn't cooperating. The past two nights I'd had dreams in which I spoke Spanish. "My brain is rebelling!" I lamented to Dr. Badawi.

"No, not at all," he said with glee. "The foreign language boxes are opening!" He had the same look of excitement I had seen more than a decade before, when he had welcomed us to the intensive program and recalled the moment the penny had dropped for him, on a London bus.

This reminded me: I had also come here to thank Dr. Badawi for his advice that day. "It really stuck with me," I said to him. "You told us that if we didn't understand, we should just make something up." I had internalized the wisdom, using it not only for Arabic, but for other languages too. It worked during political discussions, when I could nod easily in agreement (with myself) at the right spots; when the punchline of a joke arrived, I could laugh in sync, at my own witticism. I had probably taken it too far — sometimes I used the strategy when I lost track of a conversation in English.

"Oh, yes." His eyes lit up. "That's exactly how I taught myself!" While studying at Al-Azhar University — the most prestigious school in Egypt and one of the oldest institutions in the Arab world, established around the year 970 — Dr. Badawi had also enrolled in English classes at the British Council, but he had found them too slow. Back at Al-Azhar, a professor mentioned that the Islamic reformer Muhammad Abduh had learned French by reading. So Dr. Badawi followed Abduh's lead and plunged into the Trollope novel *Barchester Towers*.

"It took me eight months, and I never consulted a dictionary," Dr. Badawi told me. "If I did come to a word that was crucial for understanding a whole paragraph, I would ask someone." The books — he went on to read more in the series — were about social and religious maneuvering in Victorian England, "but really, they were like the sheikhs of Al-Azhar," with all the same politicking and currying of favor. Eventually he branched out beyond Trollope, but not before going back to reread *Barchester Towers*. The second time, with improved comprehension, he said, "it was just not as interesting."

Those books, whatever he imagined in them, had value for him — probably more than for most people who read Trollope. It didn't matter whether he'd gotten them "right," he said.

As Dr. Badawi reminisced, it dawned on me: his advice had been for *reading*. Because really, what kind of language teacher would advise you to not ask the people you're *speaking* with what the heck they mean? I had taken his advice and twisted it into something that suited my personality. I didn't like admitting I didn't know things, and I felt like a nuisance when I stopped a conversation to ask for clarification. Surely, I had rationalized, it was better to smile and nod, so my conversation partner didn't give up in exasperation.

There in Dr. Badawi's office, I didn't admit this colossal misinterpretation. He nonetheless seemed to perceive my capacity for bending reality to my will.

"Whatever you write about this meeting probably won't accurately capture me," he said with the enlightened beam of a mystic as he stood up from behind his desk. "It will really just be what *you* think." I stood too, and squared my shoulders, trying to look as if I knew what I thought. "But *I* understand what *I* think," he pronounced. "That's what makes our talk worthwhile."

And with that, the great and paradoxical Dr. Badawi, author of both the world's most wonderful dictionary and a very peculiar textbook, ushered me out the door.

See What We Did

MY NEW AMMIYA class, a level lower, was exactly where I wanted to be. The teacher, Hani, was a fireplug of a man, fairly bursting from his polo shirt and pleated khakis. "Suppose your friend says he wants to date a pretty girl," he asked the class. "What do you say to him?"

"*Fil-mishmish,*" quipped a British guy. A great comeback, in the best tradition of Egyptian banter. It meant "in apricot season," a period of time so short as to mean "in your dreams."

Hani chuckled and looked around. "Great. Anyone else?"

A Danish blonde with big blue eyes raised her hand. "I would say to him, Forget the pretty girl," she said, "you should look for a smart girl."

Hani's forehead creased in confusion. I recognized this type of language teacher: the burly, bawdy man who was seldom equipped to deal with nudges toward political correctness. He turned to his briefcase and pulled out a sheaf of papers. "We will sing a revolutionary song," he said, passing around the lyrics.

Most Arabic pop songs, and a lot of the creative output of the revolution, were sung in Ammiya. And when those lyrics were recorded for posterity, as these had been, it was a rare instance in which Ammiya was written down.

So great was the gap between high and low Arabic that even the Nobel laureate Naguib Mahfouz, who created otherwise vivid portraits of workaday Egyptians, equated dialect with "poverty and disease." In his novels, he translated colorful colloquial expressions into Fusha dialogue. The digital age had broken down some of these barriers, as Arabs began to write text messages and Internet comments in dialect, despite a lack of standardized spelling. Another breakthrough came in 2006, when an Egyptian journalist, Khaled Al Khamissi, published *Taxi*, a book of conversations with Cairo's famously colorful cabbies, written entirely in Ammiya. Compared with typical books on the Egyptian market, where selling three thousand copies was considered a success and ten thousand copies a bestseller, *Taxi* was a blockbuster. It sold more than seventy thousand copies and spawned a movie and a TV show.

Now it seemed natural that during the people's revolution, marchers brandished signs written in the people's tongue, Ammiya. And the people who documented the movement wrote down the songs and slogans in the same dialect in which they'd been sung and chanted.

Hani cued up a DVD. "Here, we will see the video too. Please sing out loud." He raised his whiteboard marker like a conductor's baton.

My hand clutched the lyrics sheet instinctively. I loved Arabic music, but singing aloud could be oddly painful, as I had discovered a few months into my college Arabic 101 class. Our boisterous Egyptian teaching assistant, the counterpoint to our stern professor, had led us in a nursery rhyme, accompanied by a tune on a whirring cassette recorder.

"*Ma-MA za-MAN-ha GAY-ya*," the assistant had directed us to sing, marking the syllables in the air with his hand. "Mommy's on her way . . ." We were singing about Mom bringing home a bag with a duck in it — a duck that said *waq-waq-waq*. That part was fun, because it called for the letter *qaf*, that little cough of a *q*. But as I sang, I felt an inexplicable sadness, and my eyes welled with tears. Everyone else in class was still happy. What was wrong with me?

Somewhere in the second verse, which involved a kid named Adel, I discerned a pattern: the poignant sensation surged each time I sang the 'ayn, that mysterious letter that was both expansive and constricted, the one that called for previously unused muscles in my throat. I *had* heard this sound before, I remembered. At the age of five or so, I had become entranced with a cassette, labeled ARABIC MUSIC in my mother's all-caps hand. She had recorded it off the radio, trying to recapture the sound of the trips she and my father had taken to Morocco before I was born. The songs' pure emotion had mesmerized me, though I hadn't understood a word. That spellbinding effect, I felt that day singing about a duck, came from the letter 'ayn. Even in those near-nonsense lyrics, it was a pure, plaintive keening.

So twenty-one years later, when Hani handed me the lyrics of the revolutionary anthem, I quickly scanned them out of habit, looking for the 'ayns. This song, I saw, was going to be a tearjerker regardless, because it was dedicated to the revolution's *shuhada'*. The word is commonly translated as "martyrs," but that puts an unnecessary religious-fanatic spin on it. Hans Wehr does list one meaning of *shaheed,* the singular, as "one killed in battle with the infidels," but during the popular uprisings across the Arab world in the past year, *shuhada'* were secular. The verb *shahida* means to bear witness or give testimony. By extension, in the current political situation, the *shuhada'* were the people who stared down the dictatorship, saw it with their own eyes, bore witness — and died. All over Cairo, the *shuhada'* were commemorated in huge murals, scribbled graffiti, and anthems like this one.

The video was a montage of earnest young men in their blurry school portraits. In the third verse, the 'ayn in the middle of "*Bawadda' ad-dunya*" — I bid the world farewell — yanked at my heartstrings. My voice broke, and I pressed my lips together and stared into the corner of the room. When I looked back to the front, I saw Hani's eyes were watering too.

In my memory, Cairo is always sepia-toned, though the brownish hue comes not from nostalgia, but from dust. Sand blows in relentlessly from the surrounding desert, coating all buildings and any car left in one spot for too long. If a sprinkle of winter precipitation manages to wash some of the sand away, the khamsin — the spring desert wind, supposedly named for the fifty (*khamseen*) days it lasts — comes every year and restores it.

So in my walks around the city after class every day, I was surprised to see that the leaves on Cairo's trees were green, even shiny, as if it had rained the night before. In the past, the sand patina on the apartment buildings had been an unbroken golden brown, but now some Cairenes had discovered bright exterior paint. Every block or so, a single balcony burst out in bright orange or mint green.

The new colors matched a dramatic change in mood I had noticed in Cairo. During the late Mubarak era, a common expression of caution was *imshi gamb al-heit* — walk close to the wall. Play it safe, to avoid the hungry eye of the police state. Now people moved freely, happily. At night on the bridges and the corniche along the Nile, they seemed to walk with a new sense of ownership, pride, and purpose. Strangers spotted my foreign face from across the street and gave me a thumbs-up, as if to acknowledge our new shared democracy. One called out in Arabic, "Hey, *amreekaniya*, you see us on TV? You see what we did?"

The palpable excitement, the pops of color, the crowds — it all did something to my brain. The language boxes were opening, as Dr. Badawi had said. With every new classroom phrase I reviewed as I walked Cairo's familiar streets, I retrieved another from my past. I felt like a medieval monk revisiting a memory palace; the whole city was my mnemonic.

South of Tahrir Square, near my old apartment, I passed a corner grocery, and its distinct smell — a mix of coffee, cumin, and washing powder — triggered shopping phrases: this one, two of those, a quarter kilo of white cheese, by your grace. These closet-size shops were a language learner's crucible, as everything had to be requested, so the youngest, smallest man could shinny up a ladder and fetch a yellow box of Bride brand tea. I had practiced my numbers here, asking for four, seven, anything but a standard dozen eggs from the stack of crates by the door. My roommates and I had even worked up the nerve to place a phone call, the most extreme test of language skill, to request that young man at the grocery to come collect our crates of empty beer bottles. In preparation, we had consulted Dr. Badawi's dictionary: "*Lamma t'uuz tishtiri biira laazim tigiib il-fawaarigh ma'aak,*" read an example in the entry for the verb *firigh,* to become empty. "When you want to buy beer, you must bring the empties with you." I imagined Dr. Badawi, in his camel-brown blazer, getting a lecture from our frog-voiced grocer.

In medieval Cairo, I wound through the narrow streets and recalled the phrases for begging someone's pardon, the polite ways to edge around donkey carts, women with massive shopping bags, and beggars with outstretched hands. Here I had learned that meaning could shift according to geography. Two miles away in downtown Cairo, a hiss from an idle man on a corner was a come-on; here, in a dogleg lane, from a man on an overburdened bicycle, it meant "Outta my way!"

As I walked, some words simply appeared in the air, untethered to a place from my past. *Badawwar* — I had said this a million times, I could tell from the way it echoed in my head for a whole afternoon. I muttered it like an incantation, then, as I passed a *kushk,* the all-purpose sidewalk kiosk bursting with newspapers, phone cards, and sandwich cookies, I remembered: "I'm looking for . . ." Kiosks were always a good place to ask for directions — or anything, really.

Badawwar 'ala sha'a, I had said to doormen, over and over, when I had arrived in Cairo for my intensive program — I'm looking for an apartment. After that, I was attuned to the phrase, and overheard it in cafés, often from one young man to another. They were looking for not just any apartment, but an affordable one to buy, on a limited income, in this overcrowded city. An apartment was a fundamental requirement for any middle-class marriage. Marriage, in turn, was a requirement for sex. So, by the transitive property, an apartment meant sex. There was a whole life plan in a single sentence.

Badawwar 'ala rihan, I had asked at the greengrocers — I'm looking for basil. That wasn't food, the bossy woman at the corner produce stand told me; it was for keeping mosquitoes away. I later found basil growing like a weed in a parking lot, and harvested great bunches of it, to the security guards' amusement.

Badawwar 'ala . . . Now I was looking for that vintage coffee bar, the one with the cloudy mirrors and the countermen in short-sleeve white shirts. I had lost my way in these streets I thought I knew so well. I should have asked directions at the kiosk.

When I finally arrived, half an hour late, Hassan was waiting at a small chrome table, reading the paper. He looked just as I had last seen him thirteen years before, on his roof terrace, swapping jokes with his friend Saad, the desert guide, and laughing his wheezy laugh.

"When I got your email," he said as I sat down, "to be honest, I was not sure who you were. Now I remember — you were friends with Susan!" My roommate, blond and charming and near fluent, had made quite an impression in Egypt. One of our teachers had taken every excuse to praise her and pat her fair skin; the rest of us, duskier and error-prone, she had pinched, squealing *"Hamawwitak!"* — I'll kill you!

Hassan ordered me a coffee and assessed me again. "You look different, really, older," he said, but kindly. I liked this aspect of Egypt, this frankness. Time passed, things changed — there was no way around it.

On closer inspection, Hassan had aged too. He still had a round, boyish face, but his fuzz of hair had turned gray. He had studied in

Belgium, married, had twin boys with his wife, divorced. He had moved out of the apartment with the wonderful rooftop long ago, he said wistfully. Now he lived on the outskirts of the city, on Pyramids Road, to save money; since the revolution, there were few Russian tourists, or any tourists at all, in need of his guidance.

"It's OK," he said, waving away my concern. "I am working also as a journalist now, to write about the revolution." Egyptians had pushed forward an amazing transformation, he said. In the early days of the Tahrir Square sit-in, he had brought his ten-year-old sons, to be sure they witnessed this moment in history.

Later, when regime-funded men charged the square on camelback, wielding whips and Molotov cocktails, Hassan had returned, passing the security cordon with a long-expired medical ID from his days as a dentist. He fought hand-to-hand against the riders, defending the demonstrators and helping the wounded. I had watched the surreal event on TV, never guessing that kind, round-faced Hassan was in the fray. Probably a dozen more *shuhada'* were made that night. The Battle of the Camel, Egyptians had dubbed that clash, both boasting and mocking — it was the same name as a well-known seventh-century battle in Basra, the first civil war in the Islamic empire. Hassan laughed a bit as he related this detail, but his eyes looked tired.

Where's Your Ear?

AHMED SEDDIK PACED the aisle of the tour bus, in showman mode with a microphone in hand. He was introducing each of us, riffing like a free-jazz genius: "Susan! The same as Arabic *sawsan*, lotus flower. When you inhale it, it heals what ails you," he called out with syncopated flair. "Ah, and we have Vivian! She is vivid, and vivacious!"

When I had met Ahmed at the Egyptian Museum a few days earlier, he had handed me a business card that proclaimed him a *Malik kalim* (ملك كلم), in mirror-like Arabic script: a King of Verbiage, a Word Lord, or, to stretch the palindromic effect into English, an Emir of Rhyme. All elbows and ears, he was slight, as though his body existed only to carry around his brain. I had jogged after him through the exhibit halls, trying to keep pace with his Pharaonic etymologies, his mnemonics for hieroglyphs, and his shameless puns.

Now we were headed southwest out of Cairo toward the fertile land of Faiyoum, which the pharaohs had first irrigated with canals more than three thousand years before. It was once the center of an ancient crocodile cult, Ahmed told us, and we would see the ruins of the temple.

Off the bus, he jammed a jaunty wide-brimmed hat on his head — instant Egyptologist. It was high noon. Soldiers with machine guns stood on nearby hills, looking serious about their responsibility to protect us tourists. (For a reason no one could articulate, Faiyoum was officially considered dangerous for foreigners, and had been so for decades.) But when we'd met our military escorts at a checkpoint twenty minutes back, I'd seen that one of them held a gun patched up with string and tape. Ahmed waved merrily and marched us down the trail.

In the afternoon, we drove to the village of Tunis, a hangout for Cairene artists and other bohemians. Our security detail, the soldiers with the taped-together guns, waved our bus down a small lane, where it promptly got stuck. As our driver engaged in minute K-turns, village residents, plus a few goats and a dreamy-eyed water buffalo, trickled in to watch. The soldiers looked on from their jeep, unapologetic.

I took the time to think of palindromes — *gumal mitsha'liba*, somersault phrases. This term I had learned from Hamdi, the husband of an American woman, Melissa, I knew from grad school. Like me, she had come to Cairo in 1997; she had met Hamdi and had lived here ever since. Hamdi was as much of a word freak as exuberant Ahmed the Word Lord, but where Ahmed quoted classical Arabic poetry and Pharaonic texts, Hamdi was entranced with the colloquial language. He had once voluntarily stayed in jail, on a minor drug charge, so he could have more time to collect the colorful stories, songs, and curse words of his fellow prisoners. Since I had told him about my idea to write a book about the joys of learning Arabic, he had been suggesting topics.

"Tell them about the old books with their rhyming titles," he said. Hamdi was an antiques dealer, and he pulled a dusty volume from a stack in his warehouse: *Takhlees al-Ibreez fi Talkhees Bareez*, a nineteenth-century travelogue about the "pure gold" (*ibreez*) of a sojourn in Paris (*Bareez*).

"Tell them about the rhythm of the language — can you mark it in musical notation?" The natural cadence of Arabic could be heard in everyday speech, and Egyptians had elevated Quranic recitation to an art.

"Tell them about the doubled roots." These proliferated in Ammiya, as though Egyptians couldn't resist repeating particularly delectable sounds. Hamdi spun through a few of the juiciest ones: *mishmish,* that impossible apricot; *masmas,* with the suitably chewy, heavy *s,* to suck the meat off a bone; *shibshib,* the Ammiya word for flip-flop or slipper, from its shuffling sound on the floor.

"Tell them about the palindromes . . ." *Himar ramih* (حمار رامح), a jumping donkey. *Walad wa-dalw* (ولد ودلو), a boy and a bucket. And wasn't there something in the Quran about *kullun fi falakin* (كلٌّ في فلكٍ), each in its orbit? The Mamluk historian Ibn Iyas, chronicler of Egypt in the fifteenth century, recalled a quip by the respected judge Qadi al-Fadil, "سر فلا كبت بك الفرس." That is, "*Sir, fa-la kabat bika al-faras*" — Go, and may your horse not fall beneath you. Ahmed and Hamdi both probably knew these, and a dozen more.

After a small lifetime, the driver extricated us from the lane and let the doors wheeze open. We ambled past adobe abodes — no sooner had I thought it than Ahmed the Word Lord said it — and cinder-block structures bedecked with gaudy balustrades. Children trailed behind us, one girl in a party dress and haphazard ponytails. A tractor came trundling along, and Ahmed shooed the children out of the road with a string of synonyms: "*Ya awlad! Ya atfal! Ya abna' wa-banat!*" Even in the face of danger, why say just "Hey, kids!" when there are three ways to say it, each more delightful than the last? They laughed at the living thesaurus and scampered off.

On the bus back to Cairo, I sprawled in my seat, exhausted. Ahmed gave up the microphone but continued to pace the aisle, dispensing wisdom. His conversation steered away from ancient Egypt and toward his other favorite subject, the English language.

A slight German woman was the only person on the bus with more pep than Ahmed. Earlier, she had complained that we were not moving fast enough; now she was determined to keep to our itinerary. "Are we going to see the waterwheels?" she demanded. Faiyoum's historic waterwheels, in various incarnations, had kept the network of canals flowing for thousands of years.

"Do you want to see the waterwheels?" Ahmed replied with a playful grin.

"Are there waterwheels nearby?" she asked.

"Which one would you like to see?" Ahmed countered.

She balled her hands into fists. "Answer my question!" she wailed.

Ahmed, still smiling, could have been Egypt's wise fool, a character called Goha who delights in confounding everyone he encounters. In one fable, someone asks, "*Widnak minein, ya Goha?*" — Where's your ear? With his right hand, Goha reaches up over the top of his head to touch his left ear. In everyday conversation, Egyptians use this question to tell someone to get to the point; the gesture alone, reaching over the head, can telegraph "You're doing it all wrong." If only the German woman had known this — she could have bested Ahmed at his own game, with a wordless retort to his maddening questions. Instead, she groaned and flopped back in her seat.

A British woman commented on Ahmed's English skills. He studied avidly, he told her. "The *Oxford English Dictionary* — it beggars description. It is ineffable!" he said. "With that one book, everything else opens up to you. The Library of Congress, everything."

I had thought the same thing about Arabic, trusting that something so vast could be contained between the covers of a dictionary. My green Hans Wehr was only a fraction of the size of the *OED*, and I had still lost myself in it.

At the edge of the city, our bus idled in a traffic jam. Ahmed quizzed us on English vocabulary words. I stared out the window, too tired to speak but playing along in my head.

Someone cut through Ahmed's swirling wordplay to ask, "What do you *mean*, exactly?" I pictured the soap-opera matron, hands on her hips, and thought, with mild satisfaction, I can say that in Arabic: *Azzzzdak eih bizzzzzabt?* The woman's throaty voice echoed in my head.

"I'm just talking about words," Ahmed replied coolly. For a moment, with his fixed grin and his overlarge ears, he resembled America's own wise fool, Alfred E. Neuman. "Not reality."

In my second week in class, my tired brain slowly recovered from Ahmed overload. Hani energized me with a batch of snappy, real-world adjectives. *Milyan,* read my notebook: fat, fleshy in a good way, "filled out"; *sha'i:* wound up, like a hyperactive toddler; *multazim:* dedicated and on the ball, and its opposite, *nayim fil-'asal:* "sleeping in honey," totally clueless. When the next weekend came, I felt *multazim* enough to leave the city on my own.

I took a local train out of Cairo, headed for a camel market. Ahmed would approve, I thought as I boarded: *qitar,* the word for train, comes from the verb for linking a line of camels together with ropes. The windows were jammed permanently open, and my car was ankle-deep in the split hulls of sunflower seeds. I was the only non-Egyptian on board, and one of the few people not transporting a huge bundle. Children worked their way down the aisle selling plastic toys, safety pins, and more sunflower seeds. The train chugged through the outer neighborhoods, past trash dumps and homely high-rises *in medias res,* bristling with rebar.

We eventually emerged in the lush delta, the area where the Nile bloomed outward — from the sky it would look like a *sawsan,* a lotus blossom. In these acres of river-blessed green, gawky egrets poked at alfalfa and women wrestled with cabbages as big as boulders. Men in the fields watched the train roll by. These were the fellahin, the tillers of Egypt's rich soil, the salt of the earth; in the popular imagination, and as I had seen them twenty years earlier, these men wore the traditional long cotton robes called galabias. Now they stood in ill-fitting T-shirts and trousers, staring vaguely, as if they'd forgotten what they'd come outside to do.

Working his way down the aisle, the conductor did a slapstick double take when he saw me. "*Ya sitt hanim!*" he said with a flourish as he gave me my ticket. His remark — My distinguished lady! — paid respect, but underscored how out of place I was. Sweaty and dust-covered like everyone else, I was nonetheless a relative aristocrat, in still-creased pants fresh from the laundry, a silk shirt, and a jaunty hat. So naturally I was deserving of the old Ottoman honorific *sitt hanim*.

The Ottoman Turks took over Egypt in 1517, and they left their mark on food, clothing, and language. They brought the hookah (*sheesha*), fezzes, and chicken kebabs, or at least the name for them, which Egyptians pronounce *shish tawoo'*. The Ottoman system of honorifics merged with the local one, and although Nasser had officially banned the terms in the 1950s, as part of his populist movement, many remained in circulation. To call a man a *bey* or a *basha* or an *effendi* could be a genuine act of kowtowing or a sarcastic gibe. It was also a conveniently easy joke.

"*Alf shukr, ya bey,*" I told the conductor — A thousand thanks, my good sir. He gave a grin and a half-salute and stepped into the next car.

Off the wheezing train in the village of Birqash, I was still a few miles from the camel market. After a little negotiation with a passing pickup truck, I was lifted into the back, which was already packed with standing passengers. As I clambered in, I snagged a pant leg and ripped it wide open, an eight-inch-long, L-shaped tear from midthigh down. The wind blew cold on my naked knee, and the only other woman on the truck made frantic gestures for me to cover it up.

The woman pulled me down to sit on the truck bed, in a forest of men's legs, and pushed the fabric into place. If only I had bought those safety pins the kid had been peddling on the train. Together the woman and I rooted through my bag for a solution. When I pulled out a long scarf, she grabbed it and, in a few quick moves, tied it like a tourniquet around my knee.

"*Ya bashmuhandis!*" I crowed, and shook her hand. I was paying the conductor's compliment forward with another Turkish-style honorific, *basha* (pasha), plus the Arabic word for engineer. The woman, a sturdy fellaha in her sixties, laughed and tugged at the leg of the man nearest her.

"Did you hear what she called me? A *bashmuhandis!*" she shouted up to him.

Word spread, and soon the whole truck rang with laughter. A man offered me a hand up. "Why are you going to the camel market?" he asked. "Are you an *ustaza*" — a professor — "of camels?"

He was playing the same game, addressing me with the term of respect for learned people, and ribbing me for being foolish enough to come out to this godforsaken place. We'd left the green delta for the desert again; the sky and the earth were the same shade of beige. The truck rolled to a stop in a cloud of dust in front of the market. Good timing, because I had only one more witty riposte.

"No, I'm a *duktoora* of camels!" A PhD in camelology. I mimed turning the page of a book and looking thoughtful as I eyed a nearby specimen of dromedary excellence.

I climbed out of the truck almost as gracelessly as I'd arrived, and walked away with my leg scarf flapping in the breeze. At least I left them laughing.

Later, leaving the market, I bantered in Arabic with a comically eloquent suitor (his pickup line: "Today there are two suns shining on us, because you are so beautiful") and, waiting at the train station, charmed some surly teens by writing their names in English. Their fast, rollicking speech confused me, and a woman sitting with her family on the next bench leaned over and said, "Don't worry, they're teenagers. We can't understand them either." We chatted lightly, eating peanuts, until the train came.

But, as on my ride in the back of the truck, these were fleeting exchanges, love-'em-and-leave-'em moments of wit. After I boarded the train with the family, conversation petered out, and I felt as if I had promised fun I couldn't deliver. The father turned to the stranger next to me and started discussing the military council, which had taken charge of the country following the revolution and was now managing the elections. I couldn't follow. Fluency flickered next to me like the telephone poles outside, ticking by the train window a bit too fast to see clearly.

Days of Rage

HANI STOOD IN front of the class and pulled at his hair, grimacing. "*Mitghaz*." He turned to write on the board: متغاظ, infuriated.

He paced, looking at his watch and scowling. "*Za'alan.*" زعلان, annoyed.

He crossed his arms and glowered. "*Ghadban.*" غضبان, irate.

You could be *mitdayi'* (fed up with) your job, he told us, or *'al'an* (anxious) about your kid not doing well in school. Or *roohak* (your spirit) could be *fi manakheerak* (in your nose) after that jerk pulled his car in front of yours on Arab League Street.

During his performance, I wrote in my notebook a dozen synonyms, plus a sketch of a hand gesture for irritation: hand in a fist below the chin, as though pulling on an invisible beard. This list of words, more than anything I'd heard about the political situation in the past three weeks, made me worried for the future of Egypt. The tear-jerking, nostalgic anthem from my first class with Hani had now given way to the frustration of daily life and the uncertainty of the future.

After his compelling performance of the subtle shades of rage, and his explanation of the situations in which they might come up, Hani turned to me. "Zora, are men in America *mitnerfizeen?*"

Were men in America stressed out? I understood the words, but I couldn't formulate an answer. Was this a question about the role of men in society? Or a question about stress and the economy and social demands? Hani wanted a quick response, not deep content. This was a conversation class, after all, and I was thinking too hard to converse.

"Men in America are *mitnerfizeen*, of course," I began. "And the women too. Some men, some women. The economy, since the year 2008 . . ." I had wandered off into abstract territory and hit a wall, as I couldn't remember the words for unemployment or depression, and couldn't begin to explain the debate over bank bailouts. The awkward pause stretched out while my head spun with ideas I could not express.

Hani broke in. "Men in Egypt are very *mitnerfizeen*, all of them. All the time. We have to make enough money for our children to go to school, and then spend time driving to work in the traffic. We must be sure our children are succeeding. And we also have to make money for our wives to go shopping, and for the bills of their mobile phones!"

At this last sentence, the Danish blonde glared and crossed her arms. "*Izzay bit'ool* 'gender norms'?" she said with a theatrical roll of her ice-blue eyes. "How do you say 'stereotype'?"

Hani looked genuinely confused. "Stereotype? *Ya'ani eih?*" he asked her. What did this word mean?

While they argued, I reviewed the vocabulary Hani had given us. *Mitnerfiz* was the most versatile word, potentially encompassing all the other shades of anger and stress. But it wasn't Arabic; it was derived from the English word "nervous." This was the brilliant root system in action, the ingenious word factory taking raw consonants and spitting out meaning. The vowels had been stripped off and the *v* turned to an *f* (there is no *v* in Arabic), then the consonants squished into the Ammiya adjective pattern. Like any other adjective, it could now take a plural ending: *mitnerfizeen*, like all the men of Egypt. Or it could be feminine: the Danish woman was *mitnerfiza*, because she had let Hani's bluster get under her skin.

Theoretically, Arabic shouldn't have any loan words. The root system, that efficient word factory, should be able to produce all the required vocabulary from local products — that is, innately Arabic letter combinations. Poets had traded on this versatility for centuries, coining words that made sense in context to anyone who grasped the patterns of word formation. If a *muthaqqaf* was a cultured person, then a *mutathaqqaf* (the passive participle of the verb form that connotes doing something temporarily) was a part-time cultured person, a poser.

The word factory had chugged along fine in the early centuries. Then, with the expansion of the Islamic empire, Arabic also expanded into territories where other languages were spoken. In the process, Arabic absorbed vocabulary from Persian, Turkish, and more. Most of these words were, as "nervous" would be later, bent to fit into the root system. In the late nineteenth century, European languages made a sudden, fresh impact, as the French and the British brought foreign technology and concepts to the Arab world. For a few concerted decades, the self-appointed reformers at the Arabic Language Academy in Cairo and the Arab Academy of Damascus attempted to supply native equivalents. But just as the Académie Française couldn't eradicate *le camping* and *le week-end*, the Arabic academies found it hard to make the official coinages stick. By the mid-twentieth century, a guy in his office, talking into his nifty new tape recorder, probably found it easier — and hipper — to say *deekta-foon* (Dictaphone) instead of the stuffy dictionary word *istiktabi* (the asking-someone-to-write-something-thing).

The academy did manage to Arabicize abstract, technical words such as *dimuqratiya* (democracy), *imbiriyaliya* (imperialism), and *ra'smaliya* (capitalism, a rare compound construction combining the words for head and money, to echo the Latin root). With their broader use, concrete nouns such as *tilifizyoon* and *radiyoo* slipped into Arabic relatively unchanged. By the time I enrolled in Hani's class, the academy had long since given up the Sisyphean struggle to keep Arabic "pure." In my Hans Wehr, there was an entry for the aberrant five-consonant root verb *narfaza,* to make nervous.

I met Hassan again, at a downtown *ahwa,* an old coffeehouse where people sucked on *sheesha*s and set their tea on rickety metal tables. It had been his regular place when I first met him in 1998. I was hoping there would be a crowd, and I could ease into Arabic, maybe hear some jokes, test my bantering skills. But when I arrived, Hassan was alone. He had his head down, looking at his phone.

"Look, Zora, here are my sons at the revolution," he said in English. He held the phone out to show me, a wistful half-smile on his round face.

The interim government, headed by the military council, had set dates for elections, a month away, yet the voting system remained opaque. No one was sure who the local candidates were, or where to cast a ballot when the time came. The Muslim Brotherhood's party was getting a lot of press, as was a far-right-wing Islamist crew, the Salafists, who seemed to have appeared out of nowhere, ranting against Israel as well as the Copts, Egypt's Christian minority. My teacher Hani wasn't the only one who was infuriated, annoyed, stressed out. In the three weeks I had been in Egypt, I had noticed a change in mood; the crowds of people out at night seemed more subdued, and I had witnessed two random fistfights. No one had given me a "Yay, democracy!" thumbs-up in a week. Hassan sucked moodily on his *sheesha,* letting the smoke leak out his nose.

"So, what will you do?" I asked him. "What do you think will happen? Can you trust the military?"

"I don't know," he said, his raspy voice trailing off. "But we'll just keep fighting. It's like a video game, when one monster comes, then another, and another . . ." He braced himself in his chair, tucked the *sheesha*'s mouthpiece under his arm, and held his hands up, karate-style, against an invisible opponent. "Now they're releasing the Salafists!"

Hassan's friend Moataza arrived. She was a bird-like woman with a huge mane of black hair and an equally huge Hello Kitty handbag. She was an actress of some repute, Hassan said as we shook hands. "People will recognize her while we are here, you'll see." Moataza spoke fluent English in a soft, high voice; she had been an exchange student in Atlanta.

She too pulled out her phone to flick through photos. In Arabic, nostalgia is expressed as *shawq lil-madi,* a craving for the past, or *haneen lil-madi,* grief for the past. Revolution nostalgia had kicked in, only nine months after the fact. On the faces of Hassan and Moataza—and so many other people I'd noticed huddled around laptops at cafés or standing on street corners peering at phones—I saw the same look of longing and sadness, as they attempted to revive the pure, uncomplicated hope of that time.

The extreme Islamic hard-liners, those Salafists whom Hassan had said he was prepared to fight, had been condemning Egyptian morals. Moataza composed her dainty features, trying to stay positive. "I went to the pub in the Marriott the other night, and it actually made me happy to see so many superficial people, listening to superficial music," she said with a rueful sigh. "Any kind of self-expression now I am so happy to see."

Hassan took a last pull on his *sheesha* and curled the hose around the bowl, readying to leave. He had another appointment.

Moataza invited me to walk with her to Tahrir Square, a few blocks away. It was Friday evening, the night that had become routine for demonstrations, though nothing special had been planned for today. "I just want to see what is happening," she said.

As we emerged on the square, a muscular young man twice Moataza's height sidled up to her. "*Foto?*" he asked, grabbing her roughly by the shoulder and trying to pull her into a pose in front of his phone. She turned on him, holding up her massive handbag as a barrier. "Don't touch me!" she hissed. "I come here as a regular person, not a celebrity." He backed away, spitting insults.

Moataza surveyed the scene on the square, and her face hardened. Clusters of guys idled, hands jammed in their pockets and shoulders hunched against the cool weather that had finally arrived with October. These were not the inspiring *shabab* of the revolution, aglow with solidarity and revolutionary ideals. These were *shabab* as defined in my old personal dictionary: aimless, frustrated, aggressive. A few roasted-nut sellers pushed their painted carts, the little chimneys on them puffing smoke, but no one was buying.

"Let's go, Zora. This is not nice," Moataza said softly, sadly. "This is people out for a picnic."

After dinner a few days later, a journalist friend checked his phone, and his face clouded. "Five dead at protests," he read aloud from his messages. "Watch yourself."

Violent protests? Where? People streamed by, belying the message and whisking away its menace. The sidewalks teemed with activity as on any other night. Vendors shilled flimsy lingerie and fresh dates, football jerseys and paperback books, cheap wigs and motley-hued headscarves. I bade my friend goodnight and started toward the metro, picking my way around the vendors.

At 26th of July Street, I heard a clamor many blocks to my left, in the direction of the Supreme Court building. A cloud of dust made it impossible to see. I was tempted to gawk, but before I had left New York, I had solemnly vowed to my family that I would never walk toward a demonstration. I had already cheated by going to Tahrir Square on a Friday with Moataza — never mind there had been nothing going on. I took a right turn, putting my back to the noise.

From behind rose more shouting, closer this time. Then the pounding of feet: men were running past, down the middle of the empty avenue. Then came one panicked driver, tires squealing as he reversed crazily away from the dust cloud.

It was not dust, I saw as I turned to look again. It was smoke. I stopped, along with all the regular shoppers out on regular strolls, and together we stared down the street. Cairo was often described as chaotic, but there was an underlying system to its churning energy. Now that system had stumbled to a halt, and a chill had settled over the empty street. True chaos was somewhere up the road, behind that smoke screen.

"*Fee eih?*" a woman near me cried, a most basic question—literally "What is there?"—that really meant, "Is there something wrong that I should know about?" In a soap opera, it would have been the neighborhood gossip lady's first line, a form of friendly prying. On the edge of this eerie scene, it was a plaintive expression of fear.

Some men running past shouted, "*Ag-geish, ag-geish!*" The army. In Hassan's video game of the revolution, the Salafists were midlevel zombies, scary but slow-moving. The army was the most dreaded beast, the highest level, the battle no one wanted to fight. I crossed to the side street, toward the metro entrance, to get out of the way. More men were running out of the smoke cloud.

Two teenage boys stopped next to me to catch their breath. One, his arms damp with sweat despite the cool night air, noticed me gazing up the street. His eyebrows arched high, his eyes widened for emphasis, as he loudly *tsk*ed, that wordless "no."

"Go there," he said in English, pointing down the stairs to the metro. "Safe." A long, searching pause. I recognized that pause, from my *mitnerfiz* freeze in class: there was more to say, but how to say it?

Finally he said, "Revolution." Not jubilant, only practical. This was the long-term reality, beyond the initial eighteen days of unity; Egypt was now in a steady, slow-burning battle. The boys turned and ran on, and I went down the stairs to the metro.

On the train, I took a seat in the women's car, where all was calm. I knew some terrible news, but I couldn't tell anyone because I wasn't sure what I'd seen. Would I say *thawra* (revolution)? Or *fawda* (chaos)? To soothe myself, I let my gaze skip across the serene faces of the women around me. Nearly every one was framed in a neatly arrayed headscarf, or in several stacked in layers. An apple-cheeked girl wore hers "Spanish style," knotted at the nape of the neck, like the poor but plucky heroine of an old Egyptian movie. A trim woman with a toddler wore a tightly wrapped tiger-print scarf, continuing the theme from her sequined Garfield sweatshirt. The only woman in the car wearing a full-face veil also sported black nail polish and a punkish silver-studded bag.

The train doors opened, snapping me out of my fashion reverie; I remembered the panic on that downtown street. Something very big, possibly very awful, was happening, but my walk home gave no clues as to what it was. I had expected to see knots of men gathered in coffeehouses discussing the news or gathered around TVs, but the sidewalks and cafés were no more crowded than usual. At my apartment, the Internet wasn't working, as sometimes happened. I crawled into bed, wondering if I had imagined it all.

In the morning, I learned that twenty-seven demonstrators, most of them Coptic Christians, had been killed by the Egyptian army and a crowd of vigilantes. Reporters on the state-run television station had summoned the mob, calling upon loyal Egyptians to "defend" the troops. It was by far the worst violence of the revolution. The words Hani had taught us welled up in me: anger, frustration, worry. Meanwhile, the sun shone, the traffic jammed, all as usual. Cairo was so big, it swallowed tragedy whole.

Hidden Fingers

A WEEK AFTER the fatal demonstration, I sat on a breezy apartment terrace with a group of resident American journalists, as well as Hamdi, the antiques dealer who had taught me about palindromes, and his wife, Melissa. The sun had set; the weather was balmy. It would have been the perfect setting for a little Hassan-style Arabic banter, some Egyptian empty talk, had the specter of needless death not hung over our conversation.

We were still trying to be lighthearted. Hamdi had rolled a joint, and it made its way around the circle. We sipped beers from big green bottles.

"Did you see the Bassem Youssef show this week?" said a lanky American woman. "The one where he went off on the 'hidden fingers'? That was a great one!"

"Hidden fingers"—unnamed, external meddling forces—were what the military council blamed for the deaths at the Coptic demonstration, and the comedian Bassem Youssef was having none of it. With a perpetually cocked eyebrow, Youssef, a heart surgeon turned

TV personality, had been commenting on the revolution since the spring. Even in the context of Egypt's longstanding love of humor, Youssef's style of explicit, cutting political satire was something new. In the past, criticism of the regime and its allies had been bundled almost entirely in structured jokes, little parables told in the third person: "Mubarak, Netanyahu, and Yeltsin are on a plane . . ." The jokes were sardonic, distancing, and ultimately powerless.

But during the revolution, the demonstrators had spoken directly to Mubarak, brandishing signs in the imperative. Hamdi, collector of colloquial wisdom, had particularly liked the ones held by children: *Leave, Already — I Have to Pee!* and *Pwease Weave, I Hafta Go Home!* Bassem Youssef was the ultimate expression of this new revolutionary humor. He was on satellite television for an hour nearly every night, staring straight into the camera and saying precisely what he thought.

On the "hidden fingers" episode, Youssef delivered a long, sarcastic rant against the military council's feeble excuses. Behind him, a trio of men in black echoed him spookily every time he said "hidden fingers." By repeating the phrase, Youssef made it sound as absurd in Arabic as it did in English translation.

"Ooooh, hidden fingers!" the American woman said, waggling hers in the light that slanted onto the balcony from the living room, and the rest of us cracked up. The exception was Hamdi, the one Egyptian among us. Hamdi was normally the gregarious one, the life of the party, telling stories in his cigarette-scraped voice. Now he had sunk low in his chair, and from the shadows he growled, "Bassem Youssef should go to hell. He is not appropriate now."

We turned toward him, in the darkest corner of the balcony.

"What do you mean? *Bass,* he's funny, *ya'ani!*" Melissa said. She and Hamdi had lived together so long, they alternated Arabic and English phrases without noticing.

Hamdi hoisted himself up and into the light. His wicker chair protested as he leaned on the arms. "By the way, don't you know people *died?*" he said, slowly and forcefully. "This is not a time for comedy and jokes!"

He glared at us, but something about his phrasing — and the weed we had smoked — sent us into peals of laughter.

"*By the way,* we know people died," the American journalist said when we were quiet again. "But isn't that just when we need the jokes?"

"*By the way,* she's right," Melissa said, reaching out to soothe Hamdi, who had slumped back in the shadows. "We're not making fun of the people who died. It's good to laugh and relieve the stress."

I could see why Hamdi was angry. Not only were we Americans lecturing an Egyptian on the value of humor, but the military council's brutality revealed a bitter truth: Egyptians had lost the power they'd held in the early days of the revolution. Or perhaps it had been an illusion and they'd never had it at all.

Although my husband, Peter, had visited Egypt several times before and was generally a happy, flexible, and uncritical traveler, he had never shared my fondness for the country. Now he was coming for a short stay, unfortunately just as political gloom had settled over Cairo. I decided we should take a weekend trip to the Coptic monasteries at Wadi Natrun. Perhaps in leaving the city, Peter might see another side of Egypt to appreciate.

At the Wadi Natrun bus stop, we were met by a battalion of Egypt's newest form of transport, the *tok-tok*. The parts came from India and the name from Thailand, but the cheap auto rickshaws had become, in a few short years, a common sight in the Egyptian landscape. The drivers, always teenage boys, souped up their *tok-toks'* beetle-black shells in ingenious ways, to resemble a Darth Vader mask, for instance, or a helicopter. My Badawi dictionary told me the verb *taktik* meant to tick or to jiggle the phone for a connection; years hence, it might be updated to include a new meaning, derived from *tok-tok:* to make the sound of a two-stroke engine, perhaps, or to pilot a vehicle without a license. Peter and I chose our ride by the best decoration, a slogan stuck on the windshield in dripping-blood letters: *Need Fur Speed.*

We squeezed into the cab, bags on our laps, and the kid gunned the motor and cranked the speakers behind our heads. "It's Amr Haha!" I told Peter. Haha was the musical sensation that fall—not the usual slick pop star, but a lower-class kid whose tight, flat beats seemed to be designed for cheap speakers. As one of the Arab world's texting youth, he preferred to spell his name "3mr 7a7a," employing the trendy chat alphabet in which numbers stood in for Arabic's unique sounds when thumb-typing on Latin keypads. One of DJ 7a7a's most popular lyrics tweaked a Fusha revolutionary chant. In 7a7a's Ammiya anthem, the people did not want the fall of the regime; the people wanted five pounds' phone credit. "And it's even better than the original slogan," I told Peter, my captive audience in the *tok-tok*, "because it rhymes!"

Peter was unmoved. He peered glumly out at sand-caked weeds and cinder-block buildings. The only signs of life in Wadi Natrun were occasional clusters of kids on the roadside, who broke into flailing dance moves when DJ 7a7a's beats washed over them. Our *tok-tok* deposited us at our hotel, a collection of shaky-looking huts edging a moat dotted with potato-chip bags and other trash. Peter looked wary; I pointed to the pristine blue swimming pool in the center.

Soon the owner appeared. He was a stout, affable man in a chambray shirt and a leather adventurer's hat. He introduced himself as the General, shook our hands warmly, and showed us to our hut, relating his story to us in smooth English. He had traveled around Africa; he'd designed the hotel himself, inspired by tourist lodges in Kenya. Exercising his right as a police officer, he had claimed the land from a local Bedouin family.

At this last fact Peter's eyes widened. I was startled too. In my little social pocket in Cairo, it was easy to believe everyone favored the revolution. Yet here, in the flesh, was a representative of the old system and its institutionalized corruption—the real "hidden fingers" that were stalling progress in Egypt.

"And have you seen the mosque I built?" the General asked, gesturing to a mud-brick structure on the far side of the property. It was elegant, but it towered over the Coptic village. "Look," I said to Peter gamely, "those holes on the top of the minaret make it look like the dovecotes you see everywhere around here."

In Cairo, I only noticed Coptic identity in an occasional cross on a chain around the neck, or a glimpse of a blue tattoo on the inside of a wrist. A young girl on the street once asked me my religion, and when I answered Christian, she turned my arm to look at my wrist, puzzled that I had no cross there. Here at the Wadi Natrun monasteries, though, some people wore their Christianity with gothic flair: large gold crucifixes set in cleavage, forearm tattoos of the Virgin Mary. A man with oiled hair sported a denim jacket with an icon hand-painted on the back, framed in metal studs.

Peter and I joined the crowd trying to enter a tiny gate in a very thick wall. Midway, the passage jammed. I felt like I was back on the bus in Faiyoum, as if I might be forever stuck in time and place.

Copts, roughly 10 percent of the population of Egypt, consider themselves the first Christians, converted when Mary and Joseph fled to Egypt with the Christ child to escape King Herod. When the Arabs conquered Egypt in the seventh century, Coptic was the dominant language. By the twelfth century it had receded to use primarily in church, where it stayed. But in those critical centuries in between, the language acted as a vessel, carrying the ancient tongue of the pharaohs, from which Coptic derived, into the Arab era. The most essential Ammiya word, *aywa* (yes), came from Coptic; so did more specific words, especially for plants (*barseem*, clover), animals (*balshoon*, heron), agricultural miscellany (an *ardabb* measured 198 liters), even bodily functions (*gees,* a noisy fart). Some Pharaonic-via-Coptic words spread all over the Arab world: *timsah* (crocodile), *waha* (oasis), *bisara* (cooked beans), and, according to some linguists, *haram* (pyramid). *Tooba,* the Coptic word for brick, traveled farther, to Andalusia, where it became "adobe," and on to the American Southwest, where it became a style.

Inside the monastery walls, the crowds thinned slightly, and everywhere wafted the smell of feet in nylon socks—as in mosques, everyone removed their shoes before entering the chapels. As we paused by an icon of a gray-haired saint, adorned in a dickey, striped like King Tut's headdress, a crew of schoolgirls spotted us, the only foreigners in the room. "Hello! How-are-you. Welcome-to-Egypt," the head girl chirped in careful classroom English. "My name is Maryam. What's-your-name?" I enunciated back, then saw a line forming, two dozen girls, each wanting to introduce herself in turn. Fortunately, a teacher intervened, and Peter and I swam against the human tide to the chapel door.

"*Dimeera* is another Ammiya word from Coptic," I told him when we were safely in the parking lot. "It means the season of the flood."

Back at the hotel, Peter and I attempted a moonlight walk. On one horizon, industrial silos glowed orange; we headed the other direction, into a dusty field, squinting up at the hazy sky in search of stars. "I don't know how you can like this place," Peter said, kicking up a puff of sand with his foot. "You need more than rose-colored glasses. You need rose-colored cataracts."

I gingerly skirted a withered garden plot. All the cultural tidbits I'd shared with Peter over the day seemed irrelevant here on this rough seam where civilization hit the desert. The problem wasn't just the General, swaggering in and claiming the land. How was anything supposed to change or grow in this harsh environment? How could a revolution stay united amid such entropy?

Behind us, car wheels crunched in the driveway. People were bundling out of a caravan of SUVs, chattering excitedly and carrying bags and boxes. Two puppies raced in circles, barking.

The General spotted us and waved us toward the house. "It is my granddaughter's birthday," he said when we stepped, somewhat reluctantly, into the circle of yellow light. "She is four years old today. Please, join us in the Bedouin tent."

Inside the black tent — "probably where the original Bedouin owners lived," hissed Peter — the General's son was fiddling with some electrical cords. In a minute, the film *Mamma Mia!* appeared, projected onto a white sheet. The irresistible beat of Abba filled the air, the General's daughter passed around finger sandwiches, and four generations settled into the cushions, tapping their toes.

We took an intermission for birthday cake. The General, who had swapped his desert explorer gear for a festive striped shirt, personally delivered slices to us.

"So, are you happy?" he asked.

How had he known we were in a funk? Could he have noticed our discomfort when we arrived? Or Peter's dismay after our stroll in the moonlight? No, the General had only literally translated a routine, casual question — *Inta mabsoot?* — that Egyptians use to ask how you're doing. Whenever I heard it in Arabic, I did the same, which gave the question an existential gravity: *am* I happy, *really?*

I caught Peter's eye, and he smiled over his fluffy white cake. "*Aywa*," I told the General in my finest Coptic turned Ammiya. "We're happy."

Yet perhaps there was something deeper in the General's question. Maybe he had meant it less for us than for himself, in this uncertain time. He had turned back to the screen, where Meryl Streep was frozen in midstep. "Whenever I feel depressed," he said, "I watch this movie. And then I feel much better."

Illuminating the House

MEDO AND I were late for lunch at his mother's house. He had insisted on picking me up downtown and driving back to his house in Heliopolis, a few miles away but now approaching an hour in the afternoon traffic. He had settled his lanky frame in for the long haul, leaning way back in his seat, one hand draped casually on the steering wheel.

"Medo, how do you say 'cool'?" We were in the habit of speaking English together, but I resolved to ask him for Arabic help. Slang was a gaping hole in my education, because for the most part, my Arabic teachers had been distinctly uncool. And what little I had learned from them had become irrelevant in almost fifteen years. This was a drawback to putting too much effort into Ammiya—unlike Fusha, it was always shifting.

"Gaaaaamid," Medo said, drawling the word with appreciation. Nice—it meant frozen. So, not just cool, but ice cold.

"Know what's *gamid*?" he asked, flashing his braces conspiratorially and raising his eyebrows above his black aviator shades. "The movie *The Fast and the Furious*. Whenever I watch it, I drive like crazy." Medo had gotten his license only nine months before.

The traffic loosened slightly, and Medo weaved between cars. "Do they do this in America?" he asked. His hands still loose on the steering wheel, he was veering almost randomly and looking over to see my reaction. I willed myself not to grip the door handle. "Egyptians don't believe in lanes!" He laughed as he settled back down, but his laughter had a bitter edge.

Medo and I had met because he was constantly reaching beyond Egypt's borders. In Egypt, everywhere he looked, he saw evidence of a country fallen apart. He seemed to keep an internal balance sheet: reasons to stay, reasons to go. Cairo drivers could fit in either column.

"OK, so, *gamid*. Thanks," I said. "And do people still say *wi-nuss?*" This was an emphatic expression my matronly Ammiya teacher had taught me my first summer in Cairo. *Wi-nuss* was an intensifier that meant "and a half," as in, "This coffee is delicious . . . and a half!"

"No way! No one says that anymore." Medo snorted as only hyper-confident youth can.

We entered a traffic circle, its center island crammed with notices for candidates in the upcoming parliamentary election. Hand-painted banners sagged down over photos of candidates, and posters were jumbles of words, names, and symbols. These icons, assigned more or less randomly to each political party, were meant to aid the illiterate in voting. They also added a surreal note to the campaigns: *Vote Toothbrush! Up with Basketball Hoop! Support Bunch of Grapes!*

Medo rolled his eyes as we inched around the circle. Even at this speed, the signs were hard to read. "This is a mess," he said. "This is not how other countries do it. These things should be comfortable for the eyes."

"So who are you going to vote for?" I asked.

"I don't know—I haven't registered yet," he said. "I might not even vote." The traffic stalled again. Since 1922, when Egypt gained independence from the British, the country had ostensibly operated as a democracy, but under each subsequent regime, elections had grown ever more symbolic and corrupt. Egyptians had long since stopped pretending their votes had any bearing on reality, and Medo was skeptical that the current revolution had changed the system. After another minute, he said, "OK, this might surprise you, but I'll vote for the Muslim Brotherhood."

All the other Egyptians I knew were firmly behind the secular reformers. Hassan, Moataza, even Hamdi, who had railed against Bassem Youssef and his satire, loved to mock the Islamists who were popping up all over the television, two weeks before the election. One night, when a prissy bearded man was lecturing on a TV talk show about the virtues of patience, Hamdi had shouted, "He must have *zibeeb* on his knees!" A *zibeeba* (raisin) was a dark forehead callus men developed, supposedly from praying; the mark had become quite popular in the past decade, though many Egyptians considered it an ostentatious display of piety, probably touched up with dirt or ash.

But as discontented as Medo seemed, he didn't have the cynical edge of my older, secular friends — nor did he have the *zibeeba* that the secularists might have assumed any Brotherhood booster would have. "The Brothers deserve it," he said. "They have been fighting for this for decades." Indeed, the Muslim Brotherhood was dogged and organized. Hamdi had shown me the slick brochures the group was distributing door-to-door. Its party, called Freedom and Justice, was assigned the inspiring ballot symbol of a set of scales.

After an hour and a half in the car, we pulled up in front of a school to collect Medo's sisters, Sara and two younger girls. As he steered toward the curb, Medo showed his first flash of irritation with the traffic. "I hate being late," he grumbled, his hand tightening around the steering wheel. "They shouldn't have to wait like this." I cringed, thinking of how late I had been to meet him and Sara at Starbucks.

Sara said hello as she climbed in, smiling shyly. Her younger sisters politely extended their hands in introduction. "I am Esraa," said one. "And I am Yousraa," said the other. The three girls, with their names spelled with the same trio of letters, were the Arabic root system in the flesh. Their names formed a matched set, a bit like the Arabic equivalent of Faith, Hope, and Charity.

At their building, we climbed a dusty, half-open stairwell to the apartment. Just as at the dentist's office — and in almost every building I had ever visited in the Middle East — the appearance of the entryway gave no indication of the quality of the interior. We walked into a spotless living room, set with curvaceous, gilt-edged, overstuffed furniture. This homegrown French-salon style was immensely popular in Cairo; Egyptians jokingly called it Louis Farouk, a nod to the glitzy tastes of the last king of Egypt.

When Medo had said, "Come to my mom's for lunch," I had pictured a kindly, gray-haired lady in an apron, rolling grape leaves with gnarled fingers. But of course Medo was much younger than me, which meant his mom was about my age. A pretty flower-print scarf framed her wide, smooth face, and a navy-blue robe gracefully draped her sturdy frame. She embraced me warmly.

"Her name is Neveen," Medo said. "In Arabic, you spell that the same backwards and forwards." By now he knew I liked these details.

"You illuminate our house," Neveen said by way of welcome. A lovely Form II hollow verb, I thought — from *nara*, to light up, made transitive by doubling the second letter in the root: *nawwara*. Then my mind went blank. Teachers didn't use that fusty old Roman-numeral verb chart anymore, I'd found out from Dr. Badawi. And grammatical analysis was not a conversation starter. Desperate, I fished in my brain and found first-day-of-class basics. What were the objects in the room? What could I say about them?

"The cat beautiful," I said haltingly, eyeing the fluffy white Persian on the seat next to me. Cairo crawled with tough street cats, but pampered house pets were not common; this one, sprawled on emerald-green velvet, was a living luxury. Neveen, perched on her own plump green chair, smiled. It was a start.

Above the sofa hung a finely rendered painting of a Chinese-style landscape on silk. "That beautiful too," I told Neveen.

"She painted it!" Medo piped up from behind me. "And those too!" He pointed at other framed pieces around the room, delicate flowers and graceful willows. Neveen smiled again, but looked down at her hands.

"*Mashallah*," I hurried to add, catching Medo's eye.

He had taught me this phrase too — or rather, its significance. "You don't believe in envy in America, do you?" he had asked, as though envy were some sort of universal force. "Here it is a big thing, a real thing. So we always say *mashallah*" — by the grace of God. Uttered after any compliment or mention of good fortune, the phrase dispelled envy and encouraged gratitude. Yet this simple bit of politeness had never come up in any of my college or grad-school classes; we had been too busy discussing grammar rules or social issues. After talking with Medo, I heard *mashallah* everywhere, punctuating every conversation. I hated to think how many social occasions I had blundered through, oblivious to the most basic ways of making a good impression.

Neveen led us to the table. As she introduced each dish, Medo removed the cover with a flourish: *mahshi*, tiny stuffed eggplants, peppers, and grape leaves; *ru'a'*, wedges of flaky pastry with meat; *batta*, roast duck, atop rice studded with duck liver and almonds; and *mulukhiya*, the essential Egyptian green, cooked up in a silky, garlicky stew.

In Hani's class we had recently practiced the various ways of communicating preferences. "I love all of these foods," I said carefully as I readied my knife and fork over my plate, "but duck is my favorite."

Neveen clapped at my statement. "You express yourself very well," she said with some relief. In the car, Medo had told me she was afraid we wouldn't understand each other.

My expression of preference may have been grammatically sound, but in terms of eating a reasonable-size lunch, it was a terrible mistake. Neveen leaned over and put a whole second duck leg on my plate.

I ate enthusiastically as Neveen beamed with pride. But soon the girls had polished off their modest portions, and then Neveen was done. Medo too. The girls carried their plates to the kitchen, and before I understood what had happened, I was sitting alone at the table.

What to do? If I walked into the kitchen with my half-finished plate, would they shoo me back to the table with a fresh round of blandishments to eat? Would I look ungrateful? While I weighed my options, I ate a few more bites. I was painfully full, but, I consoled myself, I might never be offered such good Egyptian food again, and tomorrow I would be sorry I hadn't eaten more. Finally Medo came to rescue me. "That's fine," he said gently. "It is not going to waste." His mother had put in so much work for my visit — but really, a guest was an excuse to make a lot of food. The family would enjoy the leftovers for days.

Medo gave me a tour of the rest of the small apartment, and we all settled in the girls' room, its walls a rich French blue that Sara, the eldest sister, had chosen. Over lunch, she had mentioned that she painted too, as her mother did. And now, while the rest of us sat on the twin beds, she pulled a stack of canvases from behind a desk and unwrapped the top one.

I was expecting something emotionally transparent, some expression of teenage drama. Instead, the canvas showed a lush landscape, with a bridge arching over a river and birds flitting in the sky. Sara's teacher gave them paintings to copy, she explained, and graded them on accuracy.

How narrow my experience in Egypt had been, I saw, as Sara displayed each new landscape. In college and graduate school, I had surrounded myself with people like me: my age, my political leanings, my aesthetics and religious skepticism. Without knowing I was doing it, I had followed Dr. Badawi's counsel, learning the language of one's equivalent in the foreign culture — but if I had stayed in academia, I might never have stepped out of that comfort zone. Instead, in my new, admittedly scattershot approach to Arabic, I was so desperate to converse that I'd talk to anyone, even a guy half my age who loved Vin Diesel movies. And thanks to this, I had ended up here, with him and his delightful family.

Sara gently unwrapped her last, and favorite, painting. It was not a landscape like the others, but a Spanish dancer, her back arched dramatically and a scarf cascading off her shoulder. She showed me the photograph she had worked from, clipped from a magazine. It was a literal likeness, but Sara's dancer pulsed with life.

"You have given your daughter your talent," I said to Neveen, who sat on the bed opposite. While Sara and Esraa worked together to wrap up the paintings, Neveen and I chatted directly in Arabic. She had studied law and English in college, but because she was the only daughter in her family, her father had wanted to see her married and starting a family right after graduation. She asked if I had worked my whole life. "Between you and me," she said wistfully, "I would have liked to have worked a little."

The twilight call to prayer sounded outside the bedroom window. I looked up and remembered Sara and Medo and the younger girls — I had been so focused on understanding Neveen that I had briefly forgotten about them. It was time to make my goodbyes. Neveen presented me with one of her own paintings, a small flower on satin. "I have so many!" she said with a little roll of her eyes. The girls were putting on their white headscarves to say their prayers, and Neveen nudged Medo as he readied to leave with me. "You need to pray too!" she said. "Do it as soon as you come back."

Medo escorted me to the bus stop — our long ride earlier had satisfied his driving urge. "How do you say 'nap' in Arabic?" I asked him as we walked. I'd spent so much time sleeping in the afternoon heat here, yet never learned the word for it. And I really needed a nap now, after my heavy lunch and sustained Arabic conversation.

"No special word in Egypt," Medo said. "But I've heard Gulf Arabs say *qailoola*. Isn't that a nice word?"

I said it back to him, relishing the delicate little coughing *qaf* at the start and the cute long *oo* sound, and we smiled at each other. Medo hadn't struck me as the sort of guy who cared about the relative niceness of words, or how his mother's name was a palindrome. Maybe every Arabic speaker had a little bit of that wordplay urge — or Medo was more my local equivalent than he seemed.

Graduation Day

CLASS WITH HANI was fun, but by the fourth and final week I had slipped into old bad habits: arriving late, spacing out when Hani reviewed things I already knew, and generally failing to play along with the polite fiction of class conversation. On the last day, I shook Hani's hand and took my flimsy "diploma" with relief to be done with the strictures of school.

Afterward, I wandered down to the Agriculture Museum, one of my favorite places in Cairo. It was a colonial time capsule, a museum that itself should have been in a museum, full of molting taxidermy, complex hand-drawn charts, and cobwebbed waxworks. Shuffling from vitrine to vitrine felt like browsing an archaic dictionary. One case contained all the varieties of bread made in Egypt, slowly turning to crumbs; another displayed wax models of thirteen varieties of pomegranate, arranged by size, each in its own pink plastic bowl. In front of a display of dates, I murmured their names, each as luscious as the fruit itself: *wardi* (rosy), *zaghlool* (squab), *aboo taweela* (big long guy).

I heard voices approaching. A family was making their way slowly along from the other end of the museum. We crossed paths in a room dedicated to cotton processing, and the three kids stared at me as if I too were an exhibit. Then we went our separate ways — they to the scale models of grain threshers, and I to the presentation of the Coptic months, each with a rhyming proverb.

A guard, an old man in a long galabia, appeared at my side and read for me, tracing the letters with a bony finger: "*Toot, hat al-'antoot.*" In Tut, the time of planting after the Nile's ebb, bring the plow. "*Baramhat, rooh al-gheet wi-hat.*" In Baramhat, the harvest season, go to the field and bring the bounty. Then, as though picking up a conversation we'd left off an hour before, he told me he feared the new government would be no different from the old when it came to helping Egypt's poor.

Near closing time, I walked out of the halls of eroding knowledge. It was a glittering, cool, and clear November afternoon, but I was overcome with sadness. So much had been lost, and was still being lost. In the twenty-first century, Egyptians grew only a few hardy strains of mango; bread now was mostly the standard, dark rounds sold by subsidized bakers, which was all anyone could afford. Soon Egypt's rich variety — and all the words for it — would live only in this museum.

As I headed toward the exit gate, I saw the family I had passed inside. They were having a picnic on the lawn.

"*Yalla itghaddi ma'ana!*" the mother called. Come eat lunch with us. I suppose I should have made at least one polite no-thank-you gesture, put my hand on my heart, and made to walk on. But I was hungry, and they looked so vibrant and happy.

They scooted around to make room in their circle, and the mother laid out a hand towel for me to sit on. Then she loaded up a plate for me: a jiggly wedge of pasta casserole and a whole leg and thigh of roast chicken.

Her name was Hoda. Attef was her balding husband, in a dapper plaid shirt and nylon windbreaker, and it was his forty-eighth birthday. To celebrate, Hoda had taken the day off from her job at the ministry of health, and their three children had skipped school. Mohamed, the eldest at age twelve, was studying agriculture. While Hoda talked, I nodded and ate, restraining myself from commenting on the succulence of the chicken, the richness of the casserole. By withholding praise, I was determined not to repeat the mistake I'd made with Medo's mother and her roast duck.

Dressed in a long black headscarf and a robe trimmed with a few discreet rhinestones, Hoda was a natural charmer. "Last year I did the 'umra" — the so-called minor pilgrimage to Mecca, a less strenuous alternative or addition to the haj that can be done at any time of year — "and I was scared at first to go alone," she told me. "But in the end, I met so many new friends!"

I could see why. With her big brown eyes rimmed in black liner and her easy conversation, she made me feel as if we were in the habit of meeting every week to share a picnic lunch.

With great resolve, I left a tiny bit of casserole uneaten and some shreds of chicken, so as not to provoke a second monster helping. "You like our Egyptian food?" Hoda asked, inspecting my plate.

"Of course I do!" I answered. "I'm a *bint al-balad*." This little phrase had recently popped into my head, on one of my walks down memory lane. A "daughter of the land" was a true Egyptian, a plucky native. It was a decent joke, as I was looking especially foreign that day, with a camera and a big sun hat.

Hoda burst out laughing. She tapped Attef on the knee and said, "Did you hear that? She's like us! *Dammaha khafeef!*"

Telling someone she has "light blood" might not sound flattering, but in Egyptian terms it was the very praise I had been craving. To possess, if only for a moment, the easy, bubbly jocularity Egyptians prized — it was proof I had made real progress, not just in this short time in Cairo, but from my previous life here. Back then, I had been a ball of language anxiety; now I was a light-blooded wit who could banter with total strangers. While gnawing on a chicken leg, no less.

As a bonus, I *got* Hoda's jokes. "Take these glasses and wash them," she told the children, pointing to a nearby water fountain. "And iron them!" she called after, as though giving orders to the neighborhood laundry man. The kids rolled their eyes—they'd heard that one before.

Hoda and Attef implored me to come to lunch at their house another day, but I was nearing the end of my trip. We swapped phone numbers, and the kids drew me a picture of airplanes, palm trees, and a city skyline with the lotus-like Cairo Tower to one side and the Pyramids to the other. "WE LOVE YOU!!!" they wrote in English.

Jubilant, I replayed the conversation in my head as I left the museum grounds. *I had made them laugh! I had light blood!* I folded the drawing and tucked it in my notebook. This was the diploma I'd *really* earned.

I saw Hassan one last time, the night before I left Cairo. We met at a club to see a Nubian singer he and his friends all knew. Hassan looked a bit more cheerful this time, laughing his wheezy laugh. The political situation hadn't changed. For now he was in a holding pattern in the video game.

I sat quietly in the circle of his friends, trying to find a thread in the Arabic chitchat. Ibrahim, a dark-skinned man with close-cropped curly hair, told a joke about a half-wit house servant. It wasn't the greatest joke, but I followed his every word, which made me instantly fond of him.

A little while later, I found myself seated next to Ibrahim in a booth while Hassan and the others milled around greeting friends. Our conversation was going fine, as he explained the deal he had made with his wife regarding child care, which enabled him to be out on a Tuesday night. Then it was my turn to speak. I stammered and froze, tried too-complex grammar, and blanked on basic words. My brain, in anticipation of departure, had given up.

"We can speak English," Ibrahim said—kindly enough, but I still winced. In that second, I felt I hadn't made any progress in Arabic at all.

The lights dimmed and the curtain sprang up on a seven-piece band crammed in a tiny box of a stage. Ibrahim leaned over and said, "It's like *The Mubbet Show,* right?"

Arabic has no *p* sound, which creates such things as Jaban-built trucks, the glamorous Banorama Salon, a society magazine called *Barty.* Ibrahim's Muppets reference was spot-on: the band did conjure an "It's time to light the lights" energy.

"Yeah, and we're Statler and Waldorf," I quipped. Ibrahim cocked his head, questioning. "You know, the old guys in the back," I said. The cantankerous critics who lobbed comments from the balcony were my favorite Mubbets.

"*Never* be the old guys in the back!" Ibrahim whooped, then elbowed me out of the banquette and up to dance. Nearby, a small commotion arose around an agile dancer working his way through the crowd. As he shimmied closer, I saw it was Saad, the legendary desert guide, the party conductor, the man whose jokes I had understood so well at the party on Hassan's roof, thirteen years earlier. He looked exactly the same: dark-skinned, a bit cross-eyed. Did he have gray hair? Maybe a little pudginess? I couldn't see well in the dim light and the clouds of cigarette smoke, but it didn't matter. I waved at Saad through the crowd; he grinned and waved back. Like Hassan, he probably remembered me less than I remembered him, but that didn't matter either.

It felt as if barely an hour had passed since I had last lived here. I had stepped out for a second, been distracted by some other things—New York, a job, a husband—but back in Cairo, at this moment at least, the party was still going on.

Oh, but my aching hip! I had not tried to dance this way in years. The awkward movement, not quite on the beat, nonetheless brought back good phrases. *Kan ya ma kan, fi 'adeem az-zaman* ("There was or there wasn't, back in the old days," as all the fairy tales begin in

Arabic), I had danced in the disco at the Nile Hilton, on Hassan's rooftop, and in my fellow students' grand old palace of an apartment. This scene was *zayy zaman,* like the old days.

The crowd sang call-and-response with the curly-haired frontman. For a minute I didn't worry about what language to speak or where I fit in; my earlier stumble into English with Ibrahim was forgotten. I danced, warmed by the hum of the singer's voice, the sawing fiddle, the *tet-tet-tet* of the hand drum.

When I had lived here, Cairo had been a backdrop for my drama. I had worried about my future, about what people thought of me when I opened my mouth. Once, I'd been so sick that I couldn't leave the bathroom floor, and I thought I'd grown old overnight. Now I was much closer to "old," by some world standards, but I felt so much better, so much more sure of everything. I had embarked on a grand project to revive my old life in Arabic, and at this moment it was working remarkably well. I could do this — I could keep moving, seeing new places, learning more.

In Arabic, the adjective for old, in reference to people (rather than objects), is *kabeer* — literally "big," referring to the number of years, but perhaps to more. As I danced in this crowd, I caught Saad's eye again — he was dancing at the center of a circle, a beer bottle balanced on his head. Suspended briefly in time, with the whole Arab world open to me, I felt *kabeera,* especially in my heart.

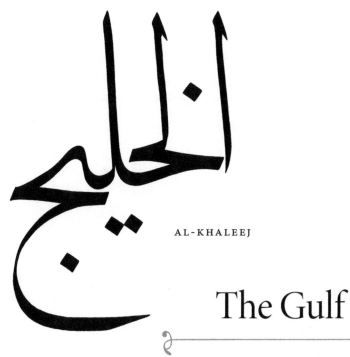

AL-KHALEEJ

The Gulf

February–March 2012

رِوِي

(*rawiya*) To drink one's fill

✦

رِوَى

(*rawa*) To tell, pass on, transmit

✦

راوٍ

(*rawin*) Storyteller, transmitter of poetry

Knowledge Village

THE ARABIAN PENINSULA is the land of the noble poets, who crisscross the desert on camelback, recounting tales of lost loves, fearsome battles, and dramatic lightning storms.

The Arabian Peninsula, where the Quran was revealed, has the purest Arabic dialect, the one closest to the classical language.

The Arabian Peninsula is so hot and sexually uptight that the people who live there consider Cairo a decadent summer vacation spot.

This was the sum of my knowledge about a landmass that measures a million square miles. I suspected it was not correct, as my sources were questionable. The poetry, which I had last consulted in graduate school, was about fifteen hundred years out of date. The assessment of the Gulf dialect was a rumor I'd heard back in the day from some fellow Arabic students. And the part about the weather and sexual mores I had deduced myself, from observing "Gulfies" two decades earlier in a Cairo nightclub, showering the famed belly dancer Fifi Abdou with crisp Egyptian pound notes.

How had I managed to study Arabic for so long while holding such confused impressions about the language's actual birthplace? It was as if I could recite *The Song of Roland* in Old French, yet persisted in thinking Parisians all danced the cancan in the streets. A major factor was a random turn I had taken in grad school. For my master's degree, I had intended to study the modern Arabic novel, but to better understand it, I found myself digging down to the bedrock of the literature: the poetry of the Jahiliya period, literally the "age of ignorance" before Islam. Contrary to the name, it was an era of poetic erudition, and themes and phrases from works composed in the sixth century could be found in the court verse of medieval Baghdad, the love poetry of Al-Andalus, and contemporary Palestinian protest literature.

My grasp of the poems came slowly. To prepare for class, I combed through all my available dictionaries, then strung together the most plausible meaning from the words I'd collected, like *Mad Libs* in reverse. The only word I reliably recognized was *habeeb*, beloved, because it was in every Arabic song ever written. In class, my professor would pick apart my "translation" for deep grammatical misreadings (oh, of course, it's a *dual imperative weak-third-radical* verb), then point out shallower pitfalls, such as my failure to recognize a long-disused term of camel husbandry. Most unfair, I felt, were place names. Arabic has no capital letters, so some nights I could spend forty-five minutes trying to find the definition for the Arabic equivalent of Moose Jaw, Saskatchewan.

Finally, though, my professor would lean forward and recite the lines again, and all the lovely words would fall into place, like pearls on a necklace. This was the payoff for the hours of logic-puzzle-like work. For a few minutes, Fusha was a true communication tool — in this case, for communing with the past. English is cut off from its roots — the original *Beowulf* is lost to all but the Anglo-Saxon specialists, and even then it dates to only the eighth century at the earliest. Arabic, though, has stayed consistent enough that it was still possible for me, in the late twentieth century, to read words that were first uttered seven thousand miles away in the year 500-something.

The place names I had stumbled over in class — the Den of the Wild Deer, the Place of the Rain-Pregnant Clouds, the Pilgrimage Site of the Circumambulating Virgins — refer to real spots in the desert. Unfortunately for me, I realized as I planned my first trip to the Arabian Peninsula, they were technically within the borders of Saudi Arabia, which did not welcome solo women travelers. But even if I could have persuaded Peter to accompany me, it wouldn't have mattered because the Saudi government did not grant tourist visas.

The United Arab Emirates, on the other hand, issued me a visa on arrival at the airport in Dubai, and let me proceed unescorted into the city. My plan was to stay in Dubai for four weeks, taking Arabic classes and trying to pick up some of the Gulf dialect. Afterward, I had another week to drive around in search of traces of the poems I had once studied. The end of my trip would coincide with a literature festival back in Dubai, where I hoped to compare old poetry and new.

When I arrived at my rental apartment, on a cool day in February, a low-grade sandstorm blurred the horizon. As familiar as Cairo, its people, and its Ammiya had been to me, Dubai was the opposite: a city where I knew no one, much less how they spoke. In the past decade, I had read plenty about Dubai's rapid transformation into a booming metropolis, but the only silhouette I recognized from my living room window was the Burj Khalifa, the world's tallest building. Beyond that stretched a hodgepodge of skyscrapers, then a gray haze of desert — the same desert that eventually crossed the border and encompassed those fabled places enshrined in verse.

The place names of Dubai are resolutely unpoetic, not fanciful but literal. The World is an archipelago of artificial islands shaped like the world; the Palm, a peninsula that resembles a palm tree. The Pearl, even as a construction site, was a bare round lot glittering nacreous in the sun. I stopped next to it, somehow lost en route to Knowledge Village, which, on the map I'd consulted before leaving my apartment, looked like a cross section of a brain.

After many long minutes, another pedestrian appeared on the wide, empty sidewalk, a teenager with milk-white skin and teardrop eyes. He was from Kazakhstan, he told me, and yes, he knew where my language school was; he was going that way himself.

On the ground, Knowledge Village resembled not a brain but an outlet mall with a Tuscan-village theme. Inside an ocher plaster building with a faux-terracotta-tile roof, my school was marked with posters of smiling students holding flags of many lands. The receptionist wore a button that said *Speak to me in English or Russian!* I chose English.

"Upstairs," she said. "In Seoul room, past Sarajevo and Cairo."

I was early, scared straight after my numerous late arrivals in Egypt. I squeezed into a desk and watched the clock. This school was the only one I had been able to find that offered intensive classes over a short period, rather than weekly meetings geared to resident expats. When I registered, I had pictured myself communing with interesting people from around the world, including an Emirati teacher, who would be my entrée into local culture. But then the group class had been rescheduled because of low enrollment. Would I like private lessons? an administrator had emailed to inquire. And would I prefer a Lebanese or a Syrian instructor? No, Emirati was not an option. I settled for private tutoring with a Lebanese teacher — at least that would help prepare me for my planned visit to Beirut, later in the year.

If I had marveled less at Dubai's architectural stunts and read more about its demographics, I might have known my initial vision was doomed. The United Arab Emirates was home to about eight million people, but only one million or so were Emirati nationals, and in the city of Dubai, they made up an even smaller portion of the population. With one of the world's highest per capita incomes, Emiratis did not take such humdrum jobs as teaching Arabic at a language school in a Tuscan-village-themed open-air mall.

The rest of the UAE's population was classified as guest workers — *wafideen* in Arabic. Literally the word means delegates, and when

I had arrived, the airport had felt like a predawn convention of international representatives: men from Kandahar in mirror-spotted caps, West Africans in bright starched fabrics, a brigade of sari-clad women, noses studded with gold. In the UAE, by far the largest contingent of *wafideen,* more than two million people, came from India, Bangladesh, and Pakistan; Indonesia and the Philippines sent major delegations as well, as did Europe.

In the few days since my arrival, the only Arabs I had encountered — or at least the only people who looked obviously Arab to me — were the airport immigration agents. They wore not the pseudomilitary uniforms of border guards the world over, but crisp white robes and, on their heads, gauzy white scarves set in place with black cords. My agent was a limpid-eyed man with wavy hair and a perfectly trimmed beard. "Good morning," I had croaked in the best Arabic I could muster after a red-eye flight.

"Morning," he had replied, in English, stamping my passport. His eyes flicked over my shoulder to the next person in line.

It was not the most auspicious beginning to my trip, but, I reminded myself as I peered down the empty hall looking for my teacher, I had added the Persian Gulf to my itinerary precisely because I knew so little about it. Asphalt-coated Dubai didn't look immediately hospitable to noble poets on camelback, and the heat I had assumed Gulfies went to Cairo to escape wasn't a factor either, at least not right now — it was downright chilly this morning. On top of it all, the map here in Seoul room labeled the water to the north the *Arabian* Gulf — a bone of contention I hadn't been aware of.

As for my notion that Gulf dialect, or Khaleeji as it was called, was somehow more pure, more true and authentic, that had been corrected before I arrived. A few months earlier, in England, I had met a Saudi police officer in a pub, and we had discussed my study plans. "Actually, I wouldn't say we speak a particularly pure Arabic," he had said, sipping his pint of ale. "We get so many people from all over the world, working, coming to Mecca on the haj, that we speak a very simple form of it." This was a relief. I had been imagining a corps of Saudi grammar enforcers, akin to the country's morality police, who beat people with sticks for not observing the Fusha rule of gender polarity in the numbers from three to ten.

I looked up at the clock in Seoul room: thirty minutes had passed with no sign of my teacher. Back downstairs at the reception desk, the Russian woman had been replaced by a man from the Philippines. I had no Tagalog to offer.

"My teacher isn't there," I said.

Thereupon ensued a process of notifying higher-ups, of placing calls, of a drawn-out telephonic rebuke. "Where *are* you?" a woman, summoned from a back room expressly for the rebuking, snipped into the phone. "The student is here, and she's *very* upset!"

I cringed and waved my hands to soften her blow. I was not at all upset. A one-on-one class was high pressure, and three days after arriving, I still felt bleary from jet lag, or perhaps from the gray timelessness of the sandstorm that had only just lifted. We rescheduled for the next day. I practically skipped out the door.

Knowledge Village was indeed an outlet mall, but for colleges. Representing New South Wales, Australia, was the University of Wollongong, where the Kazakh student had been headed. Across the way was the Islamic Azad University, in front of which stood a blond woman in a white miniskirt suit, smoking and chatting in Persian with a frail, plaid-shirted punk. It was the largest university in Iran, I read on a brochure, with more than eighteen campuses and an enrollment of 1.9 million.

On I walked, past the University of Manchester, Michigan State, and the University of Phoenix, until I reached the food court: the obligatory pizza counter and salad bar, plus an array of international options. The Lebanese counter was set up like an American Chinese takeout place, with a menu board of backlit photos. I marched up and said clearly, "*Fattet hummus.*"

This was my third attempt to engage someone in Arabic conversation in as many days. The second, after immigration, had also been at the airport, where I had asked a man at the transit desk, "If you please, where the station of metro?" He had replied in subcontinent-accented English, "Madam, you must go up one level."

After ordering my lunch, I looked for a little nod of recognition from the counterman. I had said all the tricky letters right, and at the end of *fatteh* even added the cryptic letter *ta marboota,* a *t* that was only sometimes a *t,* and in this case it was, due to the grammatical relationship between *fatteh* and *hummus.*

He gave me my change, but nothing more. Possibly he was not Arab; possibly he didn't care. In Cairo, I thought as I waited for my order, the counterman and I would be fast friends by now, holding up the line while we exchanged pleasantries. In this new city, I felt a twinge of loneliness.

The *fatteh,* a casserole of pita scraps and garlicky chickpeas, soothed me. *Fattet hummus,* I mused — not just a pleasure to eat, but a pleasure to say. It had two *shadda*s, those doubling marks that really made you pause and savor the letter. And you got the whispery, aspirated *h* in *hummus,* and the heavy, dramatic *s* that left your mouth in a thoughtful, serious pout — a substantial word for a substantial bean, the noble garbanzo.

Many centuries ago, the Bedouin who roamed the Arabian Peninsula cultivated even more complex sounds. Back then, the *dod,* that ponderous, voice-of-God *d,* had been more of a *dl* sound, made by tucking the tongue up to one side, on an incisor — rather than behind the front teeth, as lazy city slickers did nowadays. I had always considered the heart-tugging, tear-inducing *'ayn* to be the signature sound of Arabic, but early grammarians had been proudest of that complicated, asymmetrical *dod.* They dubbed Arabic *lughat ad-dod* (لغة الضاد), the language of the *dod.*

In a convenient bit of wordplay, *lughat ad-dod* sounds like *lughat addod* (لغة اضداد), language of opposites, which is equally true. English has a handful of double-edged words, such as *cleave* and *inflam-*

mable, but Arabic is full of paradoxes, enough to inspire whole medieval treatises on the subject. *Baseer* means sharply insightful, but also blind. *Sha'aba* can mean both to gather and to disperse. A now-anonymous wag quipped that every word in Arabic means itself, its opposite, and a camel. See, I wasn't skipping class, I told myself as I scraped the bottom of my *fatteh* dish; I was pondering the very essence of Arabic.

Unfortunately, no one around me was speaking it. The chatter in the food court was almost all in English, coming from Australians, Indians, Malaysians, East Africans. Dubai, in the little I had seen of it, was an exhilarating convention of global delegates. But the ancient deserts of Arabia, full of paradoxical poets who touched tongue to incisor as they recited, seemed awfully far away.

When I did meet my teacher, the following morning, she immediately set me at ease. Manal conformed to the image I held of Lebanese women; namely, that they are all elegant and beautiful. She had toasted-almond skin, ever so lightly freckled, with a fabulous nose that looked straight off an ancient vase. She removed her enormous black sunglasses, shook out her lustrous black hair, and propped the glasses atop her head, ready to work. Not to worry about my Egyptian dialect, she told me breezily. I should speak however I could, and then we'd review where I could make changes to Lebanese.

On the surface, the various dialects of Arabic vary widely, but they share key similarities in underlying grammar, which make them, oddly, more similar to one another than any one of them is to Fusha. So, no problem—all I had to do was adopt a completely new accent and learn a fresh batch of basic conversational vocabulary. *Kwayyis*—good. No, what was the Lebanese word? Right: *mneeh.*

The one-on-one conversation that I had been worried about came easily because I was genuinely curious about Manal and her life here. She had lived in Dubai for eleven years, which, in this fast-growing city, made her practically a native. She was willing to explain the social system in the crudest terms, for the sake of my comprehension: Emiratis owned things; Europeans ran things; Arabs from other countries, such as her Lebanese architect husband, designed and implemented things; Filipinos, Indonesians, Bangladeshis, and everyone else from Asia built things and cleaned things. The Danish woman in my class in Cairo would have crossed her arms and cocked an eyebrow at this stereotyping, but I was glad Manal was speaking slowly and using familiar verbs and nouns.

As we chatted, I tried to counter the advice I'd taken so wrong from Dr. Badawi. Rather than nodding when I got the general idea of her story, I asked Manal to stop and explain the specific words I didn't know. Of course, this was her job as a language teacher, and mine as a student, but I was tentative at first. In Cairo, I had grown used to talking with strangers, where, in the name of sociability, it had seemed wiser not to sweat the small stuff—and if I failed to understand, I would get a fresh start with whomever I met on the next block.

But in Dubai, I feared Manal might be the only person I would find to speak Arabic with, and I wanted to make the most of it. Fortunately, she had the ideal language teacher's outlook: genuinely amused by and interested in her own language. "Oh, that's a good word!" she would say whenever I asked her for an explanation.

My reward for asking questions was some excellent new vocabulary. *Manzoo'*, totally wrecked, came, I found later in my dictionary, from the verb that means to be in the throes of death. Also handy: *moobeeli 'am-byikharraf,* my phone is going senile. I drank up the new words eagerly—each one suggested a juicy, real-life adventure.

Practical, Fashion, Extreme

IN BETWEEN CLASSES, I vowed to squeeze as much Arabic out of Dubai as I could. Khaleeji, Fusha, Lebanese—I would take whatever I could get. Ordering correctly at restaurants wasn't getting me anywhere, so I went to the Dubai Museum. Maybe there would be a crew of school kids to tag along with, and mooch off their Arabic-speaking guide.

But the place was filled only with sunburned European tourists, so I read the Arabic labels on the displays instead. *Lu'lu'*, pearls, I murmured to myself—these treasures, collected from the Gulf waters by skin divers, had brought the city its early wealth. Then in the 1930s, the Japanese developed less expensive cultured pearls, and Dubai slipped into economic doldrums.

Daw, dhow, the hand-built wooden boat with its thin, elegant hull and its canvas sails—this vessel had plied the Persian Gulf and the Indian Ocean, connecting Dubai with Iran, Asia, and East Africa. In the museum, the dhow was presented as an artifact, but I had just walked past a dozen of the boats moored on the wharves nearby, being loaded with truck tires and refrigerators in boxes stamped MADE IN CHINA.

Tijara, trade, was illustrated with a frenetic video montage of freighters and building cranes and time-lapse construction since the 1950s. This city sustained itself not on oil, as I had assumed, but on its busy ports. The display ended on a bullish note. It had not been amended since the 2009 downturn, when construction stalled and Dubai's government-as-corporation took a $10 billion bailout from neighboring Abu Dhabi, the emirate that still drew profits from oil.

Near the museum exit, I noticed a small, dimly lit room. *Al-bedu: the Bedouin,* the sign read. And underneath: "They love good deeds and hate evil. They are proud of their customs. They have strong personalities."

This use of "they" was puzzling. My own idea of the Bedouin was a bit fuzzy, certainly not as clear in my mind as my other preconceptions of the Arabian Peninsula, the ones regarding poets on camelback and pure-Arabic speakers. But I had thought that here, on the edge of the Arabian Desert, Bedouin were all around. Yet this exhibit suggested they were some elusive race that you might glimpse only if you sat very still in the desert during the right phase of the moon.

Back at my apartment, I consulted my dictionaries. I had been conflating Arab and Bedouin, or at least assuming that here, in the *Arabian* Gulf, the two must be synonymous. The word "Arab" — or rather, an Assyrian cuneiform version of it, with the root *'ayn-ra-ba* — first referred, as far back as the mid-ninth century B.C.E., not to an ethnic group precisely, but to any desert dweller. These folk stood in contrast with the Assyrians themselves, genteel urbanites who lounged in palaces in Nineveh, near present-day Mosul, Iraq. The desert people were a thorn in the Assyrians' side, judging from their carved depictions of Arab raiders, mounted two to a camel, one at the reins while the other wielded a bow and arrow.

The raiders had some success, for later, the Old Testament referred to "the kings of Arabia." And when the Romans swept in to Petra, now in Jordan, and to Palmyra, in what is now Syria, they called the area Arabia Petraea. The Arabs led camel caravans through the desert, hauling treasures from the Red Sea in the south to the Euphrates River in the north.

Meanwhile, the word *bedu* (بدو) meant desert; it developed into a collective noun referring to the nomads who lived in this terrain. Not that these desert people called themselves Arabs or Bedouin—they identified by clan: Kindah, Banu Tamim, Quraysh. And to confuse the matter, over the centuries the root *'ayn-ra-ba* split, so the roaming Bedouin were called *a'rab* (أعراب), while more settled tribes were *'arab* (عرب). Here was perhaps the seminal example of paradox in Arabic vocabulary, the heart of the "language of opposites."

In the early seventh century, a few tribes in the Arabian Peninsula pulled together under the banner of a new religion called Islam. In less than a century, an empire was born; for convenience and prestige, the rulers moved the capital to Damascus. From new urban palaces, where fountains splashed and flowers perfumed the air, the desert-rambling Bedouin began to look like an exotic people, the Arabs' own noble savages. This image pervaded the first Arabic grammar books, which settled usage debates by citing the speech of Bedouin informants. Their Arabic was considered correct and pure, uncorrupted by the city. By the tenth century, however, this kind of fieldwork waned. City people, now in even fancier digs in the new capital of Baghdad, believed themselves superior, and the Bedouin could no longer be trusted. Some, the grammarians tutted, had been known to accept bribes to settle an argument in favor of the payee.

In the modern era, the term "Bedouin," at least when used by a city dweller, could be synonymous with bumpkin. The Bedouin accent—pronouncing the suffix *-ik* as *-ich,* for instance, and adding an extra vowel in the middle of words—sounded to some ears like a romantic cowboy's drawl or, to others, like a hillbilly's unschooled twang. And in every country where Bedouin still lived, from Egypt to Iraq to Oman, they slipped uneasily between a traditional nomadic life and a settled one. Sometimes they herded sheep around the desert; sometimes they herded tourists; sometimes they set up in cinder-block homes the government preferred they settle in. They were perpetual outsiders — outside the city, living out of doors.

Recalling the museum displays on pearls and boats, I finally saw why people in Dubai might consider the Bedouin to be "they," not "us." It was simply that Dubai faced the water. These were seagoing people and city dwellers, quite unlike the desert-tempered Bedouin. This distinction went back at least to the first century, when the *Periplus of the Erythraean Sea,* a Greek guidebook for seafarers, described the "Fish-Eaters" who occupied caves along the Red Sea coast of the Arabian Peninsula, as opposed to, inland, the "rascally men who live in villages and nomadic camps."

In 1833, a branch of the desert-based Bani Yas tribe split off in protest over the leaders' infighting. The clan established itself by the Dubai Creek, where they embarked on trade, loading dhows with goods. In less than two hundred years, rascally men from nomadic camps had become Fish-Eaters, and, to judge from their self-representation in the museum, they were not going back inland. Out my apartment window, the twinkling Burj Khalifa stretched more than two thousand feet up and away from the desert.

Loitering in the Arabic section of the bookstore, I nonchalantly flipped through a book of poetry by the ruling sheikh of Dubai. Not that I understood much of it — I was holding it only in hopes it might spark a conversation. In Cairo, I would have been swarmed by other customers, gabbing, interrogating, offering recommendations. Here, I soon noticed, my gambit was wasted, as there were no other customers.

Over on the English-language side, I perused the "local topics" section, dominated by a wall of imperiled-in-Arabia books, every cover showing a woman's face covered in an alluring veil. Nearby, I found a piece of Kuwaiti chick lit penned in "Arabeezi," part Arabic, part *Ingleezi* (English), using the numbers-for-letters chat alphabet. I browsed for useful Khaleeji phrases, but found only "*3n el na7asa*" (translated in a footnote as "Don't be mean") and "*Abi 9amonat Jeben*" ("I want a cheese sandwich"). At least the book's heroine, a pudgy ex-med student, seemed more real than the veiled women on the covers of the other books in the section. And she spoke more Gulf dialect than I might ever learn in person.

The bookstore opened into the surrounding mall, twelve million square feet of retail and thousands of shoppers, all so diverse and global that I did not attract a second glance. I passed an information desk, staffed with three men in matching black suits and one in a white Gulf-style robe. Like the crisp-robed airport immigration agents, who had seemed so incongruous in civilian rather than military garb, this man looked out of place. Then a trio of women approached and peppered him with questions in Arabic, and I understood. The robe was itself a kind of uniform, a marker of rank—and, practically speaking, a way of identifying who spoke the national language. Even more practically, here was a captive audience for small talk. I took a deep breath and headed for the man in the robe.

"Where is a store of mobile, if you please?" I asked politely in Fusha. I refrained from adding that my phone had, in Manal's words, been going senile—I didn't want to muddy the waters with Lebanese slang.

He considered me for a millisecond. "Here," he said in English, tapping a spot on the mall map. "There are many, by the Waitrose subermarket." His eyes flicked past me to the next lost shopper.

The man's linguistic snub, like the one I'd received at the airport, was probably not intentional, but it still smarted. *In Cairo* (words I found myself thinking more every day, with ever more longing), I could not walk twenty feet without someone striking up a conversation. *In Cairo*, I had been a virtual celebrity! *In Cairo*, city of extroverts, I had collapsed into bed exhausted every night, my brain full to bursting.

Now, in this more reserved city, I was like any other anonymous traveler, interacting with the usual ticket sellers, doormen, and shop-girls. Anywhere else in the world, this would have given me ample opportunity to practice the local language, but in Dubai, the service-sector workers did not, as a rule, speak Arabic. And when I encountered the rare one who did — the immigration officer, the information desk staffer — he spoke to me in English.

My phone errand forgotten, I found myself in the luxury wing of the mall, all flattering light and Italian boutiques. The ladies' restroom was equally luxurious, room upon room, with full-length mirrors and tufted settees. Older women sat amid their shopping bags, huffing and sighing and speaking too high and fast for me to understand. When two younger women entered, I turned to eavesdrop.

"_____ Fersatchi _____?" one woman said to the other, reaching over to stroke her friend's shimmery green collar, laid just so over a black robe.

"*La*, Doolchay _____. _____."

If either of them had said, "Don't be mean" or "I want a cheese sandwich," I had not heard it; all I had made out was "Versace" and "Dolce." The women stood in towering heels at the mirrors, adjusting gauzy black scarves over immense beehive hairdos and applying fresh eyeliner in dramatic swoops.

It would be fun to chat with these girls, but how to start? My first instinct was to say, "*Sheek awi!*" (Very chic!), but this was straight Egyptian dialect, and it sounded too coarse here in the mall's luxury wing. But what would I say in Fusha? "O madam, the Dolce and Gabbana is most suitable for you, with respect to its emerald-green hue"? When I considered complimenting the women in English, I realized it was not normal to make friends in the ladies' room. I patted on some lip balm and slipped out.

In a more proletarian wing of the mall, I passed a kiosk selling perfume. A sign advised me that the brand name, Shay, "in Emirati spoken Arabic means 'cool' or 'nice.'" If only I had seen this vocabulary lesson before my visit to the ladies' lounge! I rolled the word over my tongue, but it didn't feel right. Not only did I, in my sensible linen pants, button-front blouse, and colorless lip balm, not have the authority to coo "Mmm, very *shay!*" to a stranger, but in Egypt, *shay* was the word for tea, which was always served hot, the opposite of *gamid,* the word Medo had taught me for cool. It was just confusing enough to keep me from opening my mouth.

By the time I visited the Sheikh Mohammed Centre for Cultural Understanding, I had given up hopes of speaking Arabic, but at least there would be real, live Emirati nationals there, as well as a good breakfast. The center, set in an old-by-Dubai-standards stucco house from the 1940s, offered Q&A sessions for curious tourists and foreign transplants, over a traditional meal.

Our host was a tall, gregarious man named Nasif, with a sly smile and fluent-English shtick that would have killed in the Catskills: "Religions are like operating systems. 'Ooh, I'm an Apple! You're Windows!' My best friend and business partner is Jewish." Beat; theatrical shrug. "And an atheist!"

Nasif's straight man was his assistant, Muhammad, a blinky college student who stood at his mentor's elbow, pen and notebook in hand. We twenty audience members perched on carpet-covered floor cushions, arrayed around a large courtyard.

"If I shout '*Allahu akbar!*' at the bank," Nasif continued, "and you all run away, then I get to be first in line." Another perfect beat. "You got *punked!*"

Nasif's monologue ranged from the healing power of dates, the country's main agricultural product, to the UAE's hyperspeed shift to modernity: "The refrigerator, when it came, was like a precious icon," he recalled, mock-bowing before it. Early in his talk, some in the crowd had tittered nervously at the religious jokes, but by the end, they were enthralled by his stories and laughing in all the right spots.

Nasif called a break, and Muhammad served us breakfast: glistening stacks of puffy bread topped with date syrup; sweet, saffron-scented scrambled eggs with vermicelli noodles; great tureens of chickpeas in broth studded with tiny chilies. More than anything I had seen in the museum, the spices and textures of the food showed the dramatic difference from all the other Arab countries I had visited in the past. Egypt, Syria, Lebanon — those countries edged the Mediterranean and shared a common aesthetic, in food and many other details. The UAE looked north and east, spicing its breakfast with help from Iran and countries across the Indian Ocean.

The post-meal Q&A session was almost entirely about clothing. This superficial turn initially irritated me, but if I was honest with myself, I had a lot to learn. Clothing was part of the unspoken language of culture, and I had yet to feel comfortable in the Gulf's dialect. In Egypt, even when I wasn't able to communicate in Arabic, I could read other details — hand gestures, *zibeeba* prayer marks, wrist tattoos, the music on a taxi's sound system. Here, though, I was at the remedial level. I still did a double take when I saw a woman in a niqab, the black face veil that was seldom worn in Cairo; the men in their shining white shirt-front robes looked to me slightly unreal, as if they had all stepped out of stock photos.

Nasif called for volunteers to try on the niqab, as well as the abaya, the women's black top robe that was commonly paired with the *shayla,* a gauzy headscarf. The woman in the niqab posed awkwardly, her self-conscious smile visible through the fine fabric.

A man in the audience asked why, in such a hot place, Emiratis didn't wear tank tops. "Have you noticed," Nasif said, tapping his sleeve and eyeing the man's sunburned arm, "we live in a desert?"

But why did men wear white and women wear black, another audience member wondered. Wasn't that unfair, since black was hotter in the sun?

"Do you feel hotter?" he turned to his volunteer models. They shrugged; they had fallen mute as mannequins. It didn't matter whether the abaya was hot in the sun, because Emirati women were not standing around in the sun. They were walking from air-conditioned house to SUV to mall to office tower.

"Look, it's fashion too," Nasif said, indicating that the volunteers could now remove their outfits. He was right about this as well. In Cairo, the style was multicolored hijabs; here, women, like the Versace-and-Dolce ladies in the restroom at the mall, wore giant updos, with the *shayla* cascading down.

"Everything goes from practical to fashion to extreme," Nasif philosophized. In the practical era, exposing skin to the sun meant dehydration, which in turn meant certain death in the desert. With modern comforts, tradition could be tweaked. "We live in the extreme era now," he concluded. "Maybe Lady Gaga will wear the abaya and make it cool."

As for men's clothing, the standard robe, the *kandoura*, was almost always white, Nasif said, "unless you want to look old-fashioned." Here he smirked and tipped his head toward his assistant, Muhammad, who was clad in sandy brown.

"No, it is *the* fashion!" Muhammad protested. He reached up and patted his oversized *ghitra*, the cotton scarf set on his head in complex folds. Unlike Nasif's plain white gauze *ghitra*, his was a rustic red-checked design. Muhammad, wearing old-school *bedu* garb in the city, might have been a little bit of a hipster. In fact, considering what a small percentage of the population Emiratis were, any kind of *kandoura* and abaya was a marker of a subculture, a way of recognizing members of your literal tribe.

Muhammad had removed the trays of food, and now he lit an incense burner near the front of the carpet. I had noticed similar filigreed brass boxes for sale at the mall, along with the various scented woods and resins to burn in them, but this was the first time I had seen one in action. "We have a saying here," Nasif said, waving the scented smoke with his hand. "'When the smoke comes out, you get out.'" With a final Cheshire-cat grin, he gestured to the door.

When Your Ear Hears

AFTER A WEEK of classes, Manal and I had settled into an easy routine, but there was an imbalance in our communication. She usually had no problem understanding me, while I frequently had to ask her to repeat herself. And when she did, I often found she was saying words I already knew.

I wanted to blame her Lebanese accent, but really, the problem was mine. Whenever Manal's intonation suggested she'd be asking a question, my hands clenched around my notebook. Questions put me on highest alert, and I reverted to the linguistic perfectionism of my childhood. As soon as I missed a single word, my brain stalled. *Start over*, it seemed to insist, in breathless panic. *You'llneverunder standneverunderstandneverunderstand.*

"Manal," I finally said, "can you tell me some stories? Just some things that have happened in your life here in Dubai." I hoped that if she talked for long enough at a stretch, my brain would relax and stop interfering.

"About my life here? Well, OK," she said, settling down in a chair next to her desk. "Let me tell you, I'm very unlucky with maids."

For once, I had understood the words fine, but I wasn't sure why she would have said them.

"Everyone in Dubai has a maid," Manal said when she saw my puzzled expression, "so it seemed like a good idea to hire one. The first one seemed quite good. She was from the Philippines. She was with us exactly one month. And then she disappeared."

"Disappeared?" I repeated. It was not a word I had expected.

"She went out one day and didn't return that night," she clarified. According to law, because Manal and her husband had vouched for the woman's visa, they were legally responsible for her. When they reported the disappearance to the police, they were subjected to hours of bureaucracy, signing statements that they had not abetted the maid's escape. They never saw the woman again.

"The second one was Indonesian. She was good, but after a year, she got pregnant and went home," Manal went on. "And the third one . . ."

Here she paused and readjusted her sunglasses on her head. "She was Indonesian too. She had been in our house twenty-eight days when she suddenly fell ill. Very ill, with a high fever and a terrible cough. I made my husband take her to the hospital in the middle of the night. Six days later . . . *matet.*"

I had been expecting words related to health insurance and paperwork, not such a simple one as *matet* — she died.

It was septicemia, from an *ijhad.* "When a woman is pregnant, and then she is not pregnant. By choice," Manal explained as she wrote out the word on the board. Her maid had suffered a bad abortion. The doctors had been quick to say it must have happened in Indonesia — not that it mattered, since the procedure was all but illegal there as well as in the UAE. I copied the word into my notebook. I had never had occasion to discuss such a thing in Arabic before.

On the metro, I sat in a corner and stared out the window. Billboards advertising new malls and housing developments whisked past.

Reading at this speed was a good test of my comprehension. "*Koooo-loooob abaaareeeel*," I sounded out. Something about dogs? But the plural of *kalb* (dog) was usually *kilab*. And *abareel*? Was that some alternate spelling of *abreel* (April)?

The adjacent sign, in English, revealed the answer: *Club Apparel*. It wasn't Arabic; it was a phonetic transcription. Irritated, I turned away from the window. At the next stop, a recorded voice intoned over the metro speakers, "Doors closing." At first I had loved this voice — it spoke incongruously formal Arabic, complete with case endings. Now I was starting to hate it as much as the mock-Arabic billboards.

At my stop, I joined the crowd of giddy tourists streaming toward the Burj Khalifa, in hopes their cheer would rub off on me. But now I noticed the people heading in the other direction, toward the train. In polyester uniforms and ragged jumpsuits they trudged, heads down under the darkening sky, eyes dull after a day's labor. I noticed tiny cracks in building façades, unfinished curbs, one haggard bed of petunias planted in a median. The city felt precarious, suspended between fable and reality.

At the Burj Khalifa, a fresh team of jumpsuited workers was busy restoring order, vacuuming sand off the bottom of the Dubai Fountain. This thirty-acre water feature was a bit impractical in the desert, but what was practicality in the face of Arab tradition? In the Quran, after all, God says He "created every living thing from water," so a *nafoora*, or fountain, became a fixture in Islamic architecture, the center of every courtyard home. Dubai's famous *nafoora* was a bit different from other great fountains in Islamic history, such as the lion statues that had once spouted water in the Alhambra in Granada, Spain. For one thing, this fountain shot water five hundred feet high; for another, it danced along with Céline Dion songs.

A voice pierced the air, and the crowd on the plaza rustled, turned to the fountain, raised cameras in anticipation. But it was not the prelude to a pop song; it was the *adhan*, the call to prayer, a thin, airy voice emanating from speakers hidden in the lampposts.

In Cairo, the *adhan* was an assertive bellow from every mosque, and a mosque every hundred feet, or so it sounded. The *adhan* was five minutes of sonic mayhem, five times a day. *Come to—, come—, come to pray,* the muezzins urged in competing, unsynchronized rounds. *To pray, come—, to pray, come to prosper!* In response, people put aside their work and laid out prayer mats in alleys and behind shop counters.

Here in Dubai, no one in the milling crowd reacted. This was the first time I had heard the call in Dubai, I realized, and perhaps this was another reason I felt so out of sorts here. Cairo's version was cacophonous, but it lent order to the day. Its echoing song had paced my morning classes, marked lunchtime, roused me from a nap, and then, finally, beckoned me back into the cooler evening. *Adhan,* the call, and *udhun,* ear, come from the same root, a verb that means both to permit and to hear. A good muezzin (*mu'adhdhin,* one-who-is-calling-to-prayer) with a clear, true voice can cut through the background noise and deposit a harmonious ripple of syllables directly in your ear. I told myself a story to memorize the knot of the root's meanings: when your ear hears the *adhan,* you're permitted to take a break and reflect on the day so far.

I sat down on a bench to listen. Construction cranes made cryptic silhouettes in the darkening skyline. As at the airport and in the campus food court, I felt as if I had joined a great convention of delegates from all over the globe. Golden footlights illuminated faces of all shapes and shades, clothes of every type, and a dozen languages blurred together in an excited hum. The only Arabic I heard was the recorded call, still faint but distinct: *Come to pray! Come to prosper!*

With a dramatic gust of vapor, the fountain burst into action. A trill of melodious synthesizers silenced the crowd. The water, all twenty-two thousand gallons of it, burst in waves, then shimmied seductively to an Arabic pop hit. Phone screens flashed like fireflies. With each explosion of the *nafoora,* the crowd gasped in unison, as if in revelation. For a moment, I felt a shared connection — this was a language we all understood.

Then I remembered Manal's maid stories, the meaningless Arabic billboards, and the exhausted workers heading home. I stepped away from the crowd at the fountain and made my own way home. By the time I reached my apartment, I was in a deep gloom. I turned my back on the Burj Khalifa, glimmering in the dusk like the Royal Palace of Oz, and called Peter. "People here are rude," I told him. "They stare right past you."

Peter laughed. "You live in New York," he said. "You know they're not rude. They're just not interested in you. There's a difference."

"I'm so tired," I whined. "There's no one to speak Arabic to, and I'm not learning anything." Actually, I was sleeping fine, and I was learning something new every day from Manal. What had really put me in a sulk was that my plan — learn Khaleeji, crack Emirati culture, immerse myself in ancient poetry — wasn't working out.

"So if you hate it there, why don't you go somewhere else?" Peter said. "You don't have to stay in class, you know."

Right. I was an adult, and I could do what I liked. I had been planning to travel around the Emirates, maybe over the border to Oman, but not until I finished my classes. Why *not* go now?

As soon as I said goodbye to Peter, I reserved a rental car and texted Manal about my new plans. I would travel into the desert, like the poets of old.

Eau de Facebook

AL-AIN, WAY OUT east on the border with Oman, struck me at first as a pleasantly frumpy city: wide streets, low-rise buildings, serious investment in the latest neon-sign technology, circa 1980. The Hilton sported mauve leather sofas and smoky mirrors. But after parking downtown, I saw it was quite up-to-date in one respect. I had not walked fifty feet when out of the shadows sprang a black Ferrari. It screeched to a halt inches from my right leg, its engine growling like a dog straining at a leash.

Across the street, rumbling at a traffic light, was a white Lotus. Out of the corner of my eye, a Rolls-Royce hood ornament flicked up and headlights flashed as the owner sashayed over to the car, keys in hand. I looked up and down the street, and all I saw were more cars—and other men getting into and out of them. I was the only woman for blocks, as well as the only pedestrian.

Next to me was a row of shoe stores. I ducked into the nearest one, which was stocked almost entirely with slip-on sandals. As I was perusing the stock—did I want a heel of zero inches or four?—a young man in a tight striped polo shirt sidled up to me. "Berfume?"

he offered, in English, holding out a blue bottle, his finger primed to spritz. The label read FACEBOOK.

"No, thanks," I said, and immediately regretted it. What would eau de Facebook smell like—procrastination, with top notes of forced cheer? But dodging cars had made me jumpy and pushed me into default "no" mode. I backed toward the door.

"Date later?" he asked, subtly flexing his biceps. I blanched.

"No, no, ha, no!" I turned and bolted. Two doors down, past an idling Bugatti Veyron, I bought a chicken shwarma sandwich to go and dashed for my rental car.

The road to the top of Jabal Hafeet was a black swath of German engineering with generous shoulders and gracefully banked curves. I was glad it was an easy drive up the mountain, as I wasn't quite awake. I had arrived in Al-Ain the night before, too late for the sunset. Now I was aiming for sunrise.

Midway up, the perfectly spaced lights illuminating the road switched off, as the glow on the horizon shifted from gray-blue to gray-pink. It was a pleasure to have the road to myself, even if I wasn't driving a Ferrari.

After the last rise, I pulled into an enormous, completely empty parking lot. A pair of raptors circled on updrafts, and a family of fat quail skittered across the asphalt. At the far end of the lot sat a shuttered teashop; lights blinked on the claw crane arcade games out front, enticing no one at this hour. Later in the day, this place was probably lively with families—friendly families who might chat with visitors like myself. Instead, I had chosen to come at the very hour at which I was guaranteed to not meet another human being.

Worse, I couldn't even see the sunrise, because the peak of the mountain blocked the horizon behind me. So while the desert below was rapidly turning from rosy dawn to white in the full sunlight, the parking lot was in shade. I hopped from foot to foot in the cold. Better to go back to bed, I decided.

I had just turned toward my car when a white SUV cruised into the far end of the lot. I suddenly felt very vulnerable, alone and so far from the city. The SUV looped around and stopped between me and my car. The tinted window purred down to reveal a man in mirrored sunglasses and a red and white *ghitra* folded elegantly around his head.

He waved. "Good mor-ning!" he said with a heavy Arabic accent. "Where you from?"

"Good morning," I said. "From New York. The city." I tried to look stern and project an aura of urban toughness, but I had to unzip my vest to expose my mouth, and the zipper stuck a bit. While I was fussing, he cut the engine.

"America! I love America! Very good country," he said. "I want to know Americans, but . . ." He trailed off, looking a little frustrated.

I gaped. He seemed to be having trouble speaking English! Could this be my chance to talk to a real, live Emirati *in Arabic?* I felt for my car keys in my pocket and slipped my fingers through them, brass-knuckle style, just in case. "*Sabah al-kheir*," I said, walking toward his car. "*Naʿam, ana amreekaniya. Winta min hina?*"

His reaction to my basic morning greetings and paltry question — was he from these parts? — brought the kind of reaction I had been missing so far in the Emirates. The way a smile burst across his face, I would have thought I was in Egypt.

"I'm from right around here," he answered in Arabic. That settled it. I walked straight up and leaned on his window frame.

He had always wanted to meet more Americans, he went on, and this was a good sign, seeing me here this morning. In fact, he had been wanting to talk to someone. He'd been awake all night, driving around on this mountain and thinking.

"You look like a nice person," he said, taking off his mirror shades. "Can I talk to you from my heart?" He pronounced this last word *galbi*, instead of *qalbi* — just as I'd read about Khaleeji accents. He was maybe a decade younger than me, with tan skin and a neatly groomed beard. His hair was silky black and curled around the collar of his white *kandoura,* miraculously unwrinkled for someone who had spent the night in his car.

"Sure," I told him, still in Arabic. "What's the problem?" I let my hand relax around the keys in my pocket. This was not the first time in my life a complete stranger had wanted to unburden himself to me. But this was the first time it was happening in Arabic.

He had been married for five years. She was a wonderful woman, very beautiful, and they loved each other. I was listening intently, one ear trained on his story and another on his accent.

"... but there was no baby. I understood this would be our situation," he said with a sigh. This brought me back to full attention. No baby — this was a substantial tragedy. In my travels in the Arab world, people had often interrogated me on the subject of children, right after asking my name and where I was from. The Arab world didn't leave much room for those who failed to procreate, and this could doom a marriage.

The man in the car carried on, saying that he and his wife had decided to divorce; they were no longer happy together. "And then two months ago," he said, "*matet.*"

Again with the *matet!* Why did these stories end with "she died"? He was silent, glaring out his windshield, staring intently at the blinking lights by the teashop at the far end of the parking lot. After a moment, his jaw relaxed and he turned to me, his eyes shining. "I feel I was responsible," he said quietly.

"Of course you're not responsible!" I rushed to console him. "But I understand the reason why you feel like this. I very sorry. Your story, it a very sad story." My Arabic was limited, but what else would I have said in English? The social expectations for children here were high, certainly, and his story, in which two people grew apart, in which a man on the verge of divorce became a widower, could have happened anywhere.

"Now my family wants me to marry again," he said. "But all the women here are bad. Silly. All they do is talk on their mobiles and giggle."

"Right. They not serious," I said. "You need a woman who can understand your situation, a woman who will be serious."

"Exactly. Thank you for listening to me. I feel better." He sighed again. The sun was peeking up over the mountaintop next to us.

"Americans are nice people," he said after a pause. "I know this because of how you treat animals. Arabs—they're not nice to animals. If they're hurt, they just throw them away. But I saw an American TV show about how you operate on dogs and cats that have been in accidents. Once they sewed up a cat's whole leg!"

We contemplated human compassion in silence for a moment. The asphalt was warming under my feet.

He leaned toward me. "I would love to keep talking to you. Can we go somewhere and *niswalif*?"

This question made me giddy—not for the invitation, but because he had used the one distinctly Khaleeji word I knew: *soolaf*, to tell stories or chat.

I answered just so I could use the word. "Sure, let us go someplace and *niswalif*. Where is good? Is there a café open early?" My brain was racing ahead: we'd sit and sip coffee, and he'd tell more stories, and I'd drink in the new words, and I'd write some down, and . . .

"I don't think anything is open," he said. "Also, I don't think it is good for us to sit together at a café. Are you staying in a hotel?"

"Yes, the Hilton," I answered, too quickly. He wasn't taking the conversation where I thought he was, surely? "Um, there is a coffee shop in the lobby," I suggested. "We can sit there and *niswalif*."

"Oh, but someone might see. Your room is more relaxing."

He didn't *seem* lecherous. And it made sense that he would prefer to talk about his private life in private, and I would find it more relaxing to speak my bad Arabic without anyone eavesdropping. The Hilton coffee shop was always packed with *kandoura*-clad businessmen.

"I cannot do that," I said, feeling for the keys in my pocket. "You have to understand—I am married. My husband will be very upset if you come to my room." Peter wouldn't, in fact, care one bit. He trusted me.

"Please understand, you are like a sister to me!" he said, looking shocked. Maybe too shocked, fake shocked.

"Certainly," I replied, serious and formal. "But you must understand. This is a rule I have, in every place I travel. I absolutely cannot invite you to my hotel room. I mean no offense to you."

"But you are like a sister to me! I am your brother!" With his protests, his polite formulas, a false note crept into his voice. Or was it that I could no longer distinguish him from other, sleazier men who had used this "like a sister" line on me?

We went back and forth about six times—I was growing quite fluent on this point. Finally I had an idea. "Look, my hotel room has a patio in front of it. We can sit on the patio. It is private. But it is not inside my room. Will that be good?" On the way in, I would stop at the reception desk and order coffee to be delivered outside, to let them know what was going on. We would walk to the patio from the garden, without passing through my room.

"Are there trees around it?"

"Some palm trees. Other people can see if they look, but they are only other guests of the hotel." This was veering toward bargaining. It was too early for bargaining.

"OK," he said. "This will be very nice. Let's go and *niswalif.* We will meet in the parking lot at the Hilton." He seemed natural again, and somewhat cheered.

"By the way, my name is Zora," I said to him. "What's yours?"

"Saeed," he said, sticking his hand out the window. *Saeed* means happy.

All the way down the mountain, I rehearsed nice things to say to him in Arabic. What qualities he should look for in a woman. General advice for moving on: "Keep busy. Practice your English. Work hard." Did he have a job? He had said he owned land. Oh! Might he consider himself one of those mythical Bedouin? I could ask him what this word meant to him. I drove faster, eager for our conversation.

But I took the wrong turn off a roundabout and had to stop to check the GPS on my phone. By the time I arrived at the Hilton, nearly forty-five minutes had passed. None of the dozens of white SUVs in the parking lot was Saeed's.

I waited by the hotel's double front doors for another quarter of an hour. The wind had picked up. I squinted against the swirling grit and held my hair back with one hand. A woman in a black niqab sailed, unruffled, from her car to the lobby — practical fashion indeed. Saeed never appeared.

When I called Peter the next day and told him the story, he immediately said, "Of course it was all just one long pickup line."

Wait — maybe I wasn't telling the story right. But I had to admit that, the night before, while writing down what I remembered of my conversation with Saeed, I had started to doubt the man's sincerity. In my excitement to speak Arabic, perhaps I had overlooked some inconsistencies — that unwrinkled *kandoura*, for one thing.

I emailed a fellow travel writer who knew the Emirates well, requesting his analysis. He replied, "Al-Ain is notorious for sex tourism, you know." That explained the guy in the shoe store who offered to spritz me with Facebook perfume. It didn't really explain Saeed, however. What kind of a pickup line was it to tell someone, in Arabic, that your ex-wife died? If it had been pure seduction, he had managed to devise the perfect approach for me, a slightly road-weary, overly empathetic language student. And if that was the case, I was impressed.

It didn't matter what his true intentions were, I decided. It had made me happy just to talk to him.

What He Did Not Know

MY ACCIDENTAL CONVERSATION with unhappy Saeed had been pleasant, but it also underscored a flaw in my idea of a desert sojourn. This country was simply too big and empty to drive around without a plan, in search of random educational encounters in mountaintop parking lots or anywhere else. In the face of this uncertainty, I returned to what I knew best: the library.

The library in question was a two-hour drive from Al-Ain, in the city of Abu Dhabi, at the Sheikh Zayed Grand Mosque, a marvel of modern architecture that featured both the world's largest chandelier and the world's largest hand-woven carpet. Approaching the building, I longed for the empty desert roads. Abu Dhabi was a nerve-racking tangle of freeways, then an addling series of multilaned, multispoked traffic circles. Through it all, I kept my eye on the building's two minarets, which stuck up above the skyline like beacons.

The library was in the north minaret, and I had imagined the slim tower with a spiral bookcase winding up its sides, illuminated by shafts of sunlight cutting through the dusty air, tended by wizened old scribes. Instead, it was an institutionally carpeted, fluorescent-lit room, accessible by elevator and frostily air-conditioned. The desk clerk was a young, bushy-bearded man. When I described, in unsteady Arabic, my project — I was studying the importance of his fine language and its classical poetry — he blinked at me through his big glasses and exclaimed, "*Mashallah!*"

So much had been written about Arabic since I had left academia: sociological studies, specialist dictionaries, even a five-volume encyclopedia dedicated to the language. I took the Q–Y volume to read about Quranic Arabic, as well as a few reference titles about poetry. Settling at a table with my books, I pulled my mosque-issued abaya and *shayla,* required for all female visitors, around me. They were heavy polyester, and I was grateful for their warmth.

In the hierarchy of Arabic literature, the Quran is at the very top, and not just because it is a holy book. Its language is concise, precise, dense with meaning, rich with metaphors and palindromes. Even in the rare verses where I understood all the words, many of the subtleties were lost on me.

Like so much in Arabic, the Quran resists translation — in fact, it specifically defies it. The Quran is not the Quran unless it is in Arabic; versions in other languages are not considered translations, only interpretations. The logic is that the Quran is the revealed word of God, as spoken to the prophet Muhammad. This is such literal thinking that, the first time I heard it, I laughed. *Oh, God speaks Arabic, does He? Does* He *have problems remembering what makes a noun a diptote?*

The more I considered this concept, the more I saw its amazing ramifications. This was a tradition that put faith in language above all. Islam is based on the premise that one human language — Arabic — was rich and precise enough to express the very word of God, exactly as He intended.

This only partially explains why the language of the Quran is so dense and complicated. The other reason, I came to appreciate in graduate school, is the literary context into which the Quran was born. In the Jahiliya, the period before Islam, a great poet was a pop star, historian, and wizard all at once. The poets of the late sixth century commemorated battles, praised leaders, and recounted tales of love and loss. Every year before the month of pilgrimage, poets from all the tribes convened near Mecca to recite their best, most moving works.

Into this poetry-mad culture came the Quran, the direct word of God. Naturally, God spoke in the poetic style of the day. And God, being God, was more skilled with words than Imru' al-Qays, 'Antar, Tarafa, or any of His other mortal poet creations. Not that the Quran should be mistaken for the odes that preceded it. "We have not taught the Prophet poetry," the Lord made sure to specify, in sura 36, verse 69. The Quran is, the verse continues, a *revelation*.

The Quran did not follow the rigid metrical rules the poets had established, but it still followed in the tradition of poetry because it was an oral work. God spoke the verses to the archangel Gabriel, who told them to Muhammad, and the Prophet repeated them aloud to his followers, who memorized them and recited them to others. This oral tradition carried on through the centuries. I first heard verses recited in Cairo, emanating from a taxi tape deck, half sung by an idle police officer, murmured by a solo reader seated with an open book in a corner of a mosque. Everywhere I heard it, the simple, melodic chant created a little oasis of calm in the city's din. The Quran spoken aloud effectively reenacted the moment of revelation, so that the listener would hear it just as Muhammad had. Once, I heard a recording in which the reciter's voice caught and quavered, on the brink of tears; perhaps he had been gripped with this very sense of immediacy.

At the same time, the Quran was a bridge to written Arabic culture. The function is built right into its name: the word *Qur'an* comes from *qara'a*, the verb that means both to recite and to read. The first message that the angel Gabriel is said to have conveyed to Muhammad began with the imperative: "Read: Your Lord is the most generous, who has taught by means of the pen, has taught man what he did not know."

Revelation came over a period of twenty-three years, and along with it came the usual codification, canonization, and all-around paperwork essential to establishing any new religion. In the later chapters, the body of revelation is no longer referred to as a *qur'an,* a recited-thing, but as a *kitab,* a book. Revelation ended with Muhammad's death in 632, and about two decades later, the Quran was written down in a single standardized text. It was no longer just an oral, recited message but also a book that was available for all followers to read.

Along with this holy book came a need for other books about it. By the mid-seventh century, little more than thirty years after Muhammad's death, the Islamic empire had spread into what is now Egypt, Iraq, and Iran. Some of history's first intrepid Arabic students, better known as early converts to Islam, were reading the Quran and making mistakes — and this being the very word of God, any mistake was an egregious one. The second caliph, Umar ibn al-Khattab, is renowned for his love of Arabic; he is also known for beating his scribes when they made copying errors.

So grammarians established rules for Arabic, which they deduced from the Quran, as well as from poetry. Tradition holds that Muhammad was not fond of poetry, but this did not mean it was tossed aside as irredeemably pagan. This is probably because the Quran hadn't broken radically from it, but rather expanded on it.

Using the Quran as the yardstick for all of Arabic created some tricky situations. Because the Quran was God's creation, it was by definition perfect. Grammarians had to account for every variance; nothing could be dismissed as a stenographer's error or a malapropism. Every grammarian was a theologian, and vice versa. In these early examinations of the language, rational analysis constantly rubbed up against faith. A morphological mistake was also a moral misstep. So, hey, no pressure.

The Quran was a powerful force when it was revealed, and four-teen hundred years later, it was still considered, among Muslims and non-Muslims alike, the paragon of Arabic expression. In Muham-mad's time, Arabic was the language of the caravan routes from the Arabian Peninsula and north into present-day Iraq; it had probably varied significantly along the way, from oasis to oasis. The Quran was a snapshot of a certain type of Arabic — that of Mecca, of the tribe of the Quraysh, and, technically, of God. Without the scripture, Arabic would have continued to shift, adapting to the vagaries of trade and possibly splitting into new languages. Instead, the Quran preserved the language for all time.

I looked up from my pile of reference books to take a breath. The bearded librarian at the desk caught my eye and gave me an encour-aging smile.

In Abu Dhabi, I had arranged to rent a room through an online agency. The listing was scant on details, but it was the only option in my budget. When I arrived, somewhere in the generic midrise section of the city, I was greeted by a tall woman in a stretchy white headscarf. She immediately pulled me inside, locked the door, and removed her scarf. Then she chided me for having introduced myself in Egyptian dialect.

"My name is Farah. And you must speak *real* Arabic, not these accents," she said, her face breaking into a broad, gap-toothed smile. "In Libya, we pronounce every letter the way it should be." I stam-mered a Fusha reply, and we switched to English, because she spoke it brilliantly and seemed eager to practice.

I had never met a Libyan. There weren't very many of them — barely six million in the 700,000-square-mile country, and not many out-side it either. I knew only two things about Libya. One, of course, was Muammar Qaddafi, and he had recently been deposed, captured, and killed. The other was that the country's name written in Arabic makes an uncommon kind of palindrome, a visual one: ليبيا.

Farah talked with an eagerness I recognized in myself, as I was starved for company after long days of driving. She patted the overstuffed sofa in her tiny living room, and we sat down to talk. Within ten minutes, we were deep in her life story. The details tumbled out with the same generosity with which she poured my tea and ladled in the sugar. "I tried everything — pills, hormones, everything," she said, "but I could not have a child. And so we divorced." In 2000, she had remarried, to a Syrian man, and settled in Abu Dhabi. She was his second wife — or, as she put it, his "local wife."

I had never met a woman in such an arrangement. Yes, technically, in many countries in the Arab world a Muslim man was entitled to four wives, but he had to be wealthy or foolhardy to claim them. Or, I saw now, lonely — a permanent migrant, working for decades away from his family. Although she had given up her job in a hospital, Farah was no silly kept woman. In Libya, she had trained and worked as an engineer. "It makes a lot of sense," Farah told me. "Women, we can go a long time without sex. But men, they have urges. If a man isn't married, he'll be going to bad women, and that is not respectable." Then she added, almost as an afterthought, "And God would punish him."

Later, when I met her husband, Abdallah, I was momentarily abashed — I knew too much. He was a small man with a trim gray beard who spoke clear, formal Arabic and very little English; Farah played translator when necessary. Our introduction was the sort of awkward encounter that etiquette books try to save you from. I stuck out my hand; he kept his at his side, then, seeing me withdrawing mine, extended his. We settled on limply brushing fingertips. This too was new to me — I had never met a man so pious that he wouldn't shake a woman's hand.

So for several days I read at the library, and in the evenings I learned from Farah and Abdallah.

Heritage Club

THE BEARDED DESK clerk personally ushered me to my table. This time, I set aside the Quran and went further back, to the pre-Islamic poetry that I had not read in more than fourteen years — though lines of it still occasionally popped into my head.

The most famous Jahiliya poems are the seven works called the *mu'allaqat*, the "adorned" or "hanging" odes. The former meaning is probably more accurate, referring to the poems' ornate language, but the latter, a folk etymology, is more fun. In this interpretation, these seven poems were embroidered on banners and hung on the Ka'ba in Mecca after the annual poetry slam, like blue-ribbon winners at the state fair.

At first, before I could understand them well, the *mu'allaqat* had enchanted me with their sound alone. Composed for oral recitation, they proceed with stately, meditative grace, punctuated by a single end rhyme. They conjure a campfire, with faces of family visible in the warm light and the inky black of the desert swirling behind.

The more I read, the more intrigued I was by how the poems were made. Unlike the verse epics of the Western canon, which relate a legendary hero's adventures in the third person, the *mu'allaqat* are in the first person and often share the poet's emotions. Yet the poet does not simply pour out his feelings; they are contained in a formal structure that touches on set themes. Most of the poems open deep in the desert, with the poet recalling a lost love. Next comes a scene of solitary travel. Finally the poet arrives back in the circle of the tribe, and turns to a specific poetic purpose: praising a leader, eulogizing a fallen warrior, mocking a fellow poet, or simply boasting of his (and occasionally her) own talents. Shifting from scene to scene, the poems can seem disjointed, but taken as a whole, each holds the elements of any folk story: loss, quest, triumph. And like a parable or a fairy tale, they convey collective wisdom and shared values.

My own travels could fit into the structure of the pre-Islamic ode, I mused as I read. The first week in Dubai, when I had moped around dreaming of Cairo—that had been the beginning of my poem, lamenting my lost love. Now I was in the period of traveling alone through the desert. Well, at the moment I seemed to be waylaid in the city. Or was this my triumphant return? Shivering in a library, reading old books—no, it didn't seem triumphant. It was, in fact, the very activity I had sworn off at the beginning of my journey as a reformed Arabic student.

I was still in the desert-wandering phase, then. Triumph, whatever that might be, would have to wait. A new plan was crystallizing. I would leave the library and go to some isolated dune, the sort where a poet might have stood and considered an old campfire. I would take my dear old Hans Wehr dictionary, and I would sit in the sand and read the most famous of the *mu'allaqat*, the one composed by the poet Imru' al-Qays around the middle of the sixth century. Its first words, *Qifa nabki*—Halt, let us weep—are iconic, the Arabic equivalent of "To be or not to be." How much of the poem would I remember beyond the two opening words? It would be a test of my current Arabic skills, and it would give a little shape to my aimless trip.

I began copying the verses into my notebook, trying not to dwell on how much was completely unfamiliar. I'd deal with that later.

As I finished writing out the last line, I looked up to find the bearded desk clerk standing next to me. "It is time we close," he said. As if in consolation, he handed me a juice box, mango flavor.

"I have some ideas what we can do today," Farah said over breakfast. In the living room, she had pushed the coffee table to the side and laid out a bedsheet on the floor, for an indoor picnic of bread and apricot jam from her sister in Libya, and cheese from Abdallah's wife in Syria. The night before, I had told her my plan to drive into the desert and read the poem. Now she was acting as if I'd never mentioned it and offering a full itinerary for the day. We would visit the Emirati heritage club across the street from her old apartment, to see if someone there could give me ideas for my book. Then we would visit a new district of the city named Saadiyat. "It means happiness," Farah said. "It is too nice!"

Her enthusiasm was winning. I did worry that I wasn't improving my Arabic much, here in Farah's tight, fluent-English embrace. But, I reminded myself, my trip was meant to connect me with people, not books. And, as the proverb said, *Ar-rafeeq qabl at-tareeq*—Who you travel with is more important than where you go.

Abdallah came out of the bedroom in his work suit and slippers. He had been up since the pre-dawn prayer, he told me with an energetic wink. At least I could hear Arabic from him, even if a lot of it seemed to revolve around the glory of Islam.

"I get up to pray too, but I go back to sleep," Farah said as she folded up the breakfast bedsheet.

In the car, Farah looked skeptical. "How long have you been driving?" she asked as I held my breath through another one of Abu Dhabi's giant roundabouts. "I drive when we go to Syria," she said. "Abdallah gets very upset. 'You drive like a man—you drive very fast!' he says to me. No, not like a man. Like in the movies!"

"Like *The Fast and the Furious*?" I asked, thinking of Medo stuck in Cairo traffic.

"Yes! I love that movie! I watched it again last week."

The Emirati heritage club, in a dowdy office park, was a bust. The public-relations rep was Egyptian. He served us dates and coffee and loaded us up with glossy brochures about falconry, camel racing, and summer camps for schoolchildren. Then he looked expectantly at us. I wanted to know what heritage — *turath,* a weighty word — meant to Emiratis; I doubted an Egyptian could say. We thanked him and left.

Farah had more ideas. In the parking lot after we left, she swatted my arm. "You should have asked to join one of the summer camps," she said. If I wasn't careful, she would talk me into staying the next four months, until the camp started.

Saadiyat, the new city district, was more interesting, even though it had not actually been built yet. Farah and I strolled through the welcome center, a display of videos, interactive touchscreens, and renderings and models of the architectural marvels that would soon be there. Coming from America in a recession, I was struck with envy. This exhibit alone probably had a bigger budget than some midsize American cities.

In Libya, oil wealth had enabled Muammar Qaddafi to crush his country under a demented form of communism for more than forty years. Farah had called him a "barbarian," and rightly so (even if she had actually meant Berber, a source of confusion ever since the ancient Greeks had named this North African people). In the UAE, unlike Libya, the money appeared to be in the hands of rational people with vision. Saadiyat didn't have the history or splendor of Cairo or Damascus, but at least it was peaceful.

At the exit was a guestbook. A girl named Mariam had written an accidental ode to heritage: "It was my grandparent and all my family here, all my beautiful childhood. I loved the sea, it was my baradise. *Now* it's the world wonderland. I wish the most beautiful to all."

• • •

The next morning, I resolved to leave again, but Farah patted the sofa next to her. "Let me show you my pictures," she said. "Abdallah doesn't approve of photos, so we have to look while he's gone."

Farah's uncle and father had been in the political elite; in their photos, they were dapper, midcentury gentlemen with oiled hair and fezzes tilted just so. Farah's mother perched on an angular 1960s sofa. Her aunt stood regally on her wedding day, in a stiff dress embroidered with intricate silver geometry; on her chest lay a gold-and-ruby necklace as complex as a chandelier. Farah appeared as a young woman in green corduroy bell bottoms, alongside a crew of colleagues, on an engineering assignment in the Eastern Bloc. Later, with big 1980s hair, she leaned on a balcony in a red dolman-sleeved sweater.

"That is a beautiful picture of you," I said.

"Is it?" she replied vaguely, her eyes averted.

"*Mashallah!*" I remembered to add, and her face brightened.

"That was my honeymoon—with my first husband," she said. "Abdallah and I have no picture of us together married," she said. "Isn't that silly?"

As she was putting away the box of photos, a key turned in the front door. "That's Abdallah, back for lunch," Farah said. "You must stay. He has ordered food for all of us. And I made dessert."

Over a platter of spicy chicken and rice, I told Abdallah I had been reading about the Quran at the library, knowing this would please him.

"Ah," he sighed. "You can write a whole book about a single verse of the Quran and still not understand it fully." He smiled a beatific smile and pushed a chicken leg toward me.

Farah emerged from the kitchen with a tray of cake topped with jiggling fruit-filled gelatin. She cut me a piece as large as a paperback book, and when I protested, she whacked my thigh. "You *must* eat. We are the dictators—we say so!" Abdallah joined in, mock-frowning like a tyrant and modestly swatting the air an inch from my leg.

"Now you should have a nap," Farah said when I finished my cake and moved to gather my belongings. "It is not safe to drive when you are sleepy."

I would have liked nothing better than to stay here for the rest of my trip, listening to Farah's stories. But I did need to go. The structure of the poem demanded it—the open road called.

"OK," Farah finally said when she saw I was serious. "You know where you're going? Turn right outside." She put down her glass of tea to gesture. "Then go *sida* until you see the freeway."

"Sorry, what's *sida*?"

Her forehead wrinkled. "Oh, wait. That's not English. Is it Arabic?" She paused to think. "No, no — it's not. Sorry. I've been here too long! Everyone says, '*Rooh sida! Sem-sem*.' I think *sida* is from India, for straight. And *sem-sem* — well, you know that." Same-same — the great international pidgin phrase. Maybe I would learn the Gulf dialect yet.

Farah spritzed me all over with perfume she kept on a tray by the door. "Dolce and Gabbana—too nice!" she said, smoothing down my hair and giving me a hug. The scent stayed with me the rest of the day.

The Best People

THE ROAD TO Liwa, home of the most scenic sand dunes in the emirate of Abu Dhabi, was straight and dull. I stopped for cardamom tea at a gas station, the thrill of which wore off about the same time the radio signals turned fuzzy. To break the monotony, I stopped for a hitchhiker. I had noticed several men thumbing rides before this — workers, I supposed, who had no other transport than their company-provided buses. In another poem, Imru' al-Qays wrote the wise and lilting words "*Wa-kullu ghareebin lil-ghareebi naseebun*" — all strangers are kin to one another. As a foreigner here, I felt a kinship with this lone man, frail and wispily bearded, standing by the side of the road, his kurta flapping in the wind raised by passing trucks.

When he approached the car, his eyes widened with surprise. He peered in at the back seat and, seeing no one, lowered his brows in doubt. Still, a free ride was a free ride. He climbed in and arranged himself primly on the seat, his back perfectly straight. I asked him where he was from, but after a few attempts, it was clear we had no languages in common. I drove on, trusting he would direct me to stop where he needed to get out.

This man in my passenger seat, more than anything, illustrated how different the UAE was from Egypt or any other part of the Arab world I had visited. In all those places, I had never been able to forget that I was a woman. Usually this was a small pleasure, the reminders coming in the form of extra attention, compliments, or conversational flourishes: "my good lady," "sugar," "honey." Less pleasant reminders were the crude invitations from idle men on the street.

In the UAE, aside from the shop clerk who had offered to spritz me with Facebook perfume and the man who had possibly tried to seduce me by telling me about his dead wife, I felt none of this attention. On paper, this didn't make sense: the Emirates had the largest gender imbalance in the world, 2.7 adult men for every woman. But these statistics did not translate into street hassle, at least for me, a middle-aged white woman. In some parts of Dubai, I had walked for blocks without seeing any other women, but also without a single comment. The anonymity had made me lonely at first, but by now I enjoyed it. It was a luxury I didn't have even in New York.

The hitchhiker and I rode for ten minutes in awkward silence until he gestured to the side of the road. A gravel driveway led to a chain-link fence and, beyond, an oil derrick. He got out and trudged away, looking back once to confirm that he had not imagined the whole thing.

Emboldened, I looked for more hitchhikers. The next one, standing at yet another gravel road to an unmarked work site, was from Pakistan, he said in well-rehearsed English. That was his only line. He sat in the back seat, silent, like a taxi passenger. I dropped him at a bus station in the middle of nowhere and drove on.

The third hitchhiker was brimming with energy, unlike the others, who had been somewhat wilted in the heat. Better, he looked Arab—like someone I could talk to. He jumped in the front seat and gave me a toothy grin. "Where are you from?" I asked in Arabic.

"I'm Egyptian," he said, his smile stretching even wider. "My name's Hussein."

"*Ahsan nass!*" I gushed, slapping the steering wheel with excitement. The best people! This was the effusive expression Egyptians always used when I told them I was American, and it was fun to turn the tables.

More exciting still, I understood the man. It was as if I had finally tuned in to the right radio station after cranking the dial through patches of static. Hussein was from Cairo — "the capital itself," as he grandly put it — and was working here in construction.

But there was a problem. In my enthusiasm, I had picked him up while headed the wrong way — I had been looping around trying to find a turn I had missed. Hussein needed to go to Abu Dhabi, back the way I had come. I apologized and offered to drop him at the edge of town, but he directed me to the mini-market nearby.

In the store, Hussein raced around offering me things. Chips? Twinkies? Sunflower seeds? Every suggestion was an excuse to touch my arm. I was a woman again, for better and worse. I settled on an orange soda, and he went for an energy drink, as if he needed more pep. After clinking our bottles to toast our most fortuitous meeting, then shaking hands at least four times, we parted ways.

But as I drove slowly back to the highway, I noticed in my rearview mirror that Hussein was walking in the same direction. He hadn't needed to go to the market at all; that had just been an excuse to spend more time with me. It was boiling hot, and the guy had spent a portion of his tiny income on drinks for us. I made another U-turn.

"Get in," I called out my window. "I'll take you back to where you started."

When we got there, we again thanked each other profusely, and he squeezed and kissed my hand and gave me his mobile number. I nearly had to push him out of the car. He was still waving as I drove off. I was smiling too — that orange soda, and the little dose of Egyptian conversation, had hit the spot.

• • •

In Liwa, I checked in to a hotel, then drove out to the desert for the sunset. I had grown up in what people called a desert, but that rocky New Mexican scrub, punctuated by tough, pointy plants, was nothing like this. I gasped at every turn. This was proper sandy desert, the edge of 250,000 square miles known as *ar-rub' al-khali*, the Empty Quarter. The Arabic word for desert, *sahra'*, also means bleak, but now in the golden hour, the terrain looked soft and welcoming.

The road was a black ribbon curling around each dune. On a few curves, the sand had drifted onto the asphalt, creating an unnerving illusion of the road having crumbled away. I drove as far as Tell Moreeb (Horrifying Hill). The name was no overstatement; it was an intimidating mountain of sand. Two four-wheel-drive vehicles, small as tadpoles, skittered down its face; the drivers' faint, elated whoops cut through the silence. Backtracking out of sight and earshot of the dune-bashers, I found a spot to pull off the road. I gathered a few things in my bag and walked a short way into the desert, looking back frequently to check my position. I was not here to get lost, just to read a bit of poetry. I nestled down in a curve of fine sand and unpacked my notebook and my green Hans Wehr dictionary.

The burnished dunes curved all around, cutting a sinuous line to the horizon. As the sun sank low, they glowed a rosy, ferrous red. There was no other distraction—no wildlife, no plants, only the faintest breeze. I turned to my poem.

I murmured the first words of the *mu'allaqa* of Imru' al-Qays:
Qifa nabki min dhikra habeebin wa-manzili . . .

قفا نبك من ذكرى حبيب ومنزل

I traced the familiar curves, the dainty dots of the letters; the flowing cursive seemed to fit with the rounded dunes behind me.

Halt, friends! Let us weep in memory of a beloved and her campsite . . .

For a well-read Arab, the phrase *Qifa nabki* summons a flood of images, not just from the rest of Imru' al-Qays's ode, but from the whole Jahiliya canon: the abandoned campsite, marked by a few pieces of charred firewood; the lost beloved, her eyes as big and dark as a wild cow's; dramatic storms flashing over the dunes. Alongside these images are moments of bravado — oh, that saucy woman in the camel howdah! — but they are tempered with sorrow. The desert is vast, and the life of the *bedu* means always leaving a girl behind, as her tribe moves one direction and yours another.

Qifa nabki echoes through the rest of Arabic literature. Centuries later, well after Arabs had settled in cities and grown so soft they wouldn't have survived an afternoon in the desert, poems still began with an interlude of sorrow in the dunes. A poem wasn't a poem without camels, dark-eyed women, and despair. Near the end of graduate school, I wasted a couple of months trying to write a paper comparing Jahiliya poetry to American country music. I gave up when I recognized it as a desperate bid to make my absurdly narrow academic field relevant to the modern world. But the premise was sound. Jahiliya poetry had a formula, and a remarkably powerful one — as effective in evoking tears as a honky-tonk tune about cheatin' hearts and open roads. Not coincidentally, *shi'r*, poetry, comes from the verb *sha'ara*, which means both to compose verse and to feel.

The first words of the ode were crystal clear because of their endless reiteration over nearly fifteen centuries, but the rest of the opening line was foggier in my mind:

> . . . *bi-siqti l-liwa beina d-dakhuli fa-hawmali*
> بسقط اللوى بين الدخول فحومل
> . . . *at the edge of a dune between ad-Dakhul and Hawmal*

Thanks to my old grad-school professor, I remembered that ad-Dakhul and Hawmal were names of landmarks in the Arabian Desert. So I didn't have to waste time mucking around in the dictionary, then trying to figure out why this poem was mentioning "first coition in marriage" (*dukhul*) and "long-suffering" (*hamool*, the closest word in Hans Wehr to *hawmal*) right at the outset.

I was curious about the derivation of the phrase *siqti l-liwa*, though.

I remembered it meaning the dune's edge, and here I was in a place called Liwa. Had it been named for its dunes, or was it the other way around?

Hans Wehr told me that a *siqt* was a "miscarried fetus." I found *liwa* meant curvature, but was immediately distracted by the next entry, *lawa*, colic. I let out a soft laugh, which vanished in the silent desert. This was such a typical Arabic dictionary moment, like the time I had looked up a word on a Cairo restaurant menu, only to find it meant some kind of squash — or a brothel. Hans was clearly not the man for this job. I really needed to be back in the library with Lane and his eight volumes of bickering medieval sources.

If the first line was like wading into the shallows, the second one was like stepping off into the bottomless depths of the sea. I skimmed on, looking for familiar words. Oh, good Lord, there was so much left! Each *beit*, or verse, was divided into two halves — hemistichs, in poetry-nerd parlance — separated by a wide space. I was stuck on the third hemistich, the first half of the second *beit*. The rest of the poem formed two tidy columns down the rest of the page and on to a second. What hubris had made me think I shouldn't bring an English translation, or even copy down the internal vowels and case markers? I took a deep breath and muddled through four more lines. Something about weasels? Definitely animal droppings like peppercorns.

Finally it was too dark to read. I set my books and papers aside and lay back in the sand. It was silky soft, still warm from the sun. The silence settled over me like a thick blanket, and I watched the stars come out one by one. For years after graduate school, I had thought that time had been wasted, all those fruitless hours looking up names of places and precise words for camels and dunes. Yet the whole mess of it had eventually led me here, and that alone made it worthwhile.

I had intended to spend more time in the northern, less affluent emirates, the ones with names I'd never heard before arriving in the UAE: Umm Al-Quwain, Fujairah, Ras Al Khaimah. Back in Dubai,

Manal had told me, as if she had spotted a unicorn, "In Fujairah, I saw Emirati taxi drivers!" I had also wanted to drive across the neighboring country of Oman, to Al-Hadd (the Edge), the easternmost point in the Arab world, and watch the sun rise. Somehow, between my days in the library and my desert roaming, I had frittered away more than two weeks farther south, and I was due back in Dubai in a few days.

So I would hit two birds with one stone: I'd see the northernmost emirate of Ras Al Khaimah (Top of the Tent), and I'd take a day trip a bit farther north, a boat ride around the Musandam Peninsula, the proper tippy-top of the tent and a noncontiguous part of Oman. Perhaps I would see a fabled Emirati taxi driver, or an Omani one.

The capital city of RAK, as the emirate was more prosaically known, was refreshingly free of record-breaking anything. Low buildings hunkered below jagged blue mountains. The foothills were dotted with modern villas, faux castles, and hot-pink Italianate manses with blue mirror windows to block the sun.

The next morning, the bus to Musandam wound over the mountains. As soon as we crossed the Omani border, the craggy landscape seemed to shake off civilization—no more pink mansions, no more concrete-block garages, no more people at all.

On the boat, an old wooden dhow like the ones that dotted the creek in Dubai, we drifted far from the world, around the ragged edges of the land. Our Pakistani guide pointed out jellyfish, lionfish, a family of dolphins—as well as Persian saffron he was selling for a special price. With Iran only fifty miles away across the Strait of Hormuz, this area was known for smuggling; apparently everyone was involved.

Meanwhile, I had my eye on the boat captain, because I had heard him speaking Arabic, and maybe something juicier: Kumzari. I had read about this rare language of Musandam, with an estimated 1,700 speakers; the *Ethnologue*, a great encyclopedia of all the world's tongues, pessimistically categorized it as "moribund," a couple of notches above extinct. Kumzari was a natural mishmash of Persian and Arabic, a byproduct of centuries of goods and people shuttling across the water. The Arabian Peninsula may have been the heartland of Arabic, but here at the sunrise end, it nurtured many other linguistic peculiarities and trade patois: Bathari, Harsusi, Shehri, Mehri, Hobyót. According to the *Ethnologue*, Oman had 22,000 Swahili speakers too.

On the return trip, the captain tried to cajole me into steering the boat—this was my opening. "You speak Kumzari?" I asked in Arabic.

"Yes, sure. I learned Arabic in school, but at home we speak Kumzari—and here at work." His name was Jasim. His face, under a worn baseball cap, was that of a teenager, but his hands were gnarled and cut. He spun out a bit of Kumzari for me, his *r*'s rolling up from the very depths of his throat. I hung on every word—its intonation was like the little bit of Persian I had studied, and every so often an Arabic word popped out. I scribbled down transliterated phrases in my notebook. *Shai ma Khasab*—I'm going to Khasab. *Afwayyim*—sleeping.

But the strange *r*'s caught in my throat, and Jasim soon lost interest in tutoring. He pulled out his phone and showed me a photo of his brother with a hammerhead shark, then a video of a friend dancing, a lewd and subtle shaking of the behind, while from off-camera a heckler hurled bananas.

Then our boat was back in port and our group was back on the bus, winding down and down the mountain roads, out of the wild land of Oman and into the shabby outskirts of RAK. By the time I was back in my car, the sun had set. In the dark, I overshot the turn to my hotel.

All I had to do was keep driving to the next roundabout, do a loop, and come back. Except the roundabout was one of the especially huge and awful ones, with three lanes and five spokes. I gripped the steering wheel and sailed in.

As I approached the fourth spoke, I looked to my right to make sure no one was careening into the circle — just as, from my left, someone was trying to make his way out. Our two tiny cars colliding made the sound of plastic party cups meeting in a halfhearted toast.

Conveniently, there was a parking bay off one side of the circle, and we both pulled in. Five men piled out of the other car, all gesturing wildly and shouting — in Arabic! I was thrilled.

Our conversation boiled down to a simple exchange. "You have money?" the driver asked, pointing to his lightly dented back fender, where my car had clipped his.

"No. No money. Must call company of insurance," I said as cars whirled around the circle next to us. The word for insurance — *ta'meen* — I knew from reading it on scores of billboards over the years. This was the first time I had uttered it in a sentence.

"You have money?"

"No. No money. I call insurance company."

After a few more rounds of this, the men bundled into their car and drove off. I got back in my car too. Should I drive away? Was that legal? *Could* I drive? My hands were shaking badly. While I deliberated, a police SUV rolled up. The officer, in an army-green uniform, did not speak English either. I was delighted.

"I offer profound apologies," I told him in my most sincere and florid Arabic. Carefully pronouncing each word was a little meditation, soothing my post-collision jitters. "I am not accustomed to the driving in your fine country. These traffic circles — I thought . . ." I couldn't find the words to explain what I thought, but I *had* spent a lot of time thinking about these terrifying roundabouts.

"You, my good lady, were at fault," the policeman declared, likewise in grave but gracious tones. "You are obliged to stay in your lane. Go *sida, sem-sem.*"

But the other car hadn't been going *sem-sem!* Never mind, I was thrilled again, hearing the very words Farah had taught me before I left her apartment in Abu Dhabi. Anyway, my *ta'meen* would cover the damage, and I was lucky it hadn't been worse.

The next morning, I had to deliver assorted forms to the police station, a generic new building that gleamed like a car dealership. Covering one wall in the waiting area was a vinyl sign, in Arabic and English, of all the possible traffic infractions and their fines. "Misunderstanding Traffic Circles" was not listed, nor was "Failure to Go *Sem-sem*." '

My number was called. At the desk, I launched into the story I had rehearsed as I waited. The clerk's mouth dropped open. "You speak *Arabic?*" he said, and motioned for his colleagues to come see the show.

Soon six more men were crowded into the cubicle, hunched behind the desk clerk. Was this, as the poem's structure dictated, my triumphant return from the desert to society? In this case, the last section of my poem would be a boast. I continued my story, and the men hung on every word: my certain entry into the traffic circle, my cautious analysis of the confounding situation, the stunning surprise of the other car, the driver's desertion of the scene.

My papers were handled with efficiency and cheer, and the men waved when I left. *Triumph.*

Supreme Poets

IN THE END, I found all the poetry I was looking for in Dubai, not in the desert. The schedule of the annual four-day literary festival was packed with verse, starting on the opening night with the Palestinian poet Mourid Barghouti.

At the entrance to a faux tent on the Dubai Creek, past a clutch of real camels, a staffer was handing out headsets for the simultaneous translation. I hesitated, out of pride. But it was sheer delusion to think that, after one evening of browsing my Hans Wehr on the edge of a dune, I would suddenly understand everything. I took a headset.

Barghouti was Palestinian literary royalty, and the crowd of older intellectuals — recognizable by the sheen of their suits and the heaviness of their eyeglasses and costume jewelry — was engaged in a flurry of air-kissing and handshaking. When a festival spokesman stepped up to introduce the poet, the buzz took half a minute to die down. I glanced sheepishly at the perfectly coiffed matrons seated near me and put on my headset.

Barghouti's elegant, incisive poems reflected political realities as well as more existential ones. This, however, did not come through in the simultaneous translation. As Barghouti read his verses in a slow, serious cadence, the voice of a woman interpreter chirped frantically in my ear. On the one hand, it was a useful reminder of just how many words I would not have understood on my own; on the other, it made the poetry sound ridiculous. Midway through the third poem, I was undone by the dissonance and let out a small giggle. The matrons turned to glare.

I took off my headset and let the rhythm of the words wash over me, catching phrases here and there. The words I understood best were the concrete ones — a cup of coffee, a wooden table — but they were infused with grace through the elegant Fusha. In my head, inspired by Dr. Badawi, I strung together my own poems.

When that failed, I simply listened to the audience. A particularly rich and melodious line would prompt appreciative exhalations — "*Allah!*" — and a ripple of applause, the way jazz aficionados praise a fine solo. Behind me, the matrons' heavy bracelets clicked softly as they clapped or moved a hand in the air in time with the rhythm.

The next night, a panel of Emirati poets convened. It was a smaller affair, in a drab meeting room in a side hall of the hotel, but this time two interpreters were on the job. The tag-team approach produced no better results, though the source material might have been to blame.

"My eyes follow her steps from the house to the mall . . . ," a female voice intoned in my headset. The poet's microphone had a touch of reverb, so *mool* (mall) resounded in the little room.

I did my best not to laugh. This was Nabati poetry, a form composed in Gulf dialect that was related to the pre-Islamic odes I had studied. Its name came from a word with connotations of corruption and brokenness, apparently a reference to its colloquial phrasing. Bedouin culture may have fallen out of favor with these city folk, but they had not stopped versifying. Over the centuries, local poets had carried on composing poems to honor battles, great heroes, and loves lost.

"Even if she smacks me with her love," a male interpreter picked up the thread, "I will still . . . be patient for love?"

None of my professors had mentioned that the Nabati tradition existed. Perhaps they lived too far in the past, too deep in books. Or perhaps they didn't consider the colloquial language legitimate. The current poets had swapped camels for fast cars and abandoned the campsites for malls, but they were working with the same themes and the same rigid strictures of rhythm and rhyme. Poetry was very much alive, not just in this hotel conference room, but on television, in the hit show *Million's Poet,* a competition similar to *American Idol* that aired on Abu Dhabi TV. The work by the sheikh of Dubai that I had pretended to read in the bookstore, in hopes of attracting a talkative stranger — that, I realized now, was Nabati poetry. And in my drives around the desert, I had heard it on the radio occasionally, slow and sonorous, sometimes enhanced with spacy electronica in the background.

A second poet stood. He had abandoned his family for the woman he loved, he recited, and the experience tore him apart. His voice quavered with emotion, but the message coming through my headset was resolutely undramatic. Everyone else in the room sat rapt, under the spell of the words.

"And I lost weight —"

The woman interpreter broke off midline. At the podium, the poet carried on, unaware.

The other interpreter stepped in to finish. "I just want to see my family again," he said. Then came the audible click of his microphone switching off.

I turned to look at the translators' booth. Two figures were hunched over, shoulders shaking with silent laughter.

In my view, simultaneous translators were awesome, in the truest sense of the word — I could not fathom how they spoke so instinctively, acting as mere vessels for the words. Yet even with this oracular talent, they faced an impossible task in this room. It was one thing to communicate the crucial points of a rant by Muammar Qaddafi on the floor of the United Nations. It was quite another to convey the emotion in a poem. Translating poetry was a task of hours, sometimes years, not split seconds.

As I had done at the Barghouti reading, I took off my headset and listened to the sound of the syllables. The shape of these poems and the stories in them had been handed down, generation to generation, told and retold, the collective experience of a people distilled to its essential moments. Poetry — and the Quran with it — was the heritage Arabs had carried out of the desert, to the very edges of the Islamic empire, and preserved until now.

On the last day of the festival, I attended a panel on the future of the Arabic language. The panelists neatly represented all the problems Arabic faced in the modern age. Addressing the issue of early education was an elegant sheikha from the ruling family of the neighboring emirate of Sharjah. Her publishing house produced children's books featuring Arab characters and Middle Eastern settings. This shouldn't have sounded radical, but it was, because most Arabic children's books were translations of foreign stories set in foreign places, such as that blond Swiss imp Heidi.

Another panel member, an Arabic professor at the Abu Dhabi branch of New York University, laid out the problems in higher education, including a lack of good teaching materials, for both native speakers and foreigners.

The third person on the panel, a newspaper publisher, lamented the lack of Arabic in the world at large. If Arabs truly valued their language, he proposed, why shouldn't there be an Arabic equivalent of the Goethe-Institut or the British Council, teaching the language and promoting the culture around the world?

At first the discussion was proactive and dynamic — these people seemed dedicated to solving problems I had faced in trying to learn Arabic. These problems were more serious in the Emirates, where well-off children typically studied English from an early age, with little grounding in written Arabic at the same time. The sheikha had established her publishing house when she noticed that her own daughter had learned to read English before Arabic. Shutting the barn door once the horse was loose, the UAE declared Arabic an official language in 2008.

But as the panelists continued to talk, they revealed a conservative streak. "Some people hold PhDs," the newspaperman commented with a snort, pushing up his round glasses imperiously, "and what they write can't be considered Arabic. They should review the rules!"

The professor, for his part, admitted that, yes, Fusha was the language of the elite. "But when I say elite," he said, "I don't mean that in the sense of class. With education, even a farmer in Egypt can be elite."

Now it was my turn to snort. What world was this professor living in? Certainly not real-world Egypt, where social mobility was virtually nil and the literacy rate hovered around 65 percent. And not even Hosni Mubarak, the now-deposed president, had spoken Fusha. Everyone knew his Ammiya words were "translated" into the classical style when they were quoted in the newspaper.

No one on the panel entertained the idea of letting an Egyptian farmer be literate in the language he spoke. For nearly every problem over which the panelists were wringing their hands, the answer seemed to be simply this: let people write the way they talked. If Arabic dialects were written, it would make early reading easier. As it stood, children's books, including the sheikha's series, were in Fusha, but only the most devoted — and pedantic — parent would read them aloud. Fusha was the language of school and high culture, not the language of parental love and snuggling before bed. A Palestinian-American couple I knew did read to their children in Fusha, but only because the mom insisted, out of American habit; the dad, though he considered Arabic education essential, found Fusha unnatural.

If Arabic dialects were written, the newspaperman's dream of an international Arabic program would reach more people, because students could master more in a shorter time. And there would be no language of the elite, in terms of money or education. Would it be so terrible, I huffed to myself at the back of the room, if these aristocratic guardians became irrelevant, if Fusha faded away and the dialects rose up as full-fledged languages?

This was what happened in Europe, when Romance languages overtook elite Latin, and the diglossia of the Middle Ages was resolved. In the fourteenth century, Dante composed *The Divine Comedy*. His epic poem was both theologically meaty and wildly entertaining, and it legitimized the Italian vernacular in which it was written. This opened the door to greater literacy and the creative flowering of the Renaissance. No wonder Dante was crowned *il Sommo Poeta*, the Supreme Poet.

The Arab world had undergone one linguistic renaissance, starting in the late nineteenth century, when the florid medieval language was pruned to fit the more practical, populist demands of newspapers and advertisements. At the time, a pro-colloquial camp in Egypt promoted the use of Ammiya in print, but undermined itself by making its arguments in Fusha. With British and French influence rampant across the Arab world, the door on the debate closed. Fusha was a crucial unifying force, a language of solidarity against colonialism.

I couldn't help thinking Arabic needed another transformation. Every country in the Arab world could benefit from a Supreme Poet, to bring each dialect to maturity, to pull out and polish its unique vocabulary and distinctive rhythms. Or—one may as well dream—perhaps there could be one Super-Extra Mega-Supreme Poet to unite the whole Arab world, by synthesizing the ease and directness of all the dialects with the entrancing grace of the classical language.

That vision was particularly hopeless, seeing how the grumpy newspaperman headed a group called the Arabic Language Preservation Association. "It is a rich language!" he said. "We have forty words for camel. Somehow, despite this, we still need foreign terms like *tilifizyoon*."

The odd borrowed word seemed the least of Arabic's problems, and a fight that even the language academies in Cairo and Damascus had decided they wouldn't win. Yet the other panelists murmured agreement, and the newspaperman gave a final harrumph. "Arabic rests on the shoulders of every single Arab," he muttered accusingly.

By the time the floor opened for questions, I had worked myself into a snit. What if Arabs — and Arabic students — didn't want to shoulder the burden of this old, heavy language any longer? Here was my chance for another triumphant conclusion to my own poem, to stand up and dazzle the audience with my criticism. But the words coming together in my head were pure Ammiya, with the occasional Lebanese lilt where some of Manal's adjustments had taken hold. If I stood up and squawked my righteous words in a broad, broken Egyptian dialect, would anyone understand me? At the very least, I would sound silly. *This,* I fumed silently, was the very problem with Fusha and the elitists who preserved it!

An Australian woman stood up and asked, in polite and quavering Fusha, if the Emirati government was investing in teaching foreigners Arabic. She had found it very difficult to learn and would like more practice speaking and integrating into Arab society. The three panel members cooed and applauded. Humph, teacher's pet, I thought.

The crowd began to file out, and I stayed in my seat, letting my frustration ebb. The Australian woman was right to have made the effort, I conceded. I had been too concerned with my self-image, with wanting to appear as educated as the panelists. I should have stayed focused on what I wanted to communicate, the story I wanted to tell.

Develop!

ONCE UPON A TIME, there was a beautiful girl named Hamda. Her mother had died, and her father remarried. Hamda's stepmother dressed her own daughter in fine clothes and took her to parties, but she dressed Hamda in rags and locked the girl in the oven to make sure she stayed home. One night while the stepmother was out, the magical Esfaisra, a genie shaped like a fish, appeared to Hamda. She released the girl from the oven and dressed her in lovely new clothes. "Go to the party," the genie said.

Hamda danced and sang and ate, but took care to leave in plenty of time to get home before her stepmother and stepsister returned. But as she left, Hamda dropped a bracelet. The king's son found it and declared that he would marry the beautiful girl whose wrist it fit. He traveled all over the kingdom, finally arriving at Hamda's house.

The stepmother made her own daughter try on the bracelet, but it did not fit. The prince asked if there might be another girl in the house, and the stepmother said no. But the rooster was listening, and it cried out, "Cock-a-doodle-doo! My aunt Hamda, the wonderful girl, is in the oven!"

Hamda tried on the bracelet, and it fit perfectly.

Before the prince was to marry her, he came to her in the form of a dog and asked, "What would you like your dowry to be?"

Hamda answered that all she would like was a container of dates and a bag of little fish. Her stepmother scoffed at Hamda's humility, and when the dog delivered the meager gift, the woman told Hamda to eat the dates and fish and leave her in peace.

When Hamda did as she was told, she became so sick that she vomited, and out of her mouth came a stream of pearls and coral. Hamda and the prince were married and lived happily ever after.

The king's other son then asked if he could marry the stepmother's daughter. The stepmother craftily requested the same dowry of dates and little fish. The dog came and brought the girl the goods, and she gobbled them all down. But she threw up no pearls or coral, only terrible things.

So the dog ate her.

The end.

I heard this story, so familiar yet so strange, from an old woman named Um Khalaf — not sitting at her knee, but via the Internet. The tale was part of a collection of oral histories of Qatar, one of the few samples of translated Khaleeji dialect I had been able to find before my trip. Fact and fiction, the stories recalled the old days in Qatar, before its store of natural gas brought wealth, and the past of fairy tales, that mythical time of "there was or there wasn't." I wanted to meet the team of four women students who had collected the tales, so I boarded a plane to the city of Doha.

Culturally, the Gulf Arab countries are often lumped together, but after five weeks in the UAE, the neighboring country of Qatar, just an hour's flight west from Dubai, felt to me like an exotic new world. In the Souq Waqif, the city's renovated old market, the men folded their *ghitras* atop their heads in fascinating new ways, and many more women wore niqabs. The shops sold frankincense and special baskets for desert picnics. I even happened upon, wonder of wonders, street food. From a gleaming silver tureen, a woman ladled up a concoction of slippery seeds, sweetened and warmed with saffron, and then told me the price *in Arabic*. By the time I arrived for my appointment with the four story collectors at a sprawling villa, I felt a bit like Hamda myself, a stepdaughter invited to a ball.

Sara, small and slim, with nut-brown skin and coolly sculpted hair, welcomed me into a sitting room that made me feel like Alice, shrinking away in Wonderland. Its overstuffed sofas could have held eight people each; the drapes sagged under the weight of fist-size tassels.

In the center of the room, around a low table laden with finger sandwiches and coffee thermoses, our group was just four: me and hostess Sara al-Khalfan, dwarfed by her armchair; doe-eyed Shatha Farajallah; and tomboyish Mariam Dahrouj, sporting thick black bangs and a plaid shirt. They were all recent graduates of Qatar University, and the oral-history website, called Qatar Swalif, had been a project for their journalism program. We exchanged Arabic pleasantries, but these well-educated women spoke far better English than I spoke Arabic, so I was grateful to switch. Mariam, the strongest English speaker, steered the conversation.

In the Khaleeji dialect, *swalif* are the "everyday stories" people tell when they get together: childhood memories, brushes with death, I-walked-uphill-both-ways complaints, and warning parables for children. To tell these stories is to *soolaf*—the verb I had been so excited to hear from unhappy Saeed, that morning in the parking lot on the mountain near Al-Ain.

In the Gulf countries, the everyday stories had a special resonance now that "everyday" was so different. In less than two generations, just since the 1970s, lifestyles had changed drastically, from rural subsistence to highways, high-rises, and fully stocked refrigerators — those "precious icons," as Nasif at the Dubai cultural center had called them. Grandparents who had grown up in tents told *swalif* to grandkids in air-conditioned sitting rooms.

These were the stories that Sara, Shatha, and Mariam had set out to record. In the process, they also recorded a different everyday language: the Qatari dialect also had changed drastically in a few decades. "It was surprising to learn I can't understand some people in my own country," Mariam said, and the other women nodded.

"So, did you stop and ask what the words meant?" I asked, thinking of my own resolve to make this effort.

"We didn't want to do that," Shatha said, lowering her doe eyes. "Old people don't like to know young people are cut off from their roots."

So the women went home and asked their own grandparents, translating old Arabic to new Arabic. Sometimes the words were for objects that had vanished—*futtam,* pearl divers' nose clips, for instance, or *gargoor,* a woven-wire fish trap. Sometimes the dialect word was a borrowed quirk. *Dakhtur* had been the word for doctor back in the days of British influence; now Qataris were more connected to the rest of the Arab world, so most people used the standard Fusha word, *tabeeb.*

Shatha, from a Palestinian family who settled in Qatar in 1948, had been surprised to hear stories that were so different from the ones she had heard from her own grandparents. It was the first time, she said, that she had felt acutely that her roots were in a different place and culture. "But I did recognize some special words," she added. "They were very *bedu,* very rural, the same as Palestinians use."

Sara served thimble-size cups of saffron-laced tea, translating the subtle language of the ritual for me. Pouring duties for tea or coffee went to the youngest person in the room, and when I had drunk enough, I should shake my cup from side to side. "And if I fill the cup to the brim, it's an insult, like saying 'Get out!'" she explained. "My brother used to do it to a man he didn't like. You read about this in poetry too."

And in this way, I was happy to find our conversation turning, as I had hoped, to a more general discussion of the power of Arabic and literature in their own lives. How well did these women understand pre-Islamic poetry — was it as much work for them as it was for me? The *mu'allaqat,* those fine Jahiliya odes, provoked a rueful smile in Shatha. "We memorized them in school," she said, "but it wasn't that easy."

"Oof, the *atlal,*" added Mariam, eyes rolling under bangs. *Atlal,* with a deep, portentous *t,* were the campsite traces, the last sign of a departed lover, that were mentioned at the start of every poem. "You were brave to try."

I told the group about the brave, or foolhardy, interpreters at the literature festival. Poetry, the women all agreed after they stopped laughing, worked only in the original language. "It's like telling a joke," Mariam said. "Once you translate it, it's not funny. Or not as beautiful."

They held competing opinions on the value of Nabati poetry over classical Fusha writing, but they were all roundly sick of any kind of oratory involving big, elaborate words. "Old people, especially men, appreciate it," Mariam said, rolling her eyes again. As the conversation bounced from topic to topic, from Arabic rap to the relative merits of pulpy novels, I sat back and considered my good fortune to have met these smart, well-spoken women.

Statistically, the odds were in my favor, as women made up the substantial majority of college graduates in Qatar and the rest of the Gulf region. Granted, this wasn't quite as positive as it sounded, as college often represented the sole option for women; men, by contrast, could study abroad, join the military, take a government job. Still, the future, I thought, must be good, if the Gulf countries had so many women like this.

I could have stayed chatting all night, but I didn't want to get the full teacup, or, I remembered from Nasif's talk at the cultural center in Dubai, the cloud of incense. We bustled to go; I slipped on my shoes and Mariam and Shatha put on their abayas and made phone calls for rides.

At the front gate, I had some confusion with the taxi driver, and when I turned back toward the house to ask Sara for help, I was startled by a black-clad wraith. In a moment, I realized it was only Mariam, disguised in her abaya, her sheer *shayla* draped over her face. She pulled the black fabric up quickly and winked at me.

I left the taxi on the narrow waterfront park along Doha's arcing bay. I wanted to stretch my legs and think about all that the Qatar Swalif women had told me. The night was cool and windy; only an occasional jogger passed.

At the north end of the bay, new Doha was a jutting line of skyscrapers and construction cranes, telling the same fairy tale as Dubai and Abu Dhabi. Down at the south end was the original city center and the Souq Waqif. The tallest building was a replica of the ninth-century minaret in Samarra, Iraq, coiled like a snail shell, stacked like a wedding cake.

Midway along the waterfront, I came across a small, open geodesic dome. Inside stood a young man with beefy arms so big they stuck out from his sides a bit. When he saw me, he walked a short distance away and busied himself, stretching, pacing, looking at his phone.

The dome was a complex piece of playground equipment, with a touchpad at each joint. A sign detailed a number of games and patterns to play.

"It's cool, isn't it?" the burly guy said in English, still at a distance. He had looked up casually, as though just noticing me. "It's new. Two weeks only." As he walked toward me, I automatically smiled politely and turned to go.

A few paces away, I caught myself and turned back. It *was* cool.

"You want to . . . ?" he asked.

"Um, how about . . . ?" I proposed at the same time.

I put down my jacket, and he gestured to the start button. "Go for it," he said. "I'll be red. You're blue."

I pushed the button, and the dome filled with karate-chop sound effects. We raced from side to side, each trying to hit our respective colors as they lit up. In less than ten seconds, I was panting desperately. He beat me, but only 150 to 120. We crouched in the dome, breathing hard and grinning stupidly.

"That was fun," I finally caught my breath enough to say. "Thanks for letting me try it."

"No, thank *you*. I have used it only alone before this," he replied. Elaborate courtesy was the best way to avoid the awkwardness of physical exertion with a stranger of the opposite sex. In a public park. At night.

"My name's Mohammed," he said, extending his hand. Was he Qatari? What *swalif* could he tell, I wondered?

"I am Palestinian," he said. "But born and raised here. This is not my country. But I have no other." He pronounced it *uzzer,* and the word trailed away in the night. It was a poignant statement, worthy of the ancient nomadic poets crisscrossing the dark, lonely desert.

Behind us loomed a sign, a giant yellow sculpture of a single word:تطوّر. *Tatawwar,* it read, an imperative verb. *Develop!* From under its spotlights, it exhorted Doha: *You there, march forward! Play new games! Exert yourself! Don't look back!*

This growing region was gaining so much every day, yet so much was slipping away at the same time: words, dialects, stories, traditions. Still, this uprooting, and the anxiety that came with it, wasn't new. That tale was as old as the Jahiliya poets, always on the move, always longing for something. Mohammed, a relocated Palestinian, lived not too far from where a poet had stopped at a ruined camp-site and said, almost fifteen centuries before, *Qifa nabki,* Halt, let us weep . . .

"Enjoy the rest of your night," I told him.

We shook hands again, and I marched forward.

LIBNAN

Lebanon

May–June 2012

حال

(*hala*) To be transformed

✦

استحال

(*istahala*) To be impossible

✦

حالة الخطر

(*halat al-khatar*) State of readiness, alert

The New Beirut

MY FIRST NIGHT in Beirut, I was jostled out of sleep by a car horn, coming closer with that insistent, international rhythm of celebration: *honk, honk, honk-honk-honk.* I stumbled out onto the balcony of my rented room and peered down the dark street — Beirut was not a well-lit city. Past drooping power lines and shadows of trees, a black sedan had stopped under a rare streetlight. People clambered out, their shiny clothes glinting in the yellow overhead glow. A woman in a strapless white cocktail dress put her hand over her mouth and ululated — the trilling sound that signifies celebration, or, paradoxically, mourning. Was it the tail end of a wedding? Or the end of a typical night out? From this distance, I couldn't tell. Everyone hugged and kissed and squealed some more, then staggered off into the dark.

It was the end of their day, but the start of mine. There was no going back to sleep, with the sky just turning purple. In the apartment's shared kitchen, I made a cup of instant coffee. A rickety chair barely fit on the shallow front balcony, and I sat down to wait for the sunrise.

I had visited Beirut once before, in 1999. The city then, ten years after the civil war's end, had seemed brittle, muddled. People's jaws were clenched. You might get change in lira or in dollars. You never knew what language someone might speak to you. It was my first trip in the Arab world beyond Egypt, and it was the closest I had come to raw political turmoil.

When I had first enrolled in Arabic, I knew virtually nothing about the various tragedies of the Arab world. I had grown up in a semirural area, without a television. By the time Middle East disasters trickled down to me, the poison had leached out of them. Only many years later, in a media-Arabic class (the pat phrases of newspapers: preemptive strike, overwhelming majority, disaster area), did I see a montage of news clips. There was the shot-up bus that symbolized the start of the Lebanese civil war, the car-bombed rubble of the U.S. Marine barracks, and tanks firing on the Iran-Iraq border. In the barrage of images, I finally understood how Americans had come by their idea of the Middle East as a place of endless conflict — and particularly of Beirut as a synonym for war zone.

On a billboard above my balcony, the Virgin Mary emerged out of the hazy pink gloaming, her eyes cast down beneficently over the apartment blocks and out to the Mediterranean. On the building across the way, each balcony was outfitted in heavy striped drapes that hung like theater curtains. In one apartment, a slim older man buttoned his dress shirt, hooking the cuffs while he watched a black-and-white movie on a bulging-front TV set. He stepped out to his side terrace to fuss with the greenery — tiny tomatoes staked for best posture, grapevines still leafless but trained for optimal shade. The winter had been harsh and long; now, in early May, it was tentative spring.

In the past five years, Beirut had undergone a transformation. The city was *back*, glossy magazine stories proclaimed, and more swinging than ever. Cool bars, hip galleries, and fantastic restaurants — this was the kind of normal life I knew existed in the Arab world, but most Americans doubted. But in Beirut? The city had not struck me as normal, not at all. It had felt like a room where people had just stopped screaming at one another. Thirteen years after that visit, and twenty-three after the war's end, I had come again to see how the city had transformed itself and become a stylish destination.

I had come for my own transformation too — a linguistic one. While I had studied in Egypt, other students I'd known had gone to Syria and Lebanon for classes, and I envied their soft accents. Their words sounded dreamy and light, in contrast to the sometimes flat and nasal Egyptian dialect I spoke. Where Cairenes say a hard *g*, Beirutis buzz a soft *zh*, like the *j* in *bonjour*. Words have an elegant lilt, the last syllable often trailing off in a breathy *eh*. Ammiya honks like a goose; Lebanese sighs like a dove.

Much as I now loved Egypt, I thought as I drank my coffee and looked over the Beirut rooftops, we had been thrown together by chance, through the teachers I happened to have and the grants I happened to win. Ammiya was undeniably practical, my teachers told me, because it was understood across the Arab world. This was largely due to Egypt's longtime dominance in television and movie production. Arabs everywhere had been raised on Egyptian film stars and their witty banter, from the black-and-white era to modern romantic and political comedies.

But with the spread of satellite TV, Ammiya began to lose its primacy in Arab media; now people commonly heard dialects from Lebanon and the Gulf. More personally, I was still conscious of Ammiya's melodramatic, soapy intonation. I had never felt quite comfortable, quite *real* when I spoke it; I felt more like a character in one of those campy movies. Maybe Lebanese dialect was a better reflection of my true self — and I was here to try it on for six weeks, like a new outfit.

At the apartment next to the older man's tomatoes and grapevines, a woman puttered in and out from the balcony. She peeled an onion with a paring knife, letting the papery outer layers cascade down into the treetops. She hung out a skimpy nylon slip on her laundry line.

If ever there was a place to see how the Arab world's conflict-ridden reputation intersected with daily life, Beirut was it. Before the civil war, the city had been known as a liberal bastion, an intellectual and creative capital. Yet the social divisions that caused the conflict still ran deep; on this point, Lebanese society was resolutely conservative.

Just as I propped my elbows on the balcony railing, the better to watch the tiny domestic drama unfold, my neighbor-characters froze for a second. The vintage movie shrank to a pinpoint in the middle of the bulging TV screen, the tinny music died, and the neighborhood's background hum vanished. The power had been switched off.

As the woman who owned this apartment had warned, Beirut was enduring rolling blackouts of three hours per day, on a rotating schedule between 6 a.m. and 6 p.m. Spotty electricity was something I had experienced on my first visit; Israeli jets had just bombed city power plants, in retaliation for Hezbollah activity. Now, though, shaky infrastructure was apparently the norm.

The woman disappeared into her living room. The man ran his hands through his hair, shrugged on a light coat, and walked downstairs.

He seemed to have the right idea. I finished my coffee and went to grab a city map from the living room.

As I walked west through the quiet streets, more memories of my first visit returned. Humidity. Hills. Bougainvillea and staircases instead of streets. Green almonds, fuzzy and tart as stunted apricots: an epiphany that linked almonds (*lawz*) and stone fruits (*lawziyat*). French fries *in* my sandwich: just as revelatory. Armadas of gleaming new BMWs, their windows tinted black as oil, interspersed with rickety old jewel-toned Mercedes with matching hubcaps. The Ziad Rahbany album *Bema Enno*, all jaunty jazz and cooing vocals, as we cruised the coast highway in a rental car, concrete blocks and Hezbollah banners giving way to banana plantations. "Such long straws!" I marveled in my trip diary, because the other differences from

Egypt — historical, culinary, geographical, linguistic — were far too large to capture on paper.

On that trip I had stayed with a grad-school friend who had studied in Damascus and Cairo. I admired her adaptability, her gold-trimmed sunglasses, and her habit of greeting people with the groovy phrase *"Shlonak?"* — literally "What's your color?" For years, I had treasured this as my sole bit of Lebanese dialect. Finally in Dubai, in class with Manal, I had a chance to try it out. Manal had tossed her lustrous black hair and laughed: "Only Syrians say that." So here I was in Beirut, starting my language education nearly from scratch.

I arrived downtown faster than I expected — Beirut was small. Two million people in eight square miles, and less than two miles between East Beirut, where I'd started, and West Beirut. In between, I crossed Martyrs' Square, named for nationalists who were executed for leading a revolt against the Ottomans in World War I. The area had been the cultural heart of the city in the 1960s; then, during the civil war, it was the Green Line — the no-man's-land divide between the two sides of the city. Now it was a glorified traffic median.

When I had visited in 1999, this area had been consumed in reconstruction as far-reaching and complex as open-heart surgery in progress. For the most part, it was now all sewn up. Café chairs were stacked in rows, and dress mannequins stared mutely through the windows of the Hermès boutique. A Rolex-branded clock tower presided over a cobblestone roundabout. If East Beirut was, in the broadest brush strokes, Christian and West was Muslim, then downtown had been claimed squarely by capitalism.

I pressed on up a hill, past a vacant lot where the weeds smelled of the countryside, to Hamra Street. Like Martyrs' Square, this had been a swinging social and intellectual scene fifty years earlier; I had tasted a bit of it at chrome-trimmed cafés and a bar decorated with a life-size photo mural of Georgina Rizk, Miss Universe 1971. I knew many of these places had closed in the past decade — a shame, after surviving fifteen years of war — but I was appalled to see, as I walked the length of the street, that they had been replaced by Starbucks, Caribou, and Costa Coffee.

I stopped in the middle of the sidewalk, unexpectedly overcome with exhaustion and irritation. Luxury brands and coffee chains — *this* was the new Beirut everyone was so thrilled about? I turned back toward home and bed.

Passing Starbucks again, I noticed the people in the sidewalk seats. At one table, an old man in a striped dress shirt and V-neck sweater shook his newspaper flat. A woman with a meticulous titian bouffant pulled a sheaf of papers from a soft leather case. Watching them, I felt restored; these people looked as if they had been playing these roles every morning, even as the stage set had been struck and rebuilt around them. I ordered a coffee, then sat down on the edge of their tableau.

If I had studied Lebanese dialect so long ago, what would my part be in the new Beirut? Would I be a swank, air-kissing Lebanese lady, like my teacher Manal? Would I be out in the street ululating at five in the morning? Or would I be watching old movies and tending my grapevines? What would my life be like if I had gone to Beirut or Damascus in 1992, instead of Cairo? What would *I* be like?

A woman marched by in four-inch Lucite heels, silver leggings, and a frilly aqua hijab bedecked with iridescent flowers. Well, I wouldn't be like *that*, I reckoned. But perhaps if I learned to speak the way Beirutis did, some of the city's glamour would still rub off on me.

What Is the Rule?

THE TRAGEDY OF Arabic classes is that they always seem to be scheduled before noon — a time when I prefer not to talk at all, in any language. Throughout college, I had rolled out of bed for 9 a.m. dates with grammar. But the inane faux conversations — "Yesterday I went shopping. What did you do yesterday?" — sent me into a spiral of existential despair. I hoped I had adapted over the years, but my morning classes in Cairo, despite or perhaps because of exuberant Hani, confirmed my inability to chitchat early in the day. If I had stayed in class in Dubai longer, my morning time with Manal would probably have soured too.

My Lebanese classes, by contrast, were scheduled for two nights a week at 5 p.m., an hour when I felt life was worth living and words worth speaking. On my first day, I was feeling pretty jazzed up. I had clinched a deal on a cheaper place, a crash pad in a six-bedroom penthouse in West Beirut, then eaten a surprisingly sensational lunch in a restaurant by the Rolex clock tower, which made me rethink the slick downtown area. From a street cart, I bought an American-size paper cup of Turkish-style coffee, which I drank until I spilled it on myself, because the caffeine made my hands twitch.

Even after all that, I still had time before class for a stop in the school's café. "*Aseer laymoon*," I said to the bartender — lemonade.

"Fresh?" the bartender asked in English.

In these first few days in Beirut, I'd barely spoken any Arabic. Often, the person I was speaking to would switch to French. I'd repeat what I wanted in English, then Arabic again. Conversations usually ended before we reached consensus.

After a few minutes, the barkeep presented me with a glass of orange juice. I considered protesting, but he seemed busy, and the juice looked good. I sucked it down and headed to class.

A mix of Brazilians, Brits, and Italians, the group was friendly, wisecracking, and sharply dressed. Within a few minutes, we learned the cute and useful verb *talfan,* to telephone.

After the break, the teacher quizzed us on the alphabet — a sign the class was probably at a lower level than I needed. I flipped through my colorful, cartoon-illustrated book. The grammar was familiar, thanks to Manal's quick summary in Dubai, but I didn't recognize some of the polite phrases — what to say when you get into a taxi, for instance. (*Ya'teek el-'afiyeh,* I mouthed to myself — May God grant you vigor.) One page showed all the foods you could buy on the street: roasted corn, chestnuts, a sesame-covered bread called *ka'keh,* shaped like a dainty handbag. And orange juice, labeled "*3asseer laymun.*" (This was a hip school — it referred to Lebanese dialect as "urban Arabic" — so it used the hip chat alphabet for transliteration.)

A mistake, I thought. Then I remembered my café order before class. So, *laymoon,* a word that sounded like lemon, and meant lemon in Egypt and in every dictionary I'd ever seen, actually meant orange in Lebanon? I had expected basic vocabulary would be different from what I knew, but this was positively unfair. At least I had not pointed out the "mistake" to the bartender; then I might still be standing at the bar, trapped in a who's-on-first loop because, without the aid of a book, I never would have grasped that the word for orange was lemon. The few Arabic cognates were sacrosanct; I treasured them. Now one had become a *faux ami*, a false friend, as the French call these treacherous words.

After class, I cornered one of the school's staff and asked to move up a level. I didn't admit my oranges-and-lemons problem.

"I suppose," she said reluctantly. "But the night classes are full. You'll have to join the morning intensive."

"Morning?" I said weakly.

"Nine to noon, Monday to Friday," she replied with the kind of natural cheer only a language teacher can muster. "Oh, and you'll need the book." She dropped a thick, spiral-bound sheaf of pages on the table — nothing like my cartoon-filled intro text.

Five minutes early, I slipped into the last seat in the classroom, at the end of a U of tables. I sipped my coffee and stared into space, waiting for the teacher to arrive.

"Hello," the man next to me said pointedly. "I am Kaspar." He had ice-blue eyes and wire-rim glasses. In front of him on the table, he had laid out an assortment of mechanical pencils in a neat row.

Oh, right — greetings and introductions were normal in a room full of strangers. Even in the morning. There was serious, shaggy-haired Andrew from England; Nick, a tall, genial Lebanese American just out of college; Sally, with a Southern drawl; blond, British Sophie; Eliza, Lebanese raised in France; Dutch Danny, shaved bald and a shade of pink only northern Europeans turn in sunny climes; and Irene, an American woman who worked for the Red Cross.

Together they represented the whole range of Arabic experience. Nick and Eliza were the "heritage students" — early exposure to the language and culture had given them impeccable accents, loads of slang, and in-jokes, but no grammatical foundation. Kaspar's background, on the other hand, was pure Fusha, studied intently for several years in Switzerland. Danny was here for love, or post-love: he and his Lebanese boyfriend had broken up, but he still wanted to learn. Irene straddled both sides. Like Kaspar, she had studied only Fusha, but her husband was Lebanese, and she spoke dialect — or tried to — with his family.

Our teacher, a young Lebanese woman named Zaina, projected a schoolmarm vibe, despite dewy skin and a form-fitting tank top and miniskirt. Perhaps it was the pantyhose. Perhaps it was her reliance on the word "rule."

"*Wa-hayda ar*-rule" — And that's the rule — she said decisively to conclude any explanation. She pronounced "rule" as if it were an Arabic word, with a lightly tapped *r* and a pure, long vowel: *rool*.

Next to me, Kaspar's head bobbed at each *rool*. He took minuscule notes in an engineer's grid-lined notebook.

We were covering grammatical topics I already knew, roughly, but these *rools* of Zaina's were not familiar. In Egypt, my Arabic teachers had always referenced the classical language. "It's like Fusha," they would often say, to explain a detail in the dialect, "but easier." Zaina, by contrast, operated in a sealed world of colloquial Lebanese, with no reference to Fusha. This became clear when she introduced the *rools* for counting.

In classical Arabic, counting is preposterously complicated, factoring in case endings, duals and plurals, gender, and whether you're counting humans or nonhumans, and eight or eighty of them. In the dialects, most of this had been swept away. Teachers of dialects could usually say something like, "Don't bother with the case of the dual. Scratch those rules about three to ten. Otherwise, it's normal — singular nouns above ten, and four-and-twenty-blackbirds style for numbers over twenty." Students would run a couple of drills, and the class could move on.

Now, though, Zaina had started from scratch, outlining the *rools*, step by step, all the way up above one hundred. Examine the object being counted, note the gender if necessary, make the required changes. This took a while, and as she was doing it, I marveled at another habit of Zaina's: she was spelling words exactly the way they were pronounced. The Fusha word for fifteen was *khamsat 'ashar* (خمسة عشر, literally "five with ten"), but Lebanese usually moved the vowels a little and swallowed the last *r* (ر). On the whiteboard, Zaina wrote this as *khamast'ash* (خمستعش).

No, I thought, my jaw clenching and my hands tightening around my book. It's *two* words, and it's really *'ashar* at the end! I had always been a mild spelling fanatic; typos provoked a little exasperated pop in my brain. My reaction now was a visceral twist of horror in my chest. Zaina had performed battlefield surgery on the *'ayn-sheen-ra* root, just sawed its leg right off, with no anesthetic!

Zaina's phonetic spelling actually made her counting *rools* more complicated than they were in Fusha, not easier. When a Lebanese person counts an object—that is, says "fifteen pencils" rather than just "fifteen"—then the *ra* is pronounced. So, in Zaina's system, for the numbers eleven to nineteen, there was an extra step when combining the number with a noun.

"The *rool* here is to add a *ra,*" she said, tapping the whiteboard for emphasis. "*Khamast'ashr ahweh.* Fifteen coffees."

You don't have to *add* it—it's *already there,* I wanted to yell. My leg was jiggling slightly, either from grammatical vexation or the coffee I'd drunk to make sure I was awake for this morning class. I was not accustomed to the Beiruti level of caffeine intake. Fifteen was apparently a perfectly plausible number of coffees for a Lebanese person.

I wasn't alone in my agitation. Kaspar was studiously reviewing his notes, clicking his mechanical pencil as he surveyed his notebook.

"But what is the rule for two objects?" he asked.

"I told you," Zaina said, tapping the board again. "Add *-ein.*"

"But that is not a rule," Kaspar replied with the diction of a debater. "A rule has an input and an output. Where is the number? What is the output here?"

Zaina was puzzled. "You just add *-ein: kitabein,* two books, *ahwetein,* two coffees."

Kaspar muttered as he wrote in his notebook. "So, this is the output: *ahwetein.*"

The disagreement didn't dampen Zaina's spirits. Where the word *rool* didn't apply, she used her second-favorite word: excebtion. Whenever one of us raised a question about consistency, it was her default reply: *Hayda* excebtion.

By the end of class, the *rools* were close to dissolving completely. As I left the room, Irene, the American who had studied Fusha for years, fell into step next to me.

"Welcome to our class," she said with the slightest hint of sarcasm. I was glad I wasn't the only one who felt adrift.

We Don't Talk About Politics Here

LEBANON IS ONLY four thousand square miles, a skinny rectangle smaller than Connecticut, hugging the eastern coast of the Mediterranean. Beirut is at the midpoint, which puts everywhere else within just a few hours' drive. But for decades Lebanon wasn't conducive to weekend getaways. Only gradually since the civil war's end had Lebanon enjoyed longer periods of relative peace, and in this time, a number of hiking clubs had been established. They led trips out of Beirut nearly every weekend, and I joined one, in hopes of speaking more Arabic outside of class.

When I arrived at the bus, I was surprised to see that the group was not, as I had expected, a mix of tourists and locals, but almost all Lebanese, speaking Arabic among themselves. What I had been hoping for, sure — but presented with a crowd of forty strangers, I was intimidated into silence. I smiled vaguely at a few people seated near me, then fell asleep.

I woke up on the outskirts of Tripoli, Lebanon's second-largest city, on the coast north of Beirut. The bus had slowed, and I peered out the window to see what the holdup might be. We were in line at a checkpoint, and alongside the road, a row of tanks had their turrets pointed squarely at our bus.

Pro- and anti-Syrian-regime factions had been launching artillery at each other over the past few days—though not on this road, Michel, the club leader, assured us, over the bus's microphone. As we inched through the checkpoint, he pointed up the hill with a tour guide's precisely angled open hand. "Bab at-Tabbaneh, that's the neighborhood where the fighting has been," he said with a steady smile.

Michel's Arabic was as precise as his gestures, so I understood most of his commentary on roadside attractions. These ranged from a Stone Age archaeological site to a Palestinian refugee camp notorious for a grinding battle in 2007. A man leaned across the aisle to introduce himself. He was older than me, muscular but balding, dressed head to toe in multipocketed, quick-dry hiking gear. "Michel took us to the southern border this winter," he said, pulling out his phone. "I'll show you the pictures." In the photos, Michel was smiling, just as he was now, and pointing to Israeli flags, coiled razor wire, tanks at the Hezbollah war museum.

At the hotel, I was assigned a bed in a little prefab trailer with two other solo travelers. One of them, Sahar, was a woman in her late forties with an unkempt bob and freckles. Lucky for me, she didn't speak much English—and unlike most Beirutis I'd talked to, she didn't seem to mind speaking Arabic with me.

The first five minutes were awkward, though, as we explored our room together. Thanks to her heavy Lebanese drawl, I failed to recognize the word *bab*, door—the very first word I had learned in Arabic. Finally she discovered the flimsy accordion-style door that separated the toilet from the rest of the room. "*Ah, el-baaaayb hon,*" she said—Oh, here's the doooor—and we both relaxed.

Sahar steered me outdoors, chatting on in what she called *nahawi* (grammatical) Arabic, a term for Fusha that I'd heard once or twice in Egypt. There, it suggested fancy talk, putting on airs, and judging from her grin as she shifted registers, Sahar meant it in the same vein. She charged around the hotel grounds with enthusiasm and opinionated commentary. I trotted after her as she yanked green fruit off the almond trees (some for me, some for her, some for her pockets), speculated on the cost of our trailer (she wanted one for her patch of land outside Beirut), and then parked herself on the terrace next to the central stone hotel building. Together we admired the view down the rolling hills, dotted with farms, to a distant sliver of sea.

"I've traveled all over Europe and other parts of the world," Sahar said, "but in fifty years, this is the first time I'm seeing my own country."

For dinner, our group occupied one long table on the hotel's balcony, which was still sealed up against the cold. I followed Sahar like a duckling after its mother, and she parked me in a seat opposite her. Glass separated our table from the main restaurant hall, where a family was hosting a baptism party. The guest of honor, a toddler dressed in a red satin bow tie and a white tailcoat, was passed from guest to guest, squeezed by old grandpas and teenage girls in strapless taffeta dresses.

A barrage of meze landed on our table, and a man at the far end doled out bootleg arrack from a Johnnie Walker Black bottle. Sahar pointed out the tastiest dishes and made me repeat the names: *sambousek*, little pastry bundles of savory lamb; *fattoush*, salad with sour and juicy purslane; *wara' 'einab*, silky grape leaves with only the lightest stuffing of rice.

As she served us, Sahar trailed her crocheted sweater sleeve through a glossy tomato sauce. "*Il mange comme je mange,*" she said merrily, and raised her arrack glass for a refill.

Some other women at the table did not share Sahar's cavalier attitude toward clothing. They sported complete ensembles, generously accessorized with gold and full makeup. On the bus, in a sort of social triage for dealing with forty strangers, I had written off these ladies as not my sort of people. But then the most lavishly tanned woman, in a one-shoulder peacock-pattern shirt, waved her bangled wrist down the table at me. She had overheard Sahar and me speaking our "grammatical" fancy talk. "Oh, I love Fusha!" she cried. She interrogated me in mellifluous Arabic and proceeded to quote several lines of poetry.

Our half of the long table all turned to look at me, amused and expectant, as though I might offer a few verses in response. Sahar patted my hand and beamed at the crowd — I was her pet, her prize. Fortunately, the DJ for the baptism started just then, and the room filled with the pounding beat of the *dabkeh*, the traditional dance of Lebanon and Syria. I was spared.

Over the music, my conversation with Sahar dwindled to her quizzing me by pointing to nearby objects. "What's that in Arabic?" she asked. "And that?" Weirdly, in class, I *had* just learned the words for chimney (*madkhana*), up which grilled-meat smoke was billowing, and stork (*la'la'a*), of which there was a taxidermied specimen wedged in a corner of the main hall. Perhaps because Lebanon was so small, I mused over my arrack, all the words were cooped up here, and easier to catch.

By the time the meat course had been cleared, I was talking with Georges, seated next to me, because I could hear him better. He was Michel's right-hand man, and when I had noticed him on the bus, he fell victim to my social triage as well. Muttering into his walkie-talkie, he had looked officious, as well as potentially mean, with a bald skull and a handlebar mustache.

Actually, he was a softy, with a snaggletoothed grin and pretty good English. As we talked, he peeled the fruit that had been set out in a bowl in front of us. He had work-toughened hands with a few bruised nails. His day job was as an electrician, but his conversation was philosophical.

"I shouldn't say this, but Lebanon is better because of its diversity," he said, apropos of nothing. I'd encountered these same sudden transitions into politics before, as if the topic simmered steadily in the subconscious and occasionally bubbled to the surface. "It's good to know that other people think a different way. Then you can experience more." His vague statement danced around a very specific issue: Lebanon's omnipresent sectarian system, which, for legal and cultural reasons, required identification with one of eighteen officially recognized religious groups. Sectarianism cut through the whole country, though in cosmopolitan Beirut, people liked to pretend they lived beyond it.

I was relieved when Georges shifted to the topics of food and travel, because we could talk in more specific terms. "Think, in Saudi Arabia they don't have Ladurée *macarons,* because they use alcohol," he said. "Those people are missing out! Here, I don't miss pork—I don't really like it. But ham from Parma! That is something special."

Georges was a well-traveled electrician. "I went to Nigeria," he said. "Their food is yucky, just bread and yam. But I want to taste it. I *have to* taste it!" My heart swelled with warmth—to think I might never have spoken with this fellow curious eater. I could see why Sahar had introduced him earlier as Mar Jiryes—Saint Georges.

Georges had recently been to Doha, I was interested to hear. "I didn't know if I should talk to the women," he said—their niqabs had made him nervous. "Was it OK to shake their hand? Will I understand them?" he recalled. "But they were so smart, so educated. We talked about very interesting things." I eagerly told him about the wonderful Qatar Swalif team and our conversation about oral history and poetry.

In the next room, the DJ cranked the *dabkeh* louder, and the baptism party embarked on a lurching line dance. Georges wrinkled his mustache in distaste. "So boring, the same rhythm every time," he whisper-shouted in my ear. The deafening volume of the party suggested Cairo; the line dancing and my anise-laced liquor reminded me of Greece. In the greater arc of the Mediterranean, we were roughly between the two.

Meanwhile, to my left, a stern and regal *jolie laide,* distinctly makeup-free, was interrogating Samira, the other woman who was sharing the room with Sahar and me. Hiding behind lank hair, Samira had unpacked her suitcase in our room in silence, and throughout dinner she had answered questions with single words. Now she was heatedly spitting out a torrent of Arabic. Between the *dabkeh* beats, I caught something about Saudi Arabia, then "divorce" and "my babies."

After her outburst, Samira slumped back in her seat, breathing a little hard. "Excuse me," she muttered, and abruptly stood up and left the dining room.

"*Magique noire!*" the stern woman hissed at no one in particular. She was a lawyer, from a long line of Lebanese judges. "They do not respect women. Their laws are black magic."

Not long after, I excused myself. I had been waking up so early for class that by 10 p.m. I was close to passing out. I edged my way out of the dining room, thick with cigarette smoke, and around the staggering *dabkeh* line. The baptized kid was snoozing on a grandmother's shoulder.

In our trailer, Samira was brushing her teeth. I asked if she was OK — she had looked almost nauseated when she had left the table.

"I'm fine," she answered in terse English. "The medication I take makes me tired."

She arranged herself in bed, then sat watching me as I dug around in my bag for my own toothbrush.

"Do you take medication too?" she asked, almost hopeful.

"No, fortunately I don't have to." I paused. "What's your medication for?"

"I hear sounds." She lay back, pulling the sheets up to her chin. "It is terrible. I can't tell what is real."

I commiserated as best I could while brushing my teeth. It must be terrible, always having to doubt herself. Did the medication work?

"Somewhat. Sixty or seventy percent."

I climbed into my bed, next to hers. The three little beds were lined up in a row.

"Well, before we go to sleep, I have to tell you that I snore," I said. Samira hadn't shown a great sense of humor, but I risked a joke. "You won't be imagining it."

To my relief, she giggled. "Well, I'll pretend I'm imagining it — for your sake!"

"No need to be so polite," I said with mock seriousness. We both cracked up as I snapped off the light.

"This is a nice group of people," I said in the dark.

"Yes, it is," Samira murmured.

The hike itself was a bit beside the point. After a late, somewhat bleary breakfast, Michel herded us to an overlook and pointed out the day's route, down a hill and across a valley to the next village. "Are there land mines?" someone called out, and nervous laughter rippled through the crowd.

"No, no, that's just in Jezzine," Michel answered with his usual calm and even smile.

Not far down the hill, a woman sprained her ankle and had to be carried away. I briefly got lost, along with a group of Armenians. During one of the frequent rest and snack stops, someone made a joking reference to a Lebanese general. Faces froze midbite, and Michel appeared out of nowhere, still smiling. "We don't talk about politics here."

When the bus rolled up, we piled on and collapsed in our seats. Over the microphone, Michel explained that we weren't going back the way we had come; the road through Tripoli was closed.

The tanks, I recalled, and I slipped off to sleep. When I woke, we were in the clouds, with a skyline of stubby, Seussian trees — all spiky clumps and occasional rangy branches. The bus slowed to a crawl on hairpin turns. I dug a guidebook out of my bag. In the spot on the map where I guessed we must be, along the Syrian border, was empty space, no roads at all.

At the pass, an army checkpoint emerged in the fog. The black-clad soldiers waved us on. After another ten minutes, we rounded a curve and a sun-bleached valley opened before us.

An exclamation rippled across the bus: "Ah, Be'aaaaaa!"

The Bekaa Valley is Lebanon's big-sky country, an expansive stretch of fertile land that was a respite from the mountains. The bus picked up speed. I read the word *amal* spray-painted on cinder-block sheep pens. *Hope,* I thought. How nice. Then I remembered: Amal was the name of a Shiite militia.

Just after sunset, we stopped at a roadside store for sandwiches of bread and white cheese, available in a dozen subtle variations. I ordered one with honey as well, and thought how pleasant our alternate route home had been. As Michel hustled us back onto the bus, I noticed that all my tripmates were talking urgently into their phones. I had lost track of Sahar and Samira. As we turned onto the highway that headed west to Beirut, Georges made his way down the aisle. His big mustache accentuated his frown.

"Did you hear Michel? Do you understand what is happening?" he asked me, checking on my Arabic comprehension. I told him I'd understood the Tripoli road wasn't safe. Why did people seem so worried now that we were on a different route?

"A big man, a Sunni cleric, was killed today. The protests are starting. The road is closing behind," he said. His voice was low and tense, and without the aid of arrack, his English was more abrupt than it had been the night before. "But we made it. Thanks God."

As we neared the dropoff point in Beirut, Sahar reappeared, putting a commanding hand on my shoulder. "You come with me in a taxi," she said.

"No, no, she's in Hamra," a man I didn't know piped up. "I'll take her." Everyone on the bus was mobilizing, zipping zippers, setting bags on laps, jiggling a phone in one hand and car keys in the other.

As soon as the bus pulled in, the man steered me to his car. I had only a second to tell Samira I was happy to meet her, but Sahar was consumed in the scrum grabbing suitcases from under the bus.

The man's name was Ibrahim. He was a young doctor at the hospital next door to my apartment, fresh out of medical school in Houston. His mother called twice as we drove, and her panicked squawk filled the car. Ibrahim resolutely kept our conversation on small talk. What did I think of this country?

"Lebanon reminds me of Greece," I said. My cheery answer landed awkwardly in the dark. "Everyone may live in the city, but their hearts are really in their villages. They're all so proud of which village they're from."

We drove on in silence. The streets were empty.

"I know I'm not supposed to ask where people are from," Ibrahim finally said. "But as a doctor, I feel it's important information for knowing my patient."

Oh. I *hadn't* known you weren't supposed to ask. Not only was it Arabic 101 basics to ask where someone was from, but all the Lebanese people I had ever met before this trip — and there had been many, as Lebanese have emigrated all over the world — bragged nonstop about their villages. The most beautiful views, the freshest air, the most pungent herbs! But they were all Lebanese living outside of Lebanon, often for generations. Inside this country, so carved up by religion and politics, I was learning, the rules were different. This wasn't a simple case of urbanites wanting to shake off country ancestry, as in Dubai. In Beirut, the question "Where are you from?" was really asking "What side are you on?"

Ibrahim offered no details about his own roots. We sailed unimpeded over the bridge between East and West Beirut, blighted Martyrs' Square in shadows to our right.

When I looked out from my balcony the next morning, I was expecting, if not chaos, then at least some evidence of the stressful night before. Instead, I saw cars, pedestrians, the *manoucheh* bakery slinging its usual breakfast bread rounds bubbling with olive oil and mountain herbs. The produce guy, with his piles of black cherries, was in his spot next to the parking lot entrance.

It wasn't until I slid into class, a few minutes late, that things felt wrong.

"They were burning wardrobes on the highway last night," Nick was saying, in Arabic, as he teetered on his back chair legs. He was so tall, he never seemed to fit in our boxy little room.

"Burning wardrobes — it's the national sport!" Irene said, rolling her eyes. She was bundled in a pink scarf, protection against the air-conditioning blasting above her. Summer had arrived almost overnight.

"Where do they get the wardrobes?" Nick wondered. "Do they save them up until there's a crisis?"

Years ago in Cairo, my roommate had told me about her friend who, to memorize Arabic vocabulary, concocted elaborate mental scenes, the more jarring and inappropriate the better, as these stuck most firmly in the mind. For *dawaleeb,* the plural of *doolab,* he had envisioned a performer in blackface saying, in minstrel-like patois, "Dat's da way I lib," and pointing to his wardrobes stuffed full of belongings. This thirdhand mnemonic had worked all too well — not only did I know that the word *dawaleeb* meant wardrobes, but I winced a little every time I heard it.

Minstrels, wardrobes, collections of junk — none of that seemed germane to Irene and Nick's exchange, however.

"Wait — time out," I finally said. "What are *dawaleeb?*"

"Duh, tires?" Nick answered. "It's, like, the first word you learn here. Every time there's some problem, people block the road with burning tires."

"Oh, wow!" I said. Nick raised an eyebrow. It wasn't that I thought tire-burning was exciting, but Nick's translation was a clue to a secondary riddle. *Doolab* was a borrowed word, I knew from the two long vowels, which matched no pattern in the Arabic root system. In Persian, it meant waterwheel. I had always wondered how it came to mean wardrobe in Arabic. Not that a tire was a completely logical link between an irrigation tool and a storage unit, but it was a start.

Nick set his chair down with a thump, bringing my thoughts out of the dictionary and back to the here and now. His translation also explained why my fellow hikers had been so tense on the bus. I hadn't grasped that we — a busload full of Christians, I supposed, though of course we had never discussed it — might be caught on the wrong side of a flaming line, in the *Be'aaaaaa,* where Hezbollah and Amal staked claim.

"Right, *dawaleeb,*" I said to Nick, nodding.

Almost a Dead Language

ZAINA HANDED BACK our first quiz. I had thought I'd done well—only one or two words had been unfamiliar, and I had been the first to finish. But it was covered in red *X*'s, with a failing grade at the top.

The demerits were not for the words I had used, but how I had written them. But, but—I thought as I flipped the pages of the quiz. That's the way the words are *really* spelled! I felt the same visceral wrench in my chest that had seized me when Zaina had written the word for fifteen without a *ra* on the end.

In my Ammiya classes in Egypt, spelling had been a side issue, covered in one go by pointing out how the pronunciation was streamlined. In all dialects, not just Ammiya, the trickier sounds are often glossed over. The *dh* (like the *th* in "the") usually shifts to a simpler *d* or *z*. Likewise, *th* might become *t* or *s*, and the *qaf*, the delicate, coughing *q*, usually becomes an easier *g*, or just a glottal stop, a soundless stutter. Because colloquial spelling wasn't standardized, sometimes my teachers had written words the way they sounded, sometimes the way they were "really" spelled in Fusha. And they had certainly never graded on spelling.

While Zaina was introducing the day's lesson, I pulled out my pen and rescored my quiz. Disregarding the spelling "mistakes," I had missed a total of two questions. That gave me a solid A.

When I was done righting these wrongs, I tuned back in to class.

"Tell us what you did this morning," Zaina had just asked Dutch Danny. He always told a good story, and Zaina had sat down in a chair to listen, tugging her miniskirt closer to her knees.

"I woke up —"

"*Tsk,*" Zaina interrupted, jumping up. From Egypt, I knew this tongue click was shorthand for "no." But the way Zaina did it, lighter and a bit offhand, I had a hard time hearing it as simple negation; to me it sounded like the chiding of a judgmental grandmother.

Danny had spoken exactly one word, *sahsahet*. "You mean *fi'it*," Zaina said in a sharper tone than usual. Her marker squeaked as she wrote on the board. "*This* is how you say 'I woke up.'"

This was puzzling. Both words were in our book, which Zaina usually followed to the letter. Danny just nodded and continued with his story.

During our break — because, by this time, I knew that questioning Zaina's *rools* didn't yield any useful answer — I asked Danny to explain his exchange with our teacher. Surely he, who had dated a Lebanese man for years, had woken up in Beirut enough times to know what he was talking about.

"This happens with so many words," he said. "You learn one from a Catholic, one from a Shiite, and they both laugh at you. And now we are studying at a Muslim school" — we were? I hadn't thought to wonder, and I didn't know how he could tell — "so those are the words we are learning." Danny was used to navigating Beirut, crossing sectarian lines with his vocabulary learned on all sides. He told me not to worry about it.

I did worry, though. If language was as marked by sect as everything else in Lebanon, as Danny suggested, this threw my whole Arabic-study plan into disarray. When I had started classes in Cairo,

I was convinced that focusing on Ammiya rather than Fusha would free me from the unwieldy, book-learned classical language. When I had moved on to Dubai and here to Beirut, I was sure that studying dialects would get me out of my head and help me speak from my gut, or my heart. They would make my life smoother, fuller with human interaction — and in Beirut, I hoped, a bit more glamorous.

But in Lebanon, there were apparently dialects within the dialect. If I chose the wrong one, I might alienate my listener as quickly as if I had asked which village he was from, or made some remark about a political party. Perhaps in this complicated country, Fusha, though it was the language of the Quran, could be more neutral than colloquial speech, since it would give no clues as to one's sectarian affiliation. I could say *istayqathtu* — the ponderous classical word for "I woke up" — and no one would immediately guess which side of Beirut I'd been sleeping on.

I had considered Fusha an anchor tied to my ankle, dragging me to the bottom of the sea. Now, in its regimented order, logical spelling, and vocabulary that predated Lebanese identity politics, it looked like a life preserver.

More and more frequently, our class stumbled on usage disagreements. Nick cited his cousins on some piece of slang; Zaina *tsk*ed. Irene quoted her mother-in-law; Zaina *tsk*ed. We hit an impasse with the principle of continuous prefixes. These syllables attached to the front of a verb are found in most Arabic dialects, although the syllable itself differs. With the prefix, a present-tense verb takes on a sense of repetition or routine. In Egypt, *tishrab beera?* is a waiter's question: "Drink a beer tonight?" *Bitishrab beera?* is a query about habit or taste: "Do you drink beer?" Lebanese has a tiny complication, in that there are *two* prefixes, *'am–* and *bi–*. According to Zaina, they could not be used together. That was the *rool,* no excebtions.

I could have sworn I had heard Manal in Dubai start verbs with *'am-bi,* both prefixes together. I checked my notes — yes, that's what I had written.

Late one night, I burrowed into online forums on Lebanese dialect intricacies. Many posters confirmed what I had heard, while others backed up Zaina's usage, and everyone provided helpful translations. I compiled my findings into a single page, complete with citations, then reviewed them, highlighting each point. When I was finished, I paused in surprise. I had convinced myself that Zaina was a terrible teacher, with all her rigid *rools* and her unwillingness to acknowledge how anyone else might speak. But when was the last time I had been so thorough? Even if it was by accident, she had made me a much more diligent student.

The next, deeper revelation came as I was closing the tabs in my browser. For settling this *'am-bi-* argument, my Fusha grammars were no help. And there was no definitive Lebanese dialect text; all I had in print was *The Abou Abed Joke Book.* I had picked it up at a bookstore and devoured it hungrily, excited to hear the ring of a Lebanese voice in my head as I read, even if it was only little stories about ne'er-do-well Abou Abed and his scandalous wife. For explanatory references, all I had were the word nerds on the Internet and the school's spiral-bound textbook.

That textbook may have been "wrong" relative to what I had heard other Lebanese people say, but to Zaina it was right. That and all the *rools* she was teaching us reflected the way she spoke. She was teaching *her* Arabic — and according to Dr. Badawi, that was the way it should be done.

This school, it finally dawned on me, was doing exactly what I had wanted, the very thing I had had the urge to jump up and yell about at the conference in Dubai. It was treating colloquial Lebanese Arabic as a legitimate language, totally separate from Fusha. While I had been busy imagining a Supreme Poet of the People composing a masterwork that would free everyone from the shackles of classical Arabic, I had not bothered to imagine what this might look like to me, as a student of Legitimate Lebanese. Alone in my apartment, I groaned aloud at the obviousness of it all. Of course a teacher would have to present the *rools* from scratch, of course she would have to standardize spelling. So not only had I not recognized my supposed dream come true, I had spent the past two weeks fighting it tooth and nail. I felt like a jerk.

Until near the end of the twentieth century, only one kind of Arabic mattered enough to have its grammar scrutinized and written about in books. Real Arabists — and Arabs, for that matter — studied Fusha. That was that.

The various dialects of Arabic were considered mere corruptions of the classical language, simplifications that even the most dimwitted students could pick up just by conversing. Humphrey Davies, a longtime literary translator of Arabic, told me his professors at Cambridge had considered colloquial Arabic "an amiable eccentricity, to be humored." Colloquial teaching materials were rare. The Ammiya textbook I used in Cairo in 1992 covered not much more than the basics. In Lebanon, one private dialect teacher was famous for her use of course materials from a British school established in the 1960s in the village of Shemlan. They consisted of vocabulary lists: 102 key verbs, 123 professions.

English has its own distinctions between high and low speech. Responsible teachers would never instruct a student that "gotta" or "wanna" is correct, but they would accept its spoken use. Similarly, linguists accept that African American Vernacular English — or Southern American English, or Appalachian English, or any other English dialect — has its own internal logic and grammar, its own *rools*. In colloquial Arabic, people were only starting to acknowledge the same.

I went to talk to Rana Dirani, the director of my school and the developer of my textbook, to ask her: Was she doing what I thought she was doing? Was she trying to make the Lebanese dialect its own language? I felt I had my answer just from her firm handshake, her fierce black eyes, and her strong jaw. This was a woman on a mission.

"Yes, for sure," she said without hesitation, smacking the top of her big wooden desk for emphasis. "I really had this idea to codify colloquial."

In Arabic, putting colloquial on the same footing as Fusha is problematic for a few reasons. First, it is considered vaguely suspect. The logic goes like this: Arabs don't need to study the language they speak; their Arabic classes are all about classical rules and written formalities. As a result, studying dialect is something only foreigners do, and because, according to a certain paranoid view, foreigners must be in the Middle East only to gather information for some meddling government or other, studying dialect almost certainly means you're a spy. This paranoia was prevalent in Lebanon, and with good reason — that British school in Shemlan, for instance, had produced several notorious intelligence agents. A few days before my appointment with Rana at school, I had spoken with Samar Awada, a freelance teacher developing a Lebanese dialect curriculum of her own. "I get *that look* a lot," she had said. "You know, the 'you're working with spies, aren't you?' look."

Another problem with taking colloquial more seriously is that it implies taking Fusha less seriously, which in turn implies a devaluation of the language of the Quran. As Rana laid out her plan for writing the literal book on Lebanese colloquial, I asked her if she had any reservations about casting aside Fusha and all its historical associations.

Not at all, she said. Her school taught Fusha because it was still necessary for advanced reading, but in her view, it was "almost a dead language," precisely because of its association with the Quran, which rendered it untouchable. "And the reality is that people don't understand the Quran," she added. Her black bob swung along her chin as she shook her head with irritation. "Sometimes I pray and I don't understand. I sometimes have no clue! But if it were in colloquial, I could understand."

No other teacher I spoke to on my travels took such an extreme position. Even Samar Awada, a very practical teacher, had expressed a sentimental fondness for Fusha. It would be a shame if it went the way of Latin, she had said, and died out completely. It should be taught "for its beauty, not just as an obligation."

Perhaps the thorniest problem with elevating the various Arabic dialects was that it could lead to a more fractured Arab world. In the heyday of Arab nationalism, the 1950s and 1960s, Egypt's charismatic leader Gamal Abdel Nasser had managed to briefly unite his country with Syria, although they shared no border. Those days had long passed. Yet despite wars, tyrannical leaders, and significant cultural differences, solidarity among Arabs persisted across the Middle East, in large part due to a shared language, because Nasser and other nationalists had defined Arabs as anyone who spoke Arabic. Identifying as Arab first could elevate you above petty local politics and make you part of a greater culture, one that preserved the Greek classics and brought the world algebra and falafel.

Yet Rana waved off Arab nationalism — she was much more concerned with the fractures inside Lebanon. Whereas I had been spooked by the subtle divisiveness of sectarian differences in Lebanese colloquial, she saw it as a unifying force. This was because dialect countered the innate elitism of Fusha, the same elitism that had frustrated me at the conference in Dubai. Not everyone could afford a good education in classical Arabic, Rana said. "So that leaves the spoken language, the only language that can make a connection between all Lebanese people." She was building her all-Lebanese curriculum in part for American and European semester-abroad students, but more so for her fellow citizens.

"Lebanese people say to me, 'I don't know how to read.' I say, 'What, you don't know the alphabet?'" She leaned forward over her desk, conspiring. "I know what they mean, of course, but I push them. I want to create a *belief* in this language."

When I had embarked on this project to relearn Arabic the right way, I had wanted someone to congratulate me on my wise decision to abandon Fusha. It was a sign, I thought, of a devil-may-care attitude that came with true maturity, a sign that I was no longer that kid who had to get every single word just right. But with Zaina backing me up and Rana telling me to go for it, I discovered I hadn't changed much after all. I loved Fusha's rules; I had lived by them for all my years of school. I admired how grammarians had polished them for centuries, extrapolating them from the Quran and Bedouin informants, then spreading them around the Islamic empire to keep new converts and language learners from screwing the whole beautiful thing up.

Rana's mission was to do this all over again for Lebanese colloquial, for the sake of a better Lebanon. She wasn't daunted — she was more fired up when I left her office. And I felt a bit more at peace. Maybe I could relax about Zaina "correcting" my spelling; maybe I didn't have to lunge at every inconsistency in my textbook. So the *rools* weren't foolproof yet, but writing them down was the first step. Although I couldn't quite give myself over to Rana's program, I admired her for being more certain than I was.

Your Mother

I HAD CHOSEN MY school in Beirut not for its director's mission, but for a class I'd read it offered: Let's Talk Dirty, all about swearing and obscenity in a cultural context. This was exactly what had been missing from my previous Arabic instruction: not only had I skipped over polite phrases like *mashallah,* I hadn't learned any of the rude ones either.

Unfortunately, by the time I came to Beirut, the trash-talking class was no longer offered. The public outcry had been surprisingly intense, Rana Dirani told me. News stories about the class had been posted online, and readers worked themselves into a collective snit. "Instead of teaching the beauty of Arabic," one commenter lamented, "you make the dirty, low, and vile aspect of our society accessible, and you glorify it in the process." Another sniffed, "Like we need more low-class people in this country." All this, despite the fact that the cultural context for swearing in Lebanon was in fact quite rich. The Lebanese were considered the modern masters of a centuries-old tradition of colloquial poetry called *zajal* that frequently hinges on the art of insult. A *zajal* session, swapping rhymed putdowns, was as creative, competitive, and ritualized as the dozens was in English, and the Let's Talk Dirty class's final exam was modeled on this. Yet in the end, Rana said, she canceled the course, because she didn't want her place to be known only as "the school where they teach you dirty words." Outside of class there were plenty of opportunities to learn, she consoled me.

Were there ever. Taxi drivers in particular uttered streams of invective so hot the air in front of their mouths shimmered. Their profanity was at odds with the elegance of their wheels, vintage Mercedes S-class sedans that cut through the traffic like battleships.

I didn't recognize many of the words, but often the expressions were built on the same fundamental insult tactic that works around the globe: if someone says something bad to you, say their mother's got it the same. I'm a donkey? Your mother's a donkey! For efficiency, you could just answer, "*Ummak*" — Your mother. For color, implicate a sister as well.

Beyond this, I suppose I did have some basic vocabulary. Some bad words just sound bad. *'Ars*, the word for pimp, is scorn in a single syllable: a constricted *'ayn*, a nearly swallowed *r*, a heavy *s*. Other, worse words are dangerously light and easy: *kuss* for cunt, *teez* for ass, *neek* for fuck (which was why Nick went by Nicolas in class). In Egypt, *tuz feek* means "salt on you," and *zift* means "asphalt," neither of which seems rude in translation, but both are among the nastier ways to tell someone to get lost. These were all too easy to mix up, and then I learned that one of the worst possible swear words in Egypt, conveying such deep opprobrium and disgust that "fuck this fucking shit" sounds jolly by comparison, is simply *aha*, with an emphatic first syllable and a whispery *h*. I had probably exhaled that by accident, in exasperation.

I had also learned one culturally specific insult, years before in Cairo. A friend had unleashed "You look like you haven't showered in a month" on a sidewalk lecher, and he had stopped dead in his tracks. His eyes bulged with rage, then he melted into the crowd. I practiced the words like a magic spell — to make a man vanish, call him stinky — but deep down, I knew I'd never have the nerve to use it. To an Egyptian, smelling bad is a clear indicator of low class and bad character, but I did not feel comfortable establishing myself as top caste, even if many Egyptians considered me that already, simply because I was American.

Anyway, I had absorbed too much of the opposite language, the little kindnesses of Egyptian Arabic: the practice of calling someone "your presence" (*hadritak*) rather than "you," the generous use of various phrases that mean "at your service." In crowded Cairo, these were padding that softened the many points of social contact in a day.

In Beirut, those niceties seemed to have been stripped away. This made no sense to me — people were pussyfooting around what village their family came from, but they felt free to tell the guy in the next car he'd fuck his mother up the ass if he cut in. During that particular episode, I sat in the back of the taxi with my hands folded primly in my lap while my driver's neck turned red and spit flew from his mouth. The guy in the next car screamed right back about my driver's mother and her own violated behind. After several rounds of aggressive engine revving, we drove on.

"Beirut was much better during the war," my driver said after a block. His neck was returning to its normal color. "You could actually earn a living then."

We weren't coddled much in class either. Our lesson on adjectives included *nasih* (fat) and *bish'* (ugly), and then we practiced them by describing pictures of people. Almost all of them were fat and ugly. Freestyling about a photo of a bloated child in a striped shirt and beanie, Nick added, "*wi-bilit.*"

When I asked what that meant, he teetered on his chair's back legs and threw out his long arms. "I don't know, just *bilit*," he said. "Stupid, I guess?"

At the front of the room, Zaina was giggling, revealing a cute dimple. "You know, loud. Dumb," she said.

"Not as funny as they think," Nick added. "Like a *wuzz.*"

"And what does *that* mean?" I was scribbling in my notebook.

"Oh, someone who's trying to be cool but totally isn't," Nick said with assurance.

Zaina jumped in again. "*Mahbool* — that means dumb."

"And *zinnikh,* that's a good one — annoying and stupid," Nick said. "And *sa'eel.* Also annoying." He demonstrated the difference with a dismissive wave of his hand. *Zinnikh* — with a throaty *kh* as in "yech" — got a big wave; *sa'eel* got a little one.

Zaina was nodding with heartfelt enthusiasm and writing each word on the board. "Why do we need to learn all this stuff?" I asked Nick. "Who are you saying these words *to?*"

"Oh, when you're driving, of course."

Afterward, we went out to do our homework over coffee. Sally the Southerner drawled out a translation of one of the more cryptic sentences, and Nick nudged her with his elbow.

"Huh. You're not entirely useless, then," Nick said, copying her answer into his own book.

Sally knew how to hunt, sail, tie knots, and charm her way into good Internet service, a rarity in Beirut. She might have been the most capable person in our class. She looked miffed, but Irene burst out laughing. "Nick! You are so totally Lebanese!"

"Sure," he said, pleased. "But what do you mean?"

"The backhanded compliment. That is *so* typical." She had been shocked when she first heard how her mother-in-law talked to her own sisters. At a concert with Irene, I had briefly met the woman in question: short, chain-smoking, with a fabulous froggy voice in which insults would sound particularly rich. Like the rest of us, Irene was also feeling her way in Lebanese culture, but the stakes were higher: peace in her marriage rode on figuring out whether her mother-in-law really meant what she said.

Sally was laughing by now. "Oh, right, I get it. The guy I work for does that too," she said.

I was pretty sure the average cab driver was not using this rhetorical technique, but I vowed to be a bit more open-minded the next time I heard someone say something nasty.

I didn't have to wait long. A few mornings later, I was walking through Hamra when a man sidled up.

"_____ your feet," he said to me in French.

"I'm sorry, what?" I asked him in Arabic.

"Ah, you are American," he replied in English. "I wanted to say to you, your feet are quite nice." He slipped into step alongside me. "But your middle toe could be a little longer."

"Thanks for the advice—I'll work on that," I said with a big, crazy fake smile, my standard response to street weirdos. I made a hard right turn to lose him.

"Wait!" he cried out, scrambling to keep up. OK, I thought, here was a challenging opportunity to appreciate a half-assed Lebanese compliment. I turned and looked at him more closely. He was young and pudgy, with big, blinky eyes and slicked-down hair, and he fairly quivered in his freshly pressed short-sleeve plaid shirt. His khakis had a knife pleat down each leg.

"Well, you see, I have a foot fetish," he said seriously as he trotted along next to me. "So I notice these things. Women here, they don't take good care of their feet. But you clearly do."

The reason my feet looked halfway presentable was because I had shelled out way too much for a hasty pedicure at the New York airport, in a last-minute attempt to meet the high standards of grooming I had been warned I would encounter in Beirut. Never mind my disheveled hair, my shiny nose, my shapeless clothes—at least my feet would pass muster. That the admirer of my coral-pink toes was half my age, a bit soft around the middle, and an admitted pervert was inconsequential.

"Look, see—this is a nice foot, but her polish is a little chipped."

He had pulled out his phone and was thumbing through photos. I stopped and peered down, shielding the screen from the sun so I could see better.

"Oh, yes," I said. "She does have very straight toes." What was I doing? I was late for class.

"You understand!" He bounced with excitement. "Lebanese women wear a lot of makeup and do their hair, but their feet are bad. So when I see someone like you, who is pretty on top *and* with nice feet, I have to stop."

I waved my hand modestly, his mention of my stubby middle toe forgotten. *Oh, go on.*

"And you're American, so you know about this. I now understand I have this thing, this *foot fetish*." He clearly relished the phrase, the same way I rolled new Arabic vocabulary words around on my tongue.

"I'm a photographer, and I was helping a friend with a shoot, and I noticed I was" — he tugged at the collar of his white undershirt — "*very interested* in the model's feet. So I went home and I looked on the Internet, and I found these videos! And they are from *America!*" He beamed at the coincidence.

Soon he was saying he'd like to take pictures of my feet, if I had time. I demurred. I *was* late for class, and my husband, you see . . . I cast my eyes down solemnly, modestly.

"Oh, yes, married." He blinked, crestfallen. "I, I don't know what to do. I tried asking at a pedicure salon if I could take pictures there, but they sent me away. Too many married women. It would be complicated, they told me . . ."

I left him on the corner, mulling his options, and strode off to school.

Easy – but Not Good

IN BEIRUT, my conversations were still stalling, as people routinely switched to French on me, so I planned another weekend trip away in search of Arabic. I set out northward, to the seaside town of Jbeil. It was closer to Beirut than I realized, and a lot smaller. In less than an hour, I had looped through its cobblestone streets, Phoenician ruins, and wax museum (where, in a scene with John the Baptist, Jesus wore a helpful name tag: "Christ"). Unsure how to pass the hours before dinner, much less bedtime, I perched on a wall next to a church and pondered my next move. A hymn spilled out the door over the craggy stones: "*Allah* . . . ," sang the congregation.

It is a misconception in the West that Muslims worship a mysterious deity named Allah. *Allah* means "the god," or, in English convention, God with a capital *g* — a force as familiar to Jews and Christians as to Shiites and Sunnis and Druze. This is the part of the world where monotheism got its start. Jerusalem was only 150 miles south of where I sat; Jesus (excuse me, "Christ") was born in Bethlehem, a few miles farther on. Saint Paul had his conversion on the road to Damascus, fifty-five miles east.

Just inland rose Mount Lebanon, the spiritual home of the Maronite Church, established in the fourth century. In fact, the Maronite Church could be said to be the reason Lebanon existed as a state in the first place, as the church's leaders worked during the Mandate period, the two decades of French rule following World War I, to carve out a majority-Christian territory from what was then greater Syria. How well that had worked was the subject of considerable debate, to put it mildly. During fifteen years of civil war, Lebanon splintered along sectarian lines, like cracks spreading in a sheet of ice. But everyone used the same word for God.

I was pondering the oneness of it all when a ruddy-faced man approached. "*Vous êtes frensawiyeh?*" he asked.

"No, not French. *Amerkaniyeh,*" I told him in Arabic, adjusting my "American" to the more elegant way Zaina had instructed. She had *tsk*ed at my Egyptianized *amreekaniya*.

"Oh! *Btehki 'arabi!*" he said, then switched back to French. "*Vous êtes seule?*" Physically, he looked in his twenties, but a few pimples, big front teeth, and shiny eyes suggested his mental development had not quite caught up. "Do you want to walk to the harbor with me?" he asked, in Arabic again.

What else did I have to do? The port was five minutes down the hill, and his half Arabic was better than none. On the way we passed another church, where a crowd had gathered for a wedding. Two beefy men in suits greeted my escort warmly. At least I had not hitched my horse to a known lunatic. His name was Tony.

As we made the turn back up from the port he said, "Will you come to my mother's house for tea?" I weighed this offer against my earlier plan, which was nothing.

"For an *'asrooniyeh?* I would be delighted," I replied. We had just learned this word in class, and I was pleased to have an opportunity to use it. It means a social event in the *'asr*, or late afternoon; a *subhiyeh* is a pre-noon outing, from *subh*, the word for morning; *sahra*, the word for a soirée, comes from the verb that means to stay awake all night.

Tony phoned his mother and told her jubilantly, "I am bringing a friend! An *amerkaniyeh!*" His parents lived up the hill, on the other side of the highway, a twenty-minute walk. By the time we reached the highway underpass, Tony had switched from French to almost all Arabic, and I was catching about half of what he said. When I recognized words like *bhebbik* — I love you — I stopped in the middle of the road.

"Listen," I told him, speaking slowly to convey the gravity of what I was saying and to make sure I got the words right, "I am married. You are making me very nervous with all this *bhebbik* and *habibti*. My husband would be very unhappy to hear it. If you don't stop talking like this" — I paused for effect — "I can't come to your mother's house for an *'asrooniyeh.*"

He clamped his mouth shut and swallowed hard. He shifted from foot to foot. Then he looked down and said, "OK, I'm sorry. Please come."

We walked a little farther. I kept looking back, dropping mental bread crumbs along our trail: right at the cemetery, left at the bakery. "Maybe you can spend the night with me?" he finally asked, plaintive, and reached out to touch my arm. I jumped back, balled up my fist, and yelled. We were on a steep hill and I happened to be slightly ahead, so I towered over him.

It was a cruel overreaction, I sensed immediately from the way he cowered. I must have briefly impersonated someone he feared.

"I'm sorry," he whispered. "Please come."

He cheered as soon as I started walking again. Unfortunately, his blatant come-on had opened the floodgates to a conversation I didn't want to have, but he was speaking Arabic, and it was good practice. He had had sex four times in his life, he told me, while he was in the army; they had all been prostitutes. Here he switched to French, for the rhyme: *putes à la route*, he called them.

"I am *da'eef*" — weak — "and my father doesn't love me because I talk too much," he said as we walked up and up the hill. "I pray a lot, to take the devil out of me," he told me, "but my church doesn't answer. Once I went to the Greek church, though, and I really felt the light."

When we arrived at the turn to his apartment building, Tony stopped in a grocery store to buy cookies and Nescafé packets. As we climbed the last hill, he turned. "Maybe my father will be happy with me," he said, "because I am bringing you to visit. Maybe he will be proud."

In the dim apartment, Tony's mother, a plump woman with reddish hair, and his older sister were sitting in puffy armchairs watching television. Tony introduced me, then pointed to the painting of Jesus on the wall above them. "*Voilà, c'est Dieu!*" he said — as if to say, You know, the guy we were just talking about. Serving the cookies and drinks without ceremony, he was talking fast, telling the women how we had met, how I was a writer, how he was smart for having guessed I was a writer after seeing my big bag, my pen, and my messy hair. All the while, his voice increased in volume. From the depths of her chair, Tony's mother waved to shush him.

"He gets so loud," she said to me apologetically.

We watched the TV for a few companionable minutes and then Tony's father came in. I had expected more of an ogre. He was a slight, tanned man with mischievous blue eyes. He settled down on the sofa next to me and chatted as though I were a neighbor who had popped by.

Still, after seeing how Tony had cowered in the road, I didn't want to shift my loyalties, so I refrained from laughing too much at his father's jokes. Not that I understood them all anyway. I smiled and nodded, falling back on my old bad Badawi-induced habit of making up a story to fit.

"I visited _____ the family _____ argument _____ the land," he said, and I filled in the blanks with a feud among brothers, an argument over inheritance, a rocky orchard on the edge of a mountain village.

On TV, a newscaster reported that the Lebanese Shiite pilgrims who had been kidnapped in Syria were still being held.

Tony's father pointed his chin at the TV. "They're with Hezbollah, I'm sure." He said it as four syllables, *He-zib-ul-lah*.

"I have good friends in Syria," he went on. "_____ Lattakia _____ shooting. Now we do not go."

I filled in the blanks, and my eyes widened.

He leaped up. He had seen where my mind had gone: to the mounting war in Syria, and his friends in Lattakia had been shot. "No, no, my friends are safe!" he said. "We used to go shooting *birds*, hunting!" He mimed tiptoeing through tall grass with a long rifle, like Elmer Fudd, then, for the birds, he hooked his thumbs together and flapped his hands. "Syria is beautiful for hunting."

Many Lebanese did not consider Syria beautiful for anything. It was their overbearing neighbor, effectively an occupying force after the civil war. Syrian troops came in to keep the peace, then stayed for decades. In March 2005, after massive demonstrations in Beirut, the Syrian troops rolled home. Now, after a few years of relative peace in Lebanon, Syria was embarking on its own civil war, and it was creeping over the border.

Tony's father had run to the kitchen. He returned clutching something, and he gestured for me to open my hand. Into it he placed a tiny songbird, frozen solid but still fluffy in its little jacket of feathers. "These are the most delicious," he said. I was afraid the bird would defrost from the warmth of my hand, it was so slight. I handed it back.

"You eat them whole, right?" I had read about this, the Lebanese penchant for eating tiny birds, as the French did with ortolans, beaks and skulls and innards and all, though at least no feathers.

"Yes!" said Tony's father, excited that I appreciated this frozen treasure. He dashed back to the kitchen to refreeze the bird, shouting a recipe over his shoulder. "Put them on the grill with some lemon and garlic." When he came back out, he was kissing his fingers, like a cartoon Italian chef. "They're delicious."

Tony's dad had more show-and-tell: a bird, a live one, in a little silver wire cage. It was white and sidestepped nervously on its perch. "Are you going to eat that one?" I asked, laughing.

He looked a bit shocked. "*Haram,* no!" For shame! He set a blue quilted cozy over the cage. "It's time for him to sleep," he told me, patting the cover gently.

That was my cue. It had been a somewhat unorthodox *'asrooniyeh,* but my afternoon tea had given me a chance to practice Arabic for more than a minute. And perhaps I had served Tony's purpose after all.

From Jbeil and its waxwork Jesus, I returned to Beirut in the morning, and before lunch I was in the southern city of Sidon and an entirely different atmosphere. The highway was edged with billboards adorned with the caterpillar-browed face of former prime minister Rafic Hariri, assassinated by a car bomb in 2005. Hariri was a Sunni Muslim, and this was his hometown.

On the edge of Sidon's old city, I stopped at a bakery for a *manoucheh.* The bread was blissfully hot and fragrant with herbs, and I stopped and savored my good fortune. I had the whole day all to myself in a new place.

I was eating and trying to read some posters stuck on the wall when a voice at my elbow said, in English, "You speak Arabic?"

I started and turned to see a man with a shock of white hair, a chiseled chin, and fetching crinkles around his caramel eyes. He looked like an aging French film star.

"I, uh, *behki 'arabi, mais . . .*" The question was confusing (if he thought I spoke Arabic, why didn't he ask me in Arabic?), and herb-infused olive oil was dripping off my elbow.

The handsome man produced a sheaf of napkins from his suit pocket. Once I was degreased and we had established we would speak English, things were easier. Alain was a sixty-two-year-old native of Sidon who had worked in France for much of his life; he lived here with his two sons; and would I care to come to lunch?

Perhaps I should have held out for a stranger who wanted to speak Arabic, not English, but Alain lured me easily. He had just been to the library; he showed me the books, which included Mark Twain's *The Innocents Abroad.*

On the walk to his house, he told me his wife had recently left. This might have been a warning sign for a more sensible solo female traveler. But the story intrigued me ("This Facebook, it can destroy families"), and he had shown me the fresh meat he had bought for *kibbeh nayeh,* the spiced raw beef and bulgur he would prepare for lunch, so I kept following him.

At his apartment, his teenage sons were just waking up, staggering around in stretched-out T-shirts. "Marwan is a computer genius," Alain boasted, by way of introduction to the younger one.

"I am a hacker," the kid said, blinking behind his glasses.

The boys drifted away, and Alain gave me a tour of his bookshelves: Agatha Christie, Khalil Gibran, tomes on *balagha,* the art of classical rhetoric, which was still a cornerstone of Arabic education. Then we went to the kitchen, where he took off his suit coat, rolled up his sleeves, and directed me to make a salad while he prepared the meat. He had lived alone in the past, he said, and he could do it again now. "And besides," he added, "if a man enjoys life, he should take care of his stomach." He plunged potatoes into frying oil and set to carving radish flowers to garnish the *kibbeh.*

The sons made a token appearance at lunch, but they soon melted away again, to computers and friends. Alain and I cleaned our plates of the spiced meat and the last sprigs of succulent purslane. I asked Alain why he had left France.

"Life in Lebanon is easy—but not good," he said with a philosopher's sigh. "You understand?"

At first I didn't understand. If I had been asked to characterize life in Lebanon, I probably would have given the opposite answer. Life seemed hard because of the little annoyances: feeble Internet, obnoxious drivers, road closures. One of the first full sentences I had learned in Beirut was *Rahet el-kahraba'* — The power's gone out. Yet I also saw evidence of the good life, in the fresh produce, the Mediterranean breezes, the leisure time to chat after a lazy lunch. This, I would have thought, would be a reason to move home from France.

These superficial hassles and perks didn't figure in Alain's calculations, however. For him, life was easy because he was able to retire — he no longer worked as a waiter in a foreign country. Here, he lived off the income from this building; the neighboring lot, also his, was filled with fruit trees. He leaned off the balcony and picked us two flesh-red plums.

But, he had been reminded after a few years at home, life was not good in any moral sense. He was thwarted by the fundamental rule of Lebanese life, the sectarian system. The end of the civil war meant the various sects no longer battled each other outright, but the National Pact, set at independence in 1943 on principles established under the French Mandate, was still followed. The law required that government posts be parceled out according to sect: the prime minister was always a Sunni, as Rafic Hariri had been; the president was always Maronite; seats in the National Assembly were fixed at a six-to-five ratio of Christians to Muslims. This quota system trickled down to civil life, Alain told me: to get any meaningful job, one was required to show affiliation with a political party, which was virtually synonymous with sect.

Alain refused to play the game, but he feared for his sons, who would soon have to choose a side in this society. In light of this, my concern over sect-appropriate vocabulary was trivial. As an outsider, a tourist, I didn't have to choose anything. I could opt out of the whole mess, in much the same way that I had been able to sidestep revolutionary loyalties in Egypt and watch *Mamma Mia!* with a retired regime crony.

"At my sons' age, I was in France!" Alain crowed. His boast lightened the mood; the sun shone through his thick white hair. I could picture him, tanned and wiry, prowling the streets of Paris. His children were so soft, so boyish by comparison. They had the world at their fingertips — Marwan was plugged in right now, hacking into blogs in Sweden — but they seemed so vulnerable. Alain stood to adjust the curtains around the balcony.

In this shade-dappled hothouse, he turned the conversation to his ex-wife. Something had been wrong for about a year. She was depressed, messy, mean. "She forgot her sons' names," he said. "She called them Stupid, Piece of Meat, Animal." He had decided to wait it out. If she asked for a divorce first, he would not have to pay.

After she had left, Marwan looked through her files on the computer and discovered the Facebook messages between her and another man. Marwan swore never to speak his mother's name again.

I was starting to feel a bit uncomfortable. Was this a segue into some sleazy invitation? Was it unhappy Saeed of the mountaintop parking lot all over again, a seduction by tragedy?

Perhaps Alain sensed my worry. "I invited you over so I could practice my English," he said. "And *you* must do the same with Arabic." It didn't matter what sort I studied. Although, he added archly, "if one speaks Fusha, people think him a pedant." I was at no risk of that — when Alain slipped into Fusha to demonstrate, I could not respond in anything but fractured Lebanese words, still wrapped in my unshakable Egyptian accent. "Just three or four weeks a year," Alain concluded, "to keep the knowledge."

More than halfway through my travels and studies, I was starting to look ahead. How would I maintain the Arabic I had learned? I couldn't tramp around the Arab world for the rest of my life, hurling myself at strangers. I was married; I had obligations at home and other work to do. A few weeks a year, though, as Alain suggested — that seemed manageable. Together we cleared the table, and then he walked me to the bus stop.

I was always so concerned with how I spoke, I thought, as I bumped along the coast road on the bus. My Egyptian got me the wrong kind of juice, my Fusha was fading fast, and, until I had heard Alain's analysis of the sectarian system, I had been afraid of choosing the wrong Lebanese word for fear of misidentifying myself. It was slowly dawning on me that none of the people I met cared about any of that. They just wanted me to listen.

The Weird Uncle

BEIRUT, THE PARIS of the Middle East — decades had passed since this swinging-sixties cliché had been true, at least physically. Fashion had moved on from classic Chanel to more eye-searing combinations, and the colonial-era buildings were gone or slated for the wrecking ball. But the French influence was still easy to hear. Nearly everywhere I turned in Beirut, someone was squealing, "*Ah, oui, c'est chouette ça!*" into a rhinestone-trimmed phone.

As a student, I found these Francophones irritating; I needed to speak and hear Arabic. Worse, the French was not just background noise; I often overheard a conversation and grasped it easily, almost subconsciously. Which would have been satisfying, were it not also a bitter reminder of how seldom I did the same in Arabic.

After World War I, under the French Mandate, French schools were established in the territory that became Syria and Lebanon. This was one prong of a divide-and-rule strategy to diffuse pan-Arab solidarity; the other was the sectarian system of government offices. So thorough was the French education that many teachers worried that Arabic would be stamped out, and they fought vigorously to preserve the language and the culture it carried.

Even after Lebanon became fully independent of France, in 1946, the French schools were maintained for many. After close to a century of this education, the language had naturally been woven into Lebanese. When you don't know the Arabic word, I learned early on, a French one might be not just a good substitute, but the real thing.

In our class, Danny, who had learned French as part of his excellent Dutch education, was a master of this. "Yesterday I went to lunch with these lovely . . ." He fished for the word for ladies. "*Madamat,*" he concluded, flashing a convincing smile.

"*Tsk* — it's *demoisellat,*" Zaina corrected. Of course it was.

Soon I had a short list of French-derived words: *kuloon* (stockings), *mkarraz* (stressed, from *crise*), and *zhaghal* (gigolo, for a particular sort of tight-jeaned, slick-haired guy on a motorbike). Not very useful, but beggars for cognates couldn't be choosers.

After class one day, a few of us students sat in the café and reviewed our new vocabulary.

"*Tishreejeh,*" I said. "That means phone credit, right, Nick?" He was our go-to guy for real-life words.

"Yeah, like, *baddi tishreejeh bi-'ashra* — I want ten bucks' credit." He went back to talking with Eliza, the Lebanese Frenchwoman who barely spoke in class but was lively outside it. Irene reached for her big green Hans Wehr. Like me, she carried it with her always.

"I wonder what the verb is," she muttered.

I'd been doing the same mental analysis. "Right — it's sort of like a Form II verbal noun," I said, referring back to my precious college verb chart and its morphology rules. "So the root would have to be *sharaja.*"

Irene had already found the entry. She looked up, puzzled. "It's not even a verb. It just says *sharaj*, with the broken plural form *ashraj*: 'loop, ring, eyelet.'" She paused. "Oh, buttonhole too. And . . . anus?"

"What?" I reached for the dictionary. She raised her eyebrows, an unspoken I-could-not-make-this-up.

"'*Sharaji*, adjective: anal,'" I read the next line. "You have got to be kidding me." This was like that evening in the desert in Abu Dhabi, when I had looked up the word I thought meant "edge of a dune" and found "miscarried fetus."

Irene took the book back and slammed it shut. "Thanks for nothing, Hans."

With our Fusha backgrounds, Irene and I were accustomed to having to stretch our brains around surprising definitions. We even liked it. Irene maintained her own list of paradoxical Arabic words: *Taluqa* means to get a divorce, and also to jump for joy. *Siban* is childhood and sensual desire. *'Ala* is related to families and wailing. *Habasa* yields the words for wedding ring as well as prison. Those had some internal logic, if you were cynical enough. This *sharaj*, though — this was nonsense.

"How do you possibly get from anal to phone credit?" I wondered aloud. I tugged Nick's sleeve again.

He laughed cheerily, the laugh of someone unburdened by the logic of morphology. "People who talk on their phones too much are assholes?" he said.

Nick had been exposed to the singular details of Arabic from birth. To him, the language was like a weird uncle — he was never surprised by its quirks. He went back to chatting with Eliza; they had switched from English to French, as Nick had recently studied in Paris.

"Wait a minute, Irene," I said. "How would you say 'to load' in French?" The gears of the Arabic-morphology machine were turning in my head. "Isn't it *charger*? And could you use that verb to say you were loading up a phone with credit?"

Irene, who spoke French all the time for her Red Cross job, allowed that you could. And then the gears clicked in her head too. The *ch* in French was a soft *sh* sound, the *g* more of a *j*.

"*Charger.* Oh, right, the consonants are *sha-ra-ja!*" She laughed with jubilation. "Verbal noun, *tashreej,* so . . . *tishreejeh!* That's brilliant!"

Ten minutes to learn a new word, but one we'd never forget.

The burning tires had been cleared off the road to Tripoli, which was good, because I was running out of places to go on the weekends. Word on the street in Beirut was that this northern city was still dangerous, yet it was apparently safe enough that a local historian was offering a free walking tour. I decided to risk the trip.

I took an early bus so I could have breakfast at Abdul Rahman Hallab, a famous pastry purveyor that occupied a giant castle-like building in downtown Tripoli. Hallab's specialty was *knafeh,* a storied Levantine sweet of soft white cheese sandwiched between — or rather, embraced by, as the root suggests — two thin layers of semolina or fine-spun pastry threads, crisped in clarified butter and doused in sugar syrup.

I had first heard of the treat from a fellow graduate student, a Palestinian raised in Jordan who had the aspect of Droopy Dog; the only time he was cheerful was when he talked about *knafeh* — or *kunafaaaaaaah,* as he said it, a heart-rending sigh. This man's favorite pastry is said to have been invented in Nablus, in the West Bank north of Jerusalem. The cheesy delight spread around the Arab world, as did Palestinian refugees. Lebanon was home to more than 300,000 of them, about 7 percent of the population; the law blocked them from owning land and holding certain jobs. *Knafeh* had been embraced, even if those who invented it had not.

Knafeh does not indulge Proustian musing — it must be eaten quickly, before the milky-soft cheese congeals. Mine arrived molten on a small plate; the waiter pointed to the Hallab-branded squeeze bottle of sugar syrup. Within a minute, I had scraped the dish clean and slurped my coffee to the lees.

When I joined the walking tour ten minutes later, I was flushed with sugar and caffeine. I was glad to see I wasn't the only person to go against the travel warnings — three other people had made the trip from Beirut. Our guide, Elie, was as energized as I was. Like all good urbanists, he walked fast, in sensible shoes, and talked with the passion and pessimism of anyone deeply involved in local politics. As we jogged along behind him, he pointed out historic colonial buildings at risk of demolition. "And there's a nice old café," he added, "but, *pfft,* they don't use real cups anymore, just plastic."

The city buzzed with commerce. A vendor straightened a display of baseball caps with a red-and-white-check print — keffiyehs for the hip-hop set — while an older gentleman sat nearby in a fez that he had carefully wrapped in a plastic bag. Men hawked espresso and cigarettes from the backs of minivans. The chemicals in my own bloodstream had reached a perfect simmer; I grinned ecstatically at everyone we passed. *Knafeh* was good not so much for how it tasted, but for how it made you feel.

We threaded our way through the narrow alleys into Tripoli's medieval heart. This was what Beirut was missing: its own souk had been bombed to bits, its other relics torn down in the postwar real-estate frenzy. With no historic center, Beirut was unmoored — it could float off to associate with other world capitals, for better and for worse. Tripoli, though, was doubly rooted, by its souk and, on the hill above it, the Crusader fortress toward which Elie marched us with gusto.

My image of the Crusaders was partly borrowed from Monty Python: hapless knights, clomping coconut halves together, had invaded the Holy Land, and Saladin, or rather, Salah ad-Din, the sultan of Egypt and Syria, had sent them all running back to Europe at the end of the thirteenth century. In relating the history of Qala'at Sanjil (a.k.a. the Fortress of Saint-Gilles), Elie was telling a different story, about very specific French knights. Some of them had not run home, but stayed put, married local women, and learned Arabic. In Syria, I had heard jokes about redheads having "Crusader hair," but I had never considered intermarriage as a deeper reason for the Lebanese Christian affection for Gallic culture and language. Prominent Lebanese families, Elie reminded us, were named Sawaya (Savoie), Franjieh (Frankish), and Douaihy (from Douai).

By the time Elie had led us around every corner of the fortress, my blood sugar was in a dive. For lunch, our small group repaired to a specialist in *foul,* for bowls of the garlicky fava beans. Elie's exuberance had faded a bit too. As we ate, he told us about the dark side of urban preservation in Lebanon. "I'll put it very simply," he said. "There is no civil society." The instability of the civil war had driven away anyone with the means to leave. "The ones who stay simply because they don't *want* to leave, the ones like me, are rare."

He was an anomaly in a number of ways. I had just spent two awkward days in class drilling skin and hair colors, so I could decisively say Elie was the only guy with *hinti* (wheat-colored) skin and *'asali* (honey-brown) eyes in this café; everyone else's were distinctly *bunni,* coffee-toned. He was also the only person wearing shorts, which wouldn't have been remarkable in Beirut, but in this more conservative city, his bare, wheaten legs were the most exposed flesh I had seen all day. He set himself further apart by declaring his aversion to the hookah, or *argeeleh,* as it is called in Lebanon. "It's terrible for your health," he said. "And terrible for society. From eight in the morning they are smoking!" He gestured around the restaurant, where, for a change from Beirut, no one was smoking anything. "And women send their children to work lighting the pipes!"

I had seen those kids. The *argeeleh* was such a staple of Lebanese life that you could have one delivered to your apartment, already lit and ready to puff. With a phone call, two kids would hop on a moped, one driving and the other on the back holding the pipe. The coals glowed red in the breeze as the moped cruised down the street. Elie might have been fighting a losing battle against child labor — not only was *argeeleh* demand high, but that looked like a fun job.

Elie's official tour-guide duties had ended back at the fortress, but he escorted a few of us out of the central city to the abandoned Oscar Niemeyer fairgrounds. The Brazilian modernist's project aimed to put Tripoli on the world stage, shoulder to shoulder with the Paris of the Middle East down the coast. Then the civil war began in 1975, and construction was halted. Beyond the barricades were ruins of a future that never came: stark expanses of concrete, shaped into smooth, cold parabolas and domes. On the hilltop behind us, the Fortress of Saint-Gilles remained unshakable.

Pierre and His Friends

JAMEEL AND LAYAL had loved each other for a long time. He was a lawyer, and she was an employee at a company. They had a regular schedule, which was how we students first became acquainted with them, in the chapter on habitual verbs. In fact, life for Layal and Jameel, with its evenings spent watching TV at Layal's house, finishing a little work, and sometimes visiting with friends, sounded pretty boring. Then, in the next chapter, drama.

"So, *Mister* Jameel, where were you yesterday? I called you more than twenty times and you didn't answer!"

"Baby, what's up with you? Why so angry? I was with my friends at the beach."

The dialogue was titled "A Problem Between Jameel and Layal." We took turns reading, going around the table. Jameel claimed he hadn't called Layal to go to the beach because she had said she had a lot of work. In Layal's view, he had sneaked off to the Pierre et Ses Amis beach club, up the coast, to party with his friends and flirt with girls in bikinis.

Layal was willing to forgive him — this time.

"But next time you go out, you have to call me, OK?" Dutch Danny read this line in his best nagging-shrew voice, while holding his thumb and pinkie to the side of his head in standard telephone pantomime.

"Sure, love of my life, next time," crooned Nick in response. He snapped his own imaginary clamshell phone shut.

The punchline: Jameel calls Layal five minutes later to tell her he's going to the store. His laughter was written ﺍﻫﺍﻫﺍﻫ — *hahahaha-haha* — plus a smiley face for emphasis: ☺.

My classmates and I cast puzzled looks at one another. What were we meant to learn from that? This section of the chapter was labeled "Words for Daily Life," and off to the side of the dialogue, a graphic starburst highlighted new vocabulary: *ghayyura*, jealous.

Nick brought his long arm down to slap the table in defiance. "That girl is crazy!" He had said what we were all thinking. "I'd never date someone like that!"

"*Shoo, ya* Nicolas?" Zaina did the little side-to-side head-shake that means "I'm sorry — what?" Like her *tsk*ing habit, this shake, which I'd seen many other Lebanese use, was unnerving. It was too similar to how Americans indicated "no," so I had to remind myself that she wasn't disagreeing, but asking for elaboration.

"You don't like her?" Zaina persisted. "But she's showing she cares about Jameel." She wrote the word *gheereh*, jealousy, on the board in big, looping letters. "Jealousy means she loves him. Don't you all think so?"

We exploded in a storm of protests — as well as we could, given our limited Arabic skills.

"Layal crazy," British Sophie declared. She rarely spoke up, but now she seemed inspired. "Yes, my desire the man that is calling. But Layal *crazy*."

"Foundation of the relation strong is the trust," I said earnestly. "The jealousy, no."

208

"The communication between two people, this is most important of thing," Kaspar stated with his usual precision.

Zaina *tsk*ed and *tsk*ed, ever more perplexed as we struggled.

Andrew, the shaggy-haired Englishman who typically held himself a bit aloof, finally asked the question the rest of us were dancing around. "Is this," he asked dryly, "a *normal* situation in Lebanon?"

"Oh, yes, pretty normal," Zaina answered. "This is a very important concept." She turned back to the whiteboard.

"*Ghar 'ala*—He was jealous for her. This is good jealousy, jealousy that shows you care. But *ghar min*"—here, she wrote the verb with a new preposition—"this is bad jealousy. Like, she was jealous of his new car." It seemed similar to the distinction between jealousy and envy in English, with a difference: "Thou shalt not covet" was going strong here, and a jealous girlfriend was adorable.

"But Sophie is *ghar 'ala* Nicolas for his good grades in class," Zaina continued. This was a good thing in her estimation, but a new spin for me. Sophie was "jealous of" Nick's grades, which meant she wanted him to do well. So a solicitous pride in one's friends was jealousy too?

The root of the verb *ghar* is especially flexible. It produces many other verbs, including one that means to haggle. From Zaina's explanation, I saw the root's internal tension, as well as its broader use. Layal was, in a way, haggling with Jameel over her right to keep tabs on him; Sophie, through friendship, had negotiated a share in Nick's success. People had been *ghar 'ala* me, in a good way, too: I was theirs, they'd staked a claim. In Cairo, Medo had asked me to spend all day at the mall with him; on my hiking trip, Sahar had seated me next to her and shown me off to the rest of the group. Multiple phone calls and demands on my time were ways of showing investment and love.

"Well, I think he was cheating anyway," Danny declared, to move us back to the juicy stuff. "Why would he not call her? He clearly wanted to go to the beach to talk to girls. Or to boys." He wiggled his eyebrows.

For the first time, Zaina agreed. "Yes, he was probably cheating."

Casting the blame on Jameel tapped a new spring of vaguely unpleasant vocabulary, and Zaina wrote the words on the board with relish. Betrayal. Cheater. To yell.

"Stop!" Eliza, the French Lebanese woman, threw her hands up. This was a rare outburst; she spoke even less than Sophie. "I have fragile ears here. These are terrible words."

"*Tsk*, they're very important words," Zaina insisted, still writing. "Womanizer, *niswenji*."

This *was* a good one! The *–ji* suffix is from Turkish, and it basically means "the guy who does," referring to whatever noun it follows. I knew it from Egypt, where it was pronounced *–gi*, with a hard *g*, and used for the *makwagi* (the guy who does the ironing) and the *kababgi* (the guy who does the kebab).

Zaina was using the suffix in a somewhat more figurative, more judgmental way: *niswen* means women, so a *niswenji* is "the guy who does women." She listed other juicy examples: *sakarji* (the guy who does booze), *'amarji* (cards), *hakwaji* (stories, hence a gossip), and the even more abstract *maslahji,* or moocher, an expert at benefiting his own interest (*maslaha*).

"Well, maybe Layal was texting so much because she was worried," Irene allowed, with her usual calm, even enunciation. She was trying to make peace. "If Jameel had just texted back immediately, this would not have happened."

Zaina let out one last *tsk* and hustled us on to the next lesson.

Nick's parents had put him in touch with a Lebanese "uncle" — some older cousin or other — who owned a seafront restaurant, so Nick arranged an afternoon outing for the whole class, complete with two purring late-model, chauffeured Mercedes, a nice change from the rattletrap old ones that circulated in the city. We bundled in and cruised north up the coast. The day was splendid, the first lazy lick of high summer, with a cloudless sky and a soft breeze.

As we were descending a hill toward the restaurant, I noticed flags fluttering on each lamppost: white with a green-and-brown geometric cedar tree. These flags — this icon, as well as a dozen other ones — represented political parties, and they were another part of the intricate code of Lebanese identity. I had noticed them, silently marking territory and allegiance around Beirut. So far, my symbol vocabulary was limited, but I did recognize this blocky cedar, and it gave me a chill. It represented the Phalange, which in its previous incarnation as a militia had orchestrated the massacres at the Palestinian refugee camps south of Beirut in 1982.

It was irrational to fear the Phalange more than anyone else. Atrocities had been committed on all sides. And now the Phalange was a political party, nothing more, like all the other disarmed militias. Still, the Phalange commanders had never been brought to trial; no one had. Instead, the postwar government passed the 1991 General Amnesty Law, which absolved everyone involved in the war without a single hearing. Lebanon would, as the local saying had it, *yitwe saf-het el-madi* — turn the page of the past. The militias didn't even have to rebrand themselves with new symbols.

When I had arrived in Beirut, I had believed that the page truly had been turned, that the past had been sorted out, bundled up, and neatly stowed on a shelf. After all, more than twenty years had passed since the war. Looking at American history, though, I saw how laughable that expectation was. Our own civil war was a century and a half behind us, and it still caused trouble — often over a flag, in fact.

Nick's uncle, barrel-chested and tan as a coffee bean, greeted us with outstretched arms. Behind him was a giant table, and then the calm, blue Mediterranean. I held back briefly. But on what grounds? I knew nothing of his history. He only happened to reside on a road with some flags that reminded me of a past I had not even lived through.

We ate fish in order of size, from finger-length sprats to dense, white-fleshed bass, and swiped salty french fries through thick, sour *labneh*. Aloof Andrew, behind his shaggy bangs, revealed secret knowledge of wine, ordering a different bottle of white with each course. In short order, we were all cheerfully buzzed.

After lunch, Nick's uncle led us to the nearby harbor for a boat tour. I felt cool climbing into his inflatable rubber raft, as it was the sort of boat that, in spy movies, the secret agents use to sneak into the hidden bay. And Nick's uncle was the captain to end all captains, with a big gold cross nestled in his chest hair, a cigarette clamped between his lips. He grinned around the cigarette and raised a glass of whiskey to us, his awestruck passengers, then steered us out of port.

From the boat, I could better see how the mountains met the coastline, almost pushing toward the water. Construction zigzagged up their steep slopes, following a meandering road. Where the rocks met the sea, they flattened out into large water-level tables. The occasional fisherman stood, surrounded and seemingly suspended by the water, flinging a long pole into the surf. Far behind, the cars on the highway zipped along, small as bees.

Nick's uncle slowed the boat to half speed and nosed it toward a stretch of pebbly beach. A palm-frond awning shaded a long wooden bar, and lounge chairs sat in a line. Irene pointed to the handful of people perched on bar stools. "I wonder, do we look incredibly cool to them or really dorky?"

Her question was answered when we jumped out and headed for shore, flailing against the tide and slipping on algae-covered rocks. This could have been my Ursula Andress moment. Instead, I clambered up the beach doubled over, clutching my bikini bottom.

Beers in hand, we gathered at a table to bask in the truly excellent turn the day had taken. After the second round, I looked down at the napkin under my bottle: PIERRE ET SES AMIS. Why did that ring a bell?

In a second, I had it. We had arrived at the very beach club we'd read about in class, the one at the heart of the problem between Jameel and Layal.

Kaspar was standing next to me. I nudged him and pointed at the napkin. Together we coolly surveyed the beach club, like detectives inspecting a crime scene. We had debated the case in class, but we had been missing this critical piece in the mystery that was Jameel and Layal's relationship.

"You know what?" Kaspar said. "I've been here for hours and I haven't thought of my phone once. I don't even know where it is." We toasted: To Jameel and Layal! To jealousy!

And maybe this was the normal Lebanese behavior that Zaina had been talking about. Until now, Beirut had struck me as hard, unrelenting, too flashy. Here was the antidote: You cruised up the coast in your silver Mercedes for a lavish fish lunch with a variety of local white wines. Then you zipped across the water in a boat that made you feel, fleetingly, like a Bond girl. You chilled out at the beach, under the wing of a man who looked like Tom Selleck.

I had been harboring a slight disdain for Beirutis' beer-and-bikinis standard of fun. It seemed too simple, too escapist — how could people be more concerned with their tan lines than with the state of their country? But if everywhere you turned you were confronted with some signal or symbol of conflict, maybe you'd want to escape too. Standing here in my two-piece, with a cold bottle in my hand, while the late-afternoon Mediterranean sun washed over me — this kind of fun felt good.

Our captain rallied us back to our trusty craft. We left as awkwardly as we had arrived. I flopped into the boat backwards, like a tuna. Nick's uncle grabbed Sally under the armpits and hoisted her up like a rag doll. Andrew momentarily lost his shorts.

We buzzed off merrily into the sunset, leaving Pierre and his friends to their more graceful life.

We Have Not Taught the Prophet the Price

I LIKED RANA ABOU RJEILY as soon as I met her. "Let's go some-where else," she said when we convened in front of the Hamra Star-bucks. It was evening; the dapper older set that I had seen there on my first morning in Beirut, and every morning after, had concluded their performance for the day. "How about a communist bar?"

By now, approaching the end of my time in the city, I had to ad-mit my personal transformation had failed. I had not picked up a breathy Lebanese accent, and the more I saw of flashy Beirut fashion, the happier I was with my shapeless clothes. Style-wise, communists would be more my speed.

The communist bar was not filled with the lumpen proletariat af-ter all, but with the usual assortment of young, tight-T-shirted Bei-rutis. The lighting, at least, was mellow, and 1960s jazz was playing at an unobtrusive level. "I know, there's nothing communist about it," Rana said, pointing to an old French ad poster. Stalinist propaganda it was not. "It's just what we call places like this." She turned to peruse the beer list.

I had expected Rana, a graphic designer, to be different too, clad in black and imperiously cool. And here she was, pink-cheeked, pretty, and nice. I had contacted her because I was curious about how type designers created Arabic fonts, wrestling flowing, cursive handwriting, a traditional art in itself, into the modern, mechanical world of print.

In design school in London, Rana told me as the waitress brought us our drinks, she had thought she could whip up a good Arabic font set in a day. At a glance, the Arabic alphabet doesn't seem too hard to render in type. The twenty-eight letters are made up of eighteen basic shapes. You could knock out *ba* (ب), *ta* (ت), and *tha* (ث) in practically one stroke, plus most of *noon* (ن). And no capital letters—that was a bonus.

She took a sip of her ale and sighed. "But then it got complicated."

The alphabet's complexity developed over centuries. The first Arabic writing, in the early fourth century, was a simple adaptation of the Aramaic alphabet, via Nabataean. It didn't have enough letters to reflect all the tricky Arabic consonants, so it used the same shape for similar sounds—there was no distinction between *s* and *sh*, for instance. The letters were stiff and spidery, made for carving in rock.

Up through the dawn of the Islamic era, in the early seventh century, Arab culture was primarily oral, so imprecision in the alphabet wasn't a big deal. The written word was more a memory aid than a direct communication tool. When you read, you understood that the word was *shi'r* (poetry), not *si'r* (price), because you already knew it all by heart, or because you knew Arabic well enough to understand that, in this context, you were reading about verse, not money.

The first wave of Islamic expansion brought new Arabic speakers (and readers) into a growing empire. These clueless foreigners did not necessarily understand the context, so they could easily misread *shi'r* as *si'r*, for example, and think the Quran said, "We have not taught the Prophet the *price*." This could lead to a whole misinterpretation about God disliking money, perhaps, when the verse actually read, "We have not taught the Prophet *poetry*," and was understood as a comment on the Quran's linguistic style.

So in the late seventh century, Abu al-Aswad ad-Du'ali, the first persnickety grammarian in a long chain, devised a system of dots to distinguish ambiguous letters and indicate short vowels. Later writers refined the system, keeping ad-Du'ali's dots on the letters and developing the vowel marks used today. Ad-Du'ali's three dots still distinguish poetry — شعر — from price — سعر. Additionally, the vowel marks ensure that poetry — *shi'r*, or شِعْر, with full vowels — is not mistaken for hair — *sha'r*, شَعْر. These innovations turned a loosey-goosey, you-get-the-idea system into one in which every possible Arabic sound was represented. That was great for the goof-prone newcomers to the language, but down the road, for typographers like Rana, all these extra marks would mean more work.

Meanwhile, the shapes of the letters were developing too. In the mid-eighth century, the Arabs learned how to make paper, probably from Chinese prisoners taken in Central Asia. In 794, the first paper mill was built in Baghdad and began churning out reams (from the Arabic *rizma*, bundle) of the stuff. A few decades later, the caliph al-Ma'moun founded the translators' institute Beit al-Hikma, the House of Wisdom. Copyists, scholars, and calligraphers sharpened their reed pens and went to work on paper's inviting, smooth surface.

Until then, the dominant style of formal writing, called Kufic, was spare and angular, still showing its roots in rock inscriptions. Parchment had enabled some flourishes, especially in copies of the Quran, but paper was an even more versatile medium. In the early tenth century, with the House of Wisdom in full swing translating Greek scientific treatises and the Islamic empire still expanding, the grand vizier Ibn Muqla set down the first rules of proportion for calligraphy. His *naskh* (copying) script was an elegant, legible handwriting that was suitable for both religious and secular material.

Because standardization across a polyglot empire and consistency of the Quran were both critical, any substantial changes in writing were not organic, but official. Each innovation was debated by the leading clerics and the caliph, then a decision was made, decreed, and disseminated. This charged context made calligraphy high-stakes work. In the course of palace intrigue, Ibn Muqla's tongue was cut out and his hand cut off. He strapped a reed pen to his stump and carried on.

In the Siege of Baghdad in 1258, while the Mongols sacked the city, the calligrapher Yaqut al-Must'asimi is said to have holed up in a tower, bent on refining the rules for *naskh* script. While he toiled in seclusion, Hulagu Khan's troops tossed the contents of the House of Wisdom, by then the world's largest collection of books, into the Tigris; according to legend, the river ran red with blood, then black with ink. (Fortunately many books were hidden before the battle; the Greek translations eventually made their way to European libraries.) Al-Must'asimi survived, and his perfected *naskh* was so fine, clear, and well proportioned that it became the default for all copies of the Quran. It also formed the basis of most modern typefaces.

Despite al-Must'asimi's focused efforts in Baghdad, *naskh* script could not be instantly transformed into a typeface. The crucial difference between calligraphy and type is both physical and philosophical. "Good Arabic script," Rana told me in the communist bar, "isn't necessarily all on one baseline."

Elegantly written Arabic can dip, swoop, cascade, or curl into the shape of a bird or a flower; words become decorative art, on a page in a manuscript, on a wall of a building, or in a standalone inscription. Even simple handwriting can flow diagonally, each letter set a little lower than the one before it. How to render all that grace and flexibility in type? The mechanics of printing demand a baseline, one place to set all the letters.

The other difficulty is the cursive nature of Arabic writing—how each letter is linked to the next. Blocky, standalone Latin letters have only uppercase and lowercase. In Arabic, a letter can have up to four forms, depending on where it sits in a word.

For example, at the beginning, on the right side, the letter *'ayn* looks a bit like an English *c*, an open mouth:

عين

In the middle of a word — say, *ta'ima*, which means to taste or savor — that mouth closes up into an angular loop, a little polyp:

طعم

At the end of a word — such as *isba'* (finger) — the loop grows a graceful tail:

إصبع

Standing alone, as at the end of *dhira'*, the word for arm, the *'ayn* opens its mouth again:

ذراع

Perhaps because of all these nuances, as well as the reverence given to the calligrapher's art, Arabic typography was still a small field, even in the digital era. Word-processing software came loaded with Latin font fripperies like Britannic Bold, Castellar, and Comic Sans, but only a dozen or so Arabic options. Signage in the Arab world was not always legible, books could be hard on the eyes, and, my particular peeve, movie subtitles could be too cramped to read quickly.

When I had seen creative Arabic type design, though, I noticed that much of it came from Beirut. There was a historic reason for this, Rana explained. The first printing press in the Arab world was imported from England to a Maronite monastery on Mount Lebanon in 1585 (Christians were exempt from an Ottoman ban on printed books); it used Syriac letters. In 1734, some of the region's first printed matter in Arabic letters was produced in the same area.

Further, Rana said, calligraphy had traditionally been the domain of Muslims — the art of it was intimately linked with copying the Quran. Because monks had brought in the printing presses, type design fell to Christians. "Not that I think that's the way it *should* be," she said. "Calligraphy is my heritage too." The communist bar's lights had dimmed a bit for the evening, and the music grew louder. Rana's voice carried over the background Afropop. It was refreshing to hear someone speak so evenhandedly about yet another sectarian division.

Rana, like Hamdi in Egypt and many other Arabs I had met, had hated her childhood Arabic classes. She was not taught good handwriting, she made spelling mistakes, and she never felt comfortable reading. "When they asked for volunteers to read passages from the Bible, I hid behind the other students," she recalled with a grimace. "Maybe I was dyslexic and my parents just didn't know."

In fact, it was her own trouble with reading that later inspired her type designs. For her first project, she had interviewed children learning Arabic as a second language. They all complained that it was hard to distinguish the letters — the same problem she'd had as a kid. Out of this came a design for a stylized cursive for use in children's books.

Then Rana moved on to the general-use font she named Mirsaal, from the root *rasila,* which means to flow and communicate. In Mirsaal, each letter has only one form, like in the Latin alphabet, but it has a little tail on either side, so it can be joined to its neighbor or, if the designer prefers, stand alone. In standalone mode, Rana said, she found the letters far easier to distinguish. To my non-native eye, the Mirsaal alphabet took getting used to, but a whole paragraph in Mirsaal type looked much less intimidating than a typical Arabic newspaper column, perhaps because Mirsaal has more of the breathing room around the letters that I was accustomed to in Latin type.

Rana was far from the first to try to revamp the Arabic alphabet. In the 1930s, the Arabic Language Academy in Cairo created a few additional letters to represent foreign-to-Arabic sounds such as *p* and *v,* although they never became standard on Arabic keyboards. In the 1950s, a Lebanese American named Nasri Khattar, a trained calligrapher, developed a set of all standalone letters. It was never adopted, but it remained an inspiration for many future type designers, including Rana.

The history of type design was littered with even more outlandish reform attempts, all failed. These included Arabic alphabets built out of the shapes of Latin letters (î for ﺙ, for instance); new letters to represent short vowels; a new letter to represent nunnation (*tanween*), the indefinite case ending; symmetrical letters that could be read from the left or the right; and a "condensed alphabet" with fewer shapes. This last innovation was promoted by Saddam Hussein in Iraq, then abandoned; its developer went into exile in Paris.

Since Rana had left school, she barely used Arabic in her professional life. "Sometimes I find it difficult to remember the alphabet!" she said. Her Lebanese colleagues often spoke English together, and the design classes she taught were almost entirely in English too, because the students would later use it for work. "Basically, everything encourages you to use another language," she said with real frustration.

In this respect, Lebanese were wrestling with the same problems that Emiratis and Qataris were. Above a certain level of education, in a certain globalized realm, Arabic of any kind — Fusha or colloquial — was no longer relevant. Many Lebanese in the diaspora had come back after the war, not all speaking Arabic fluently, and prosperity brought guest workers from Ethiopia and Bangladesh. Beirut was one-tenth the size of Cairo, but it was a visibly more mixed city, and an audibly more polyglot one.

No wonder the tongue-in-cheek Beiruti greeting was "Hi, *keefak, ça va?*" And no wonder that, in order to actually practice my Arabic, I had had to take bus trips out of town. For Beirutis, the linguistic mishmash was a source of pride, even for Rana. "But," she cautioned, correcting herself, "when I say everyone in Lebanon is trilingual, of course it's not everyone. It's really a certain class."

Rana's frank attitude encouraged me to share my own Arabic difficulties. I told her about my plan for a dialect makeover in Beirut, and how I felt stymied by the sectarian differences I couldn't help but notice everywhere. Whose language should I learn, exactly?

She didn't deny there were different ways of speaking in Lebanon, but, just as Dutch Danny had, she told me not to worry about it. "So you won't say it like they say it in Kaslik," she said gently, waving a slim hand. "It doesn't matter."

"Kaslik—what does that mean?"

"It's an expression," she said. She let out the tiniest exasperated sigh. "Kaslik is, like, the ultimate Christian street in the ultimate Christian town in the ultimate Christian governorate."

Lebanon, where every acre was spoken for, would have a place like this. I imagined some picturesque spot on Mount Lebanon, the Christian core of the country: a narrow lane in a tiny village, a gnarled old olive tree, church bells pealing as two aged monks bent over their canes by a weathered stone wall. I bade good morning to the black-clad men—and they recoiled, as I said some obviously Muslim phrase. Oh, well.

Rana drove me home in her creaky, sun-bleached Volvo station wagon ("my communist car"). I immediately went to my laptop and looked up this mythical Kaslik. It was a real place, but instead of a historic mountain village, I found it was a town on the coast north of Beirut. The photos showed red Ferraris, beach clubs, and women sporting surgically inflated lips and tiny halter tops. Rana was right: I was never going to say it like they say it in Kaslik.

Land of Thorns

IN MY LAST week of classes, Peter arrived for a visit. At the snack stand across from our apartment, he somehow circumvented all Beirut etiquette, within minutes bonding with the counterman over their shared religion. "That's the first time in my life I've gotten a high-five for being Greek Orthodox," he said with a laugh, as he bit into his little handbag-shaped *ka'keh* sandwich.

When classes ended, Dutch Danny hosted a party at his place: Lebanese pop on a small boom box, smoking on the balcony, a mix of nationalities chatting on the spare furniture of his temporary apartment. Irene's Lebanese husband was at the party. He gave us a lesson in folding pita bread properly for use as a hummus scoop, and asked us our plans. Peter and I were going hiking in the Chouf Mountains east of Beirut.

"Oh, the Druze area," Irene's husband said. "They say the *qaf* there." One of his uncles was from the Chouf, and they all made fun of him. "We call him a duck. *Waq-waq-waq*," he chortled, making the sound I recognized from the Egyptian song I had learned long ago, the one about Mom bringing home a bag with a duck in it.

"Hey, knock it off," Irene spoke up. "I love the *qaf!* It might be my favorite letter."

The *qaf* is one of the more elegant letters in the Arabic alphabet, as it exhales in a delicate pop from the back of the throat. Unfortunately, most dialects don't pronounce it. Egyptians make it a glottal stop; many Gulf Arabs make it a *g.* I gave Irene a nod of solidarity, for defending the *qaf* and for having a favorite Arabic letter in the first place. I decided the hiking trip would be a quest for the *qaf.*

Just as Peter and I were saying our goodbyes to my classmates, a band of teenagers delivered *argeeleh.* The last thing I saw as I looked back through the door was Kaspar sprawled out on a mattress smoking the pipe, like a bony odalisque.

Our first afternoon hiking, outside Jezzine, Peter and I got lost. We thrashed and cursed our way through a gully filled with dense, fragrant yellow broom before we discovered our error. My invectives came more from fear than from frustration. The trail book had suggested the faintest possibility of encountering land mines, and encouraged hiring a guide. But after more than a month of Arabic classes in busy Beirut, I craved the solitary quiet of hiking. And I had faith in my navigation skills. Peter and I didn't need help, I decided.

But here we were in this canyon, no trail to be seen. Hadn't Michel, the tour guide on the weekend hiking trip up north, said there were land mines here in Jezzine? Or had he said Janine, some other village down here in the south? As I walked and scrabbled and clambered, I replayed the scene in my head, the group laughing nervously at the edge of the overlook. Then Peter and I thrashed and cursed our way back the way we had come. When we finally reached the safety of a dirt road, I confessed my fears to Peter, and the stupid choice I'd made by not hiring a guide.

"Oh, we'll be OK," he said, unfazed, although his arms were scratched and bleeding. "Besides, it would have been annoying to talk to someone all day."

As penance, I practiced my Arabic as we walked. Aside from calling myself an *amerkaniyeh*, I had not managed to adopt much of a Lebanese accent at all. In fact, my Egyptian pronunciation seemed stronger than ever. Nor had I been able to shake my Cairo-learned habit of saying *inshallah* after every future-tense statement, though Zaina had *tsk*ed every time. In Egypt, it was so common that it meant not so much the literal "God willing" as a routine "hopefully," but to Zaina's cosmopolitan Beiruti ears, I must have sounded like a superstitious hick.

In my head, anyway, Lebanese sounded lovely. *El-jebel*—the mountains—I murmured. The *j* was soft and languid, like a French *g*. *El-'anzeh*, the goat—it had just a hint of an *'ayn* at the start, and a lovely drawled *-eh*. The goat in question, which we encountered in the middle of the road, was tiny, knock-kneed, and belligerent. *Showk*, thistle. These were everywhere, in possibly as many varieties as there were sects in Lebanon. Some radiated out in complex fractals; others ended in silver, spiky heads like medieval weapons; still others glowed bright purple, flowers, stems, and all. I wished I knew their names. My favorite thistle, the artichoke, was *kharshoof.* When I had ordered one in a Beirut restaurant, the waiter corrected me: I wanted an *ardishowki*. The Arabized English almost made sense. In Arabic, *ard* is land, *showk* is thistle. Lebanon, land of prickly things, I thought, remembering the taxi drivers of Beirut, who cursed their way through the thickets of the city.

Descending from the ridge to what our guidebook told us would be the Shrine of Nabi Ayoub, a Druze pilgrimage site dedicated to Job, of Old Testament fame, we found the trail covered in two large carpets. A grill was set up, and a family picnic was under way. The patriarch greeted us with a handful of dates and an ice-cold can of Pepsi.

Peter and I had been hiking in solitude for almost eight hours, interacting only with goats and scratchy plants. Now we stared in wonder, like aliens fresh off our UFO, at the lavish picnic, the gleaming white domed building topped with a multicolored star, the crowds bustling all around. Who were these dazzling people and their exotic ways? And most important — I remembered my mission — were they saying the *qaf*?

We crossed the spotless white patio to the shrine, removed our dusty boots, and entered. The Druze are an eleventh-century off-shoot of Islam, led early on by a preacher named Muhammad ad-Darazi — hence their name, though they call themselves *al-Muwah-hidoon*, the Unitarians. Their rituals are secret and practiced only by select members of the community. Men in the religious elite wear black trousers, baggy to the knee then tight to the ankle; women wear capacious white veils covering the head and the face below the nose. Inside the shrine, which was edged with floor cushions, I looked for people in these clothes — the most promising, I figured, for eaves-dropping for *qaf*s.

But most people in the shrine were dressed in jeans and T-shirts and talking so quietly I couldn't hear. Peter and I sat for a while to rest our feet. With the low murmuring and the light slanting in through a stained-glass star in the wall, the place felt like a large, comfortable waiting room. There was Job himself, presumably, in a large marble tomb in the center.

Back outside, we laced up our boots. The hillside below the shrine was terraced with picnic spots occupied by more carpets, grills, and extended families. We edged our way between carpets, past clouds of meat smoke. I kept my ears open for the *qaf*, but mostly I heard *"Itfaddaloo"* — Come, please join us. It had a distinctly perfunctory tone — Peter and I, scabby and reeking from exertion, were not ideal guests.

After a steep descent, we arrived in a village. It may have been charming once, but now it featured a radically paved town square, with asphalt right up to the doorsills. A young tough in a fast car was driving loops around the central fountain, tires squealing and muf-fler ripping through the still mountain air. He revved past us, then slowed to a crawl. In his rearview mirror he looked us up and down, then returned to a nonchalant slouch. He drummed his fingers on the steering wheel. He stole a glance over his shoulder.

"I think he's hoping we'll ask him for directions," Peter said. "We must be the most interesting thing to happen here all week."

The guy's driving had forced me up against a wall, as far out of the street as I could be. I was so irritated I couldn't bring myself to speak to him, though I knew I was shirking my duty as a visitor. The villagers had done their part, saying "*Itfaddaloo*" and giving us food. My obligation, like that of travelers anywhere in the world, was to supply entertainment. And this village needed some badly. The teenager finally drove away.

We asked the next old man in baggy pants for directions to the guesthouse. He too was hugging the wall of a building. "The kids always drive like that?" I asked the man with a sympathetic eye roll. Tires squealed in the distance.

He chuckled affectionately. "Oh, *'am-byimbistoo*" — they're just enjoying themselves. He used the double verb prefix, the *'am-bi* that Zaina had claimed was against the *rools*. But damn, no *qaf*.

Along the trail, we met two people who had been maimed by land mines. One worked in the welcome hut at the nature reserve where we were hiking, and happened to run the guesthouse where we were planning to stay that night. He called his wife to tell her to expect us; his fellow ranger dialed for him and held the phone to his ear, as he had no arms below the elbows. That night, he adeptly laid the table, balancing the plates on his stumps, and served us a hearty dinner.

The other man was blind. He wove cane chairs in the corner of his wife's preserves shop, surrounded by jars full of pickles and candied fruits. In excellent English he told us how he had stepped on a mine while out hunting with friends, years after the civil war had ended. He had learned cane weaving at a school in Beirut, and in the process he had reconsidered his religion. Now he took a little bit from each, he said — he liked Catholic confession, for instance, and Orthodox frankincense. He was more content than he had been in his old life, as an architect.

On the last day, in the last village, I finally heard the elusive *qaf.* On the main plaza, paved over like all the others, I poked my head into a women's clothing shop to inquire about the bus schedule. "Yes, *biyoqef hon,*" the woman said — it stops right here.

The bus was small, and a woman squeezed my arm as she scooted toward the window. "Sit here, sit here," she said in English, patting the adjacent seat. She wore a white Druze-style face veil, showing only her eyes and nose.

Nahida, she introduced herself. Born and raised in Chicago. She fished in her slouchy purse and pulled out an American passport. The photo showed a rosy-cheeked woman with chin-length, mousy-brown flyaway hair.

"This is me," she said. Her veil covered her mouth, but I could hear that she was smiling as broadly as she was in the picture.

She was thirty-four, and she had moved to Lebanon about eight years ago. Her aunts and uncles were here, in Beqtaa, where she lived, and in villages nearby. (Of course she pronounced the *qaf* in Beqtaa!) Her English faltered a bit as she tried to explain why she had left the United States.

"I wanted to live . . . behind my god," she said. "You understand?"

I did, in an abstract way. It was an odd preposition — maybe she hadn't meant it, as prepositions are difficult in every language. But it did suggest a relationship with the divine that seemed right for these mountain villages, as if God hovered in the clouds along the edge of the Mediterranean.

"And I wanted to wear these clothes," she said, gesturing at her robes. "But I just couldn't in America. You know, 'Ooh, terrorist!'" She laughed as she said it and wiggled her fingers in the air in comic fear. She didn't even go to Beirut now; she was sure someone would pull the veil off her face. Would anyone go that far? I couldn't picture it, but Nahida's Druze clothing was a breach of nonsectarian Beiruti etiquette.

"Did you like living in the United States?" I asked. "Or do you prefer it here?"

"Oh, I *loved* America! Life there is more free," Nahida answered immediately. "But I cannot wear this — what is the word for this?" She gestured at her white scarf.

"Veil, I guess." I wanted to apologize that there wasn't a better word. Like Arabic, English has no shortage of super-precise vocabulary, yet, in a surprising failure of imagination, "veil" is commonly used for every kind of head and face covering: a hijab, a niqab, a nun's getup, a bride's accessory, a belly dancer's frippery.

And I wanted to apologize for the absurd quandary she had faced in my — no, *our* — country. While still in Chicago, Nahida had made the choice to become a practicing Druze, a member of the religious class. Then, after she donned the required clothing, she didn't feel comfortable in America, land of religious freedom.

Peter had heard her talking and turned around in his seat. "Where did you live in Chicago?" He had grown up in the city. Nahida reeled off her house number and street as though she had just come from there. "Oh, near the Mexican area," Peter said. "Do you like Mexican food?"

This was a silly question, I thought, for the real, live English-speaking Druze woman we could be peppering with far deeper queries about religion and culture.

Nahida's eyes lit up. "Oh! Mexican food," she said with a longing sigh. "Let me tell you something." She took my hand in hers and looked intently at me. I met her gaze and settled in my seat to listen. The bus careened along the road. This side of the mountains, facing the sea, was lush and draped here and there in fog. I thought back to the confessions of unhappy Saeed at the top of the mountain, of Tony and his *putes à la route;* what secret would Nahida share with me?

"Right now," she said, with sincere emotion, "I want a taco."

She had tried to cook Mexican food here, she said. But it never tasted right. She couldn't find the right kind of peppers. "And the —what is the word? The Mexican bread . . ."

"Tortillas?"

"You can't get tortillas. Well, there is one supermarket in Beirut that has them, but they're seven dollars for a small package."

We agreed that this was highway robbery.

"Oh, yes—I love burritos too. And en-chi-la-das!" She savored each word as if it tasted of the thing itself.

We were approaching another paved-over town plaza. "My stop is here," Nahida said. "You are welcome at my house anytime. Give me your number."

The next day, my phone beeped with a message from Nahida: HI BABY.

When Peter and I returned to Beirut, the city felt different. The traffic buzzed far away from us. We took a taxi, and the remarkably old and polite cabbie drove as if by pantomime, wiggling the steering wheel from side to side. After the days we'd spent in the austere and quiet mountains, the gratuitous French and the gaudy fashions of the city struck me as rather sweet. Were all the gold bangles and obvious facelifts so different from traditional Druze clothing in the end? They were the markers of the flashy Beiruti clan, a sect of its own, striving for its own transformation to a resolutely secular existence.

I still couldn't speak like these people, but maybe that was fine. I had been striving for a total transformation in Arabic, a dramatic new identity. I hadn't made much progress, largely because I had been so overwhelmed by the culture's little codes, the clues and symbols that exposed sect and allegiance. I couldn't learn them all, but without knowing where I fit in, I couldn't decide what to learn. Being an outsider here was easier than being an insider. I was excused from knowing the most proper behavior, all the minute courtesies (or discourtesies) and the complications that lurked under the glamour that I had admired from afar.

Maybe the blind man weaving the cane chairs, the one who had lost his sight to a land mine, was on to something. Rather than identifying with one group, he had picked all the good parts from various Christian sects. Outside of Beirut, I had picked through Arabic the same way. The language didn't have to be anything mysterious or dogmatic, just a tool to make my point, or to make sure we were on the right trail. Then I could dress it up with whatever I liked. The more I traveled, the more I collected. I could say *inshallah* as much as I liked. I could tell my *swalif,* my stories, Gulf style. And I could pronounce my *qafs* from the back of the throat, as they were meant to be.

Excellent rationalizing, I told myself as Peter and I waited for the plane. I needed it, because I was headed to Morocco soon, and this would only add to my Arabic identity crisis.

AL-MAGHRIB

Morocco

September–October 2012

أصُل

(*asula*) To be firmly rooted

✦

تأصّل

(*ta'assala*) To derive one's origin

✦

أصول

(*usul*) Principles, axioms, guidelines

Daddy, Mommy, Gramps

IN THE AIRPORT gift shop, buying New York City knickknacks for my host-family-to-be, I imagined a heartwarming intercultural exchange. We would gather around a table in a cozy room somewhere deep in the medina of Fes, Morocco's historic former capital. Flipping through a picture book, we would compare modes of transport — taxis in New York, donkeys in Fes. My host father would chime in with a rhyming proverb about donkeys. Two days later, after successfully navigating my way home through the medina's web of alleys, I would find the occasion to work the proverb into conversation. This would make my host parents' charming, well-behaved child laugh with delight. Everyone would beam — I was making *such progress!*

What really happened: My host mom, Btissam, was sporting an I ♥ NY T-shirt when I arrived. She thanked me for the candies and the books and stashed them away somewhere. My host family wasn't impressed by my big-city life — a fresh American tramped through their house every few months. And forget learning donkey proverbs from Dad. Btissam and her husband, Yacine, lived in the French-built *ville nouvelle,* the new city a mile away from the old medina, in a modern house. Yacine listened to my stumbling Fusha — wrecked after all my country-hopping — and switched on the TV.

It wasn't that they were unfriendly. It was that I was hardly an ideal host daughter. Being forty years old was the first hitch.

"Think of me as your mother," Btissam, a decade my senior, said gamely as she showed me to my room. Over the bed hung a big poster of Fulla, the Muslim equivalent of Barbie, looking chic in pink plastic heels, a pink plaid skirt, and a black abaya with silver brocade sleeves. A deflated party balloon drooped from another wall, and schoolbooks were wedged in a cheap bookcase. Everything in the tiny room — the sofa, two chairs, my bed, the curtains — was done in the same pink-and-orange zigzag fabric.

What had happened to the girl who lived here? If Btissam had mentioned her, I had not heard it. She was giving me the house tour in rapid-fire Darija, as Moroccan dialect is called, her voice occasionally rising to a squeak, like a bath toy — a disarming tendency of women I remembered from my previous visits to Morocco. I caught roughly every seventh syllable. In a leap of illogic, one even Dr. Badawi would have considered too inventive, I spent my first night in the villa convinced I was occupying the bedroom of Btissam and Yacine's recently deceased daughter.

So I was relieved to meet Amal the next afternoon, when she returned from a school trip. She was a perfectly healthy, slightly pudgy fourteen-year-old, with big eyes and thick black hair. The only family tragedy was that I, as a paying guest, had temporarily booted her from her bedroom.

The other thing that made me an undesirable host daughter was that I knew too little Arabic to have a real conversation — but also too much to be treated like a child, which at least would have been entertaining.

After dinner the second night, Btissam reminisced fondly about the previous guests, two students who had arrived not even knowing the alphabet. The pair had provided hours of free comedy by sitting around the house practicing all the funny Arabic sounds. "The best was the *qaf,*" she told me, letting out a gale of giggles. "Oh, how we loved that! They sounded like chickens!"

I understood this story primarily with the help of accompanying gestures, as Btissam hooked her thumbs in her armpits and flapped her stubby wings, and a bit of onomatopoeia—she used the familiar *waq-waq-waq,* which I knew from the old Egyptian children's song. Otherwise, most of what she and Yacine said sailed right over my head.

I wasn't helpless, because I could make myself reasonably well understood in my Egyptian-Lebanese-Fusha mélange. The communication did not run the other way, however. Every time Btissam or Yacine spoke, I felt as if I had strapped myself to a bucking bronco. I could usually grab hold of the first word, but after that, the rhythm jumped and rolled.

"Tonight _____." One second, and I hit the ground.

"When you go out _____." Barely two seconds.

"This is the dog. *Shut up, dog!* You should _____." Good. Longer. But whatever it was I should do sounded really important. That was one cranky-looking German shepherd.

"Oh, that Amal! She _____ such a _____. If she says _____." I'd been thrown, but my boot was caught in the stirrup and I was being dragged along the ground.

It was fitting that I was able to arrange a homestay with a family during my month of classes in Morocco, as this country was woven into my own family's history, via objects and anecdotes from my parents' travels there. And, of course, my name.

The first time I had visited Morocco was a few years after I left graduate school and twenty-eight years after my mother named me for her neighbor near the Tangier hotel where she and my father had stayed. On that trip, I had felt simultaneously bewildered and right at home. I recognized the earthenware bowls I'd eaten out of as a kid, as well as the pillow-strewn salons, like my own living room. And in Marrakech, I saw that my parents must have settled in New Mexico for its same red-brown adobe, jagged mountains, and turquoise sky.

Yet that familiarity had sometimes refracted and sent me reeling. There's my dad, I thought one afternoon as I fell into step behind a man in the exact same dark brown djellaba my father owned. And there's my dad. And *there*. Several days passed before I stopped expecting to see his face peering out from a wool hood. And whenever I heard someone call *"Aji"* — Come here — I felt a sudden intimacy with the person, because that was how Beverly had summoned me all through my childhood. She spoke no other Arabic, but she had kept this word as a souvenir.

My current homestay was also appropriate because it was preparing me not just for Arabic class, but for the two weeks after, when my parents would arrive and we would visit their old haunts together. Granted, my duties as a host daughter seemed to consist mainly of showing up for meals. As a real daughter, I would be expected to do a lot more, such as pick out restaurants, get us to trains on time, and, above all, translate. The trip had been my harebrained idea — half a gift to my parents, who had not been back to Morocco since the late 1960s, and half a gambit to satisfy my curiosity about their lives before I existed, when they were younger than I was now.

The train schedules and restaurants I could handle. It was the translating I was worried about. I had to agree with the general attitude across the rest of the Arab world: namely, that Moroccans are impossible to understand. On my previous trips, I often communicated more successfully in French than in Arabic. "Good luck," an Egyptian friend in New York had scoffed when I told him my plans to study Darija. "I hear a Moroccan, he sounds like a Scottish does to you. No, worse — like a Jamaican." I would have to retune my Arabic ear, to turn the impenetrably foreign into the familiar. My time with my parents depended on it.

Fortunately, my Darija class was excellent, beginning with the classroom itself. A riot of geometrical tiles, intricately carved white plaster, and beveled-edge mirrors, it was like studying inside a pastry. My two teachers were energetic, methodical, and committed to teaching only in Arabic — or, where necessary, charades. Mohamed, who taught the first session, was a meticulously groomed man with a system of hand gestures for grammatical points (masculine: stroking an invisible beard; feminine: flipping hair up at the shoulder). Taoufik took over after the midmorning break. Tall and thin, with a gray caterpillar of a mustache, he employed a three-part move to explain the word *tawledt* (I was born), hand curving over a pregnant belly, downward gestures with both hands between his legs, then his fingers up to pop his droopy eyes wide open.

My fellow students were American, which answered my nagging question about where my compatriots were studying now that Egypt was in a fresh uproar, Syria and Yemen were firmly out of the question, and the situation in Lebanon was growing more dubious by the day. Most of the students expressed an interest in politics, and one was tackling a dissertation on, as he stated in Fusha, "the intersection of Islam and politics across North Africa, the Middle East, and Asia."

"A big project," Taoufik said dryly, and directed us to open our books to something more manageable: a drawing of a family tree.

Arabic is full of complicated words for family members. Your maternal aunt is different from your paternal one, and one type of uncle can be used figuratively, as a term of respect, but not so much the other type. And in-laws, according to Taoufik, will always be in-laws. "You have to specify," he said. "Like, 'He's not my *uncle*, he's my uncle because he married my mother's sister.'" And here he made a slight pushing-away gesture.

By Middle Eastern standards, my family was pitifully small, so I didn't have an opportunity to use many of the words, and thus had a terrible time remembering them. To complicate matters, I had noticed that even the most common terms could be used creatively. Egyptian parents called their kids *baba* (Daddy) and *mama* (Mommy) to get their attention, and Lebanese granddads had a curious habit of calling all their grandchildren, regardless of gender, *jiddo* (Gramps).

Taoufik was working his way around the room, asking the other students to describe their siblings, their parents, their aunts and uncles. When he came to me, I said my family was *ana w-rajli* — me and my husband — and in the pause when I wondered whether to start next with my mom's side of the family or my dad's, he nodded and gestured to the next person.

Taoufik was not snubbing me, I understood after a second, or recoiling at my terrible pronunciation. It was likely due to the fact that, at age forty, I was expected to be the center of a household, not a little satellite of a larger one, the way the college students in my class were. Plus, I didn't have children. Taoufik was probably just being polite, skirting the terrible tragedy he assumed must have befallen Peter and me.

My family may have been small, but it was complicated in ways that not even Arabic had words for. No term for ex-stepfather, for instance — for my mother's second husband, father of my half brother. And when I alluded to my parents' divorce ("My mother lives in the state of New Mexico," I would say in simple sentences, "and my father lives in the state of California"), people had looked sad. This wasn't so much because of the split itself, as divorce was not considered a disaster, but because I lived so far from my parents.

And I never bothered to explain the no-children thing. Peter and I just didn't want them, and most people, anywhere in the world, were puzzled by this. Often, Arabs were much less tactful than Taoufik, demanding, *Why* no children? You *must* have children! There is still time! The kindly owner of a bicycle shop in Aleppo offered a free bike to our firstborn — blue for a boy, pink for a girl. Another man, in Abu Dhabi, offered a cruder solution: he would be happy to do what my "weak" husband could not.

Still, I would need to explain the basics of my family while I was here. I looked at the diagram of the family tree in my textbook and mentally composed the Darija phrases I would need while escorting my parents around the country: "This is my mother, and this is my father. They lived in Morocco before I was born . . ."

The Place Where the Sun Sets

I HAD A CRUSH on Darija from day one. I was taking an introductory class, which is always the phase of dizzy infatuation with any language, when every vocabulary word is thrilling, standards are low, and the learning curve has nowhere to go but up. Moreover, Darija was so alien to me that it reminded me of the days — first in college, then in Cairo — when Arabic had been simply strange and wonderful rather than a complex chore. Completing the throwback effect, my teachers used cassettes for listening exercises. One *ka-chunk* of a button and it was 1990 all over again.

Darija was an adaptation of Fusha that I might have made up myself. First, the precious *qaf*, that wonderful, delicate letter I had chased around Lebanon, was still pronounced, at least in Fes. And some fussy grammar business had been streamlined — for instance, no dual. All Arabic dialects scrapped the verb conjugation for two people, but Darija was the first I'd learned that didn't have a specific noun form for two items. The dual was a Fusha eccentricity that I did like, in theory, but on a day-to-day speaking basis, it was a nuisance. Besides, the Darija word for the number two was *zhuzh*, a fun, buzzy

word, two sibilants that were a pleasure to say. Such a pleasure that I
didn't think to be mad that Darija had a whole different word for two.
It came from the Fusha word *zawj*, which meant pair (of pants, socks,
people, or, oddly, pigeons), and how cute was that?

Darija had much of the same formal elegance that I appreciated
in Fusha. Men were addressed as *Si*, and women were *Lalla* — I liked
the sound of "Lalla Zora." Some terms were gloriously ornate. To illustrate the term for natural light, Si Mohamed gestured to sunbeams
streaming into our cream puff of a classroom — this was *ad-daw
d'rabbi*, the light of my Lord.

Some of the most common words were artifacts from centuries
back. To say "I want," for instance, was *bagheet*, which I recognized
as a grand old verb that, in the Quran, meant to seek or to covet. (In
a typically Arabic way, the root had since taken on other meanings:
ibtagha is to strive for God's grace, while another variant means to go
whoring.) Thus a visit to the corner store became, in my mind, a noble quest: "I seek water with gas," I told the man behind the counter.

Even the writing was pleasingly odd and old-fashioned. Si Taoufik
and Si Mohamed wrote in careful, even letters on the whiteboard in
an unfamiliar combination of curves and angles. Sometimes the letters were short where I expected them to be tall, or bent back when
they should have gone forward. In this contrary way, the writing
echoed the bucking, contorted Darija accent. Eventually I recognized
this handwriting, as well as the loopier typeface and calligraphy styles
that signaled "traditional Moroccan": they were descendants of Kufic
script, that early Arabic writing style in which the first Qurans were
recorded.

To leaven all this old-time formality, there were phrases that
sounded sweetly pidgin. As in the Gulf, "same-same" was an essential phrase, though Darija translated it to *kif-kif* or *bhal-bhal*. "Sometimes" was *mra-mra* — time-time. Plenty of borrowings from French
added a patois vibe: a tire was a *bnu,* and a plumber was a *plombiyi.*

Given Morocco's history and location, this pragmatic mix of formal and informal made sense. As the westernmost end of the Arab world, Morocco is hardly part of the Middle East. Its name in Arabic is al-Maghrib, literally the place-where-the-sun-sets. In fact, it is farther west than all of Europe except Ireland. At the height of the Islamic empire, the "center" of power in Damascus (and later Baghdad) considered Morocco the fringe. But this corner of North Africa was a crossroads for armies going in and out of Islamic Spain, as well as the endpoint for trade routes from sub-Saharan Africa. So naturally the kinks of Fusha were smoothed out, to make it easy for a Timbuktu salt dealer to haggle in the market or an exiled Andalusian to buy Berber carpets for his new home.

What I could not grasp about Darija was its near-total absence of vowels. Each word seemed to erupt in a burst of consonants, which was why listening to Btissam and Yacine felt like riding a wild horse. Si Taoufik's preferred metaphor was the accordion, which he played in pantomime to illustrate the Moroccan tendency to squeeze words, then occasionally expand them and trail off at the end.

I could usually follow him and Si Mohamed, with their moderate, careful teachers' pronunciation, but when they pressed play on the tape deck, the syllables whisked past in a jumble. On the second pass, I might recognize one or two words I knew from other countries, but which had eluded me the first time because the em-PHA-sis was on a different syl-LA-ble.

To illustrate the subtlety of Darija vowels, Si Taoufik made us practice two phrases. *Allah ykhalleek* means "May God be pleased with you," and it is what one should say to request something politely. *Allah yakhleek*, on the other hand, means "May God abandon you," and it is what one should pretty much never say.

To avoid the damning phrase and properly enunciate the requesting phrase, Si Taoufik advised us to "open up" the second syllable, expanding his pantomime accordion to illustrate. Contrary to what he advised, however, Si Taoufik kept his own syllables clamped down tight. I knew the distinction he was making—I could see how the words were spelled differently and how they ought to be pronounced. In his rendition, though, *Allah ykhalleek* sounded exactly like *Allah yakhleek,* no matter how many times he said it.

Much as I admired Darija otherwise, I decided that flawless pronunciation should not be one of my principal goals. In the case of *Allah ykhalleek,* where I risked giving a grave insult if I said it too briskly, perhaps it was better not to embrace Darija tightly. For compliments, I was sure no one would mind if I doled them out in plodding, clearly articulated Fusha.

It was the second week of September, and a street fair near my house was busy selling books, backpacks, polyester uniforms, and other gear for kids headed back to school. I opted for the less scholarly cotton candy on offer at the entrance.

"One of those, please," I told the man awkwardly in Fusha. I held out a handful of coins so he could pick the right amount. He gave me a cloud of pink caught on a fresh green reed, a natural touch that almost made the stuff seem like a health food.

As I walked away, I kicked myself for such a feeble interaction. What was the point of loving my class so much if I couldn't use the words in the street? I had been in Morocco nearly a week, yet I was still stammering and playing the bumbling tourist when I spoke. Everywhere I went, Darija was rushing by, and I hadn't worked up the nerve to jump aboard. I could have greeted the man politely. I could have asked him the price. Those were phrases I knew from class. I could have asked him what cotton candy was called in Arabic. That might have been illuminating, I thought as I strolled, because the English words "cotton" and "candy" both came from Arabic.

I passed a stall selling pretty handmade keychains, thin slices of wood with Arabic names painted on in black calligraphy. Here, for the first time in my life, was my chance to find a personalized souvenir!

Midway through college, it had dawned on me that my name

might be Arabic—I was named after a Moroccan woman, after all. It had taken me a while to make this leap, because, in my mind, Morocco had always been separate, an almost mythical setting for my parents' adventures, while the Arabic I was learning came from a place much farther east. Until I made the connection with my studies, Zora had just been *my name*. I hadn't even particularly liked it, though my mother assured me my namesake was a great role model, a savvy single mom who had run her own business, a hand laundry service. Beverly had admired Zora's independence—rare not only in Morocco at that time, but in America too—and hoped to confer that spirit on me.

Whatever. Zora, I thought, clashed with my Irish last name. The movie *Zorro the Gay Blade,* released when I was in fourth grade, inspired jokes for years. When the Valley Girl craze hit, I missed out because I couldn't spell my name with an *i* and dot it with a heart. And I never once found a personalized mug, bumper sticker, or keychain.

"I think it's supposed to be Zahra," I had proposed to Beverly during a phone call home in college. "That means flower."

Not only did it mean something, but it was more fun to write. Spelled phonetically, as my Arabic professor had taught me the first week of class, Zora was a dull string of standalone letters with no option for fun cursive loops: زورا. Zahra, by contrast, had a squiggly *ha* in the middle and a *ta marboota,* that cryptic, usually unvoiced *t,* at the end: زهرة. (I was especially fond of that last letter, which looked like its name, a "tied-up *ta,*" or a little cartoon mouth, open wide in alarm.)

"Honey," Beverly had replied, "I'm pretty sure I know my friend's name. It was Zora."

"But you don't speak Arabic," I persisted. "You could have misheard. They have a weird accent in Morocco." At the time, I knew this only through hearsay.

"*Honey*, your name is Zora."

The next semester, I read a fascinating Lebanese novel called *The Story of Zahra*, by Hanan al-Shaykh. When Beverly asked what I was studying, I sent her a copy. The protagonist was a neurotic mess of a woman who fretted and picked her scabs while the Lebanese civil war raged.

She called me a week later. "I've been thinking. Maybe your name *is* Zahra." I tabled the topic.

Years later, when I went to Morocco for the first time, I tried a new variation on my name every time I introduced myself: Zahra. Zohra. Zorrrrrra, with a lavish trilled *r*. Everyone stared at me blankly. In Tangier a day before I was set to leave, I ran out of toothpaste. At the pharmacy, a bustling, middle-aged woman behind the counter gave me the usual friendly interrogation that is part of any business transaction in the Arab world. Where was I from? Did I like Morocco? Was I married? And what was my name?

"*Ismi* Zora," I said, barely thinking. I was already mentally on the plane home. So no flair, no trills. Just the way I'd said it my whole life.

The woman broke into a wide smile, then reached out and clapped her hands to my cheeks. She looked deep into my eyes, as though she recognized me from long ago.

"*Zweeeeeeyna!*" she practically squealed, opening up the vowel as far as it could go. Looooooovely!

Her hands still cupping my face, she turned to introduce me to her fellow pharmacists. "This is Zora," she told them. "She's Moroccan!" She stroked my cheek and hair and beamed at me.

Despite all that drama, I still didn't know how my name was spelled. In my rush of excitement at being recognized, I had not thought to ask the pharmacist to write it for me. At least my mother had the grace never to say, "Honey, I told you so."

At the keychain stand at the school fair, I picked through the pile of girls' names, scanning for familiar letters. Aisha, Hakima, Khadija, a very long one, Fatima-something. But nothing resembling Zora, in fact nothing at all starting with ز, the letter *za*.

When I arrived home, Yacine was in the dining room, watching TV as usual. He waved me in. "There. Are. Some. Problems. For. Americans?" he said, slowing down his Arabic to a glacial pace to make sure I understood. "Something. Happened. In. Libya?" He saw my blank look and gave a big shrug. I was dismissed.

When I checked my email, I had a message from a reporter, asking me for a quote on how I, as a traveler in the Middle East, was handling the trouble.

Problems? Trouble? I checked the news online. The U.S. embassy in Benghazi had been attacked—two days earlier. And rioters had been tearing up downtown Cairo, also for two whole days. This was the first I had heard of any unrest. It made a pleasant change from Lebanon, where neighboring Syria's strife had pricked the skin every day. I was "handling the trouble," it seemed, by being far, far off to the west of it.

You Pour the Tea

BACK IN BEIRUT, my teacher Zaina had *tsk*ed me out of tacking *inshallah* onto the end of a sentence. In Fes, I had to get back in the habit of invoking God at every turn.

Si Mohamed was vigilant—future plans required *inshallah,* and when they didn't, he looked genuinely pained. Even more important was proper gratitude. "Always, always you must say *lhamdullah,*" Si Mohamed admonished my sleepy-eyed classmate who had praised his powerfully strong coffee. After any good fortune, one must always, always thank God.

I liked this aspect of Arabic. These phrases were a pleasant ritual; they also paced out a conversation and bought me time. Pausing to thank God, a phrase I could say without thinking, gave my brain a free moment to race ahead to find the next substantive words I needed. Unfortunately, just because I admired this aspect of Arabic didn't mean I was any good at it. I had the basics—*min fadlak* (please) and *shukran* (thank you)—but they were tiny drops in a sea of gracious phrases.

On our first day in Darija class, we were given a confusing heap of formulas, many of which were subtly different from what I already knew. "These are very important," said Si Mohamed, himself the picture of politeness in a crisp caftan. "When you say *shukran*, you're saying thank you with your brain. When you say *barak allahu feek*, you're saying thank you from the heart."

At the class break later in the week, I sipped mint tea with another student. She showed me her notebook, in which she had dedicated the back page to a list titled "God for All Occasions." The next time we drank tea together, at the end of the second week, the list was already spilling onto the next page.

I had not been so diligent. Although Si Mohamed had warned us that these phrases were essential, each day I had assumed that surely this would be the last batch of them. And then came the phrase for when you offered to pour water for hand-washing at lunch and the phrase for "when a bad smell comes out of you," as Si Mohamed tactfully put it. Soon I was neck-deep, flipping desperately through my notebook for the right words.

Barak allahu feek.

Tbarak allahu 'aleek.

Allah ybarak feek.

Which meant which, again? I wanted to believe it didn't really matter, but of course it did, the same way it mattered to say "welcome" instead of "you're welcome" in English. On every occasion, both in class and out, I stumbled and stammered. My heart was not fluent.

The GAOs (as I had begun to refer to my classmate's back-of-notebook list) maxed out the day our class did a unit on eating lunch at a Moroccan friend's home. It came early in the curriculum because most students faced the situation immediately. In fact, many students complained of being overfed, returning from the midday break groaning about the meat and couscous and bread their host families had forced on them. This was not a problem I had — Btissam was an indifferent cook, and after Yacine saw how inept I was at eating with my fingers, he stopped nudging chicken legs toward me, to spare us all the mess. Still, in light of previous hospitality dilemmas, such as the enormous duck lunch with Medo's mother, I was eager to learn some ritual ways of managing the situation.

The textbook conversation involved our two American protagonists, Ellen and Dan, dining with their hostess, Lalla Zohra. (Hey, my name! Or not? If it was common enough to be a textbook name, then why had I found no keychain? Hmph.) As the scene opened, Lalla Zohra was encouraging her guests to eat more: "Don't be bashful!" she told Ellen.

I skimmed through the words, looking for substance amid the formulaic niceties. I found none. The whole conversation, which filled a two-column page, was back-to-back GAOs, imploring God to increase the blessings, strengthen the goodness, and plenty more. In an underhanded move, Lalla Zohra even swore by God that her guests must eat. Si Taoufik paused the tape to explain that when someone broke a sworn promise, he or she was obliged to fast for three days. Would Ellen really be so selfish as to make Lalla Zohra renounce all food for that long?

On the recording, Ellen made an audible gulp. "This one bite is because you swore, may God increase the blessing."

Our next important lesson was the process of making mint tea. Si Mohamed shaped the key items in the air: teapot, small glasses, serving tray, giant sugar bowl. I knew them all from home, where Btissam had one filigreed silver set, gathering dust on a sideboard, and a battered tin version that she used morning, noon, and night.

Si Mohamed demonstrated the verbs to stir, to pour, and to mix by transferring from pot to cup and back again (*qleb w-sheqleb*, a singsong combination of syllables that reminded me of the word for heart; as a mnemonic, I pictured mint tea bubbling through my veins). Then it was our turn.

The student who aspired to write a dissertation about Islam and politics everywhere in the world went first. When he reached the step of pouring, Si Mohamed coughed. "Ehherrm. It's *kaykhwi. Nta kaykhwi al-atay.* You pour the tea."

"Oh, not *kayhwi?*" the student replied. Si Mohamed coughed again.

I knew from reading the word that the distinction was one letter: the fricative *kha* (خ), as in "yech," rather than *ha* (ح), the aspirated *h,* the one for hissing "Hey!" like a spy. But as when Si Taoufik had demonstrated how to "open up" the vowels, I was having a hard time hearing the distinction — the word was too compressed.

"Because that's what I thought you said," the student continued. "Oh, yes, it's printed here in the book. I just didn't see the dot. Of course, *kaykhwi,* not *kayhwi.*"

Si Mohamed had turned quite pink from coughing. "Noooo, this is very important," he managed. "*Kaykhkhkhkhwi* is correct. The other way is . . ." He smoothed down the front of his pristine muslin djellaba unnecessarily. It was Friday, the start of the weekend, and he was dressed especially well.

I felt bad for Si Mohamed, but I had my pen poised over my notebook, eager to hear the meaning of this Darija profanity that was making him lose his composure. My store of vulgar Arabic words was still meager, even after Lebanon.

"It is . . ." Si Mohamed began, in English, which meant the word must be too terrible to explain via pantomime. He looked out the window, avoiding our eyes. "It is . . . what adult man and woman do in the mattress."

Every day that passed, Darija showed new, subtle pitfalls. The sleepy-eyed student, the one who thanked God for coffee, had studied in Tunisia, but when he used the word for bread that he had learned there, Si Mohamed again had to supply an evasive English gloss. "That," he said, "is a word boys shout at each other on the playground."

After class, another student, a woman who was doing research with sex workers, explained in more detail. The Tunisian word came from the one for oven, and, well, if we thought about female anatomy, and insults kids used . . . and had we seen *Pink Flamingos*, where Divine shoplifts the steak and keeps it warm in her own "private oven"? "Also," she said, crossing her arms sagely, "don't tell anyone you're allergic. Here, it means gay."

Taken individually, these cough-inducing Darija words were hilarious — oh, Morocco, land of a thousand linguistic embarrassments! Taken together, they were faintly demoralizing, especially when combined with other, more mundane words that, I eventually discovered, did not mean what I thought they meant.

"OK, I'm finished in the bathroom now. You can turn off the water heater," I cheerily told Btissam my first night at the villa. I did this four nights in a row, until my class did the unit on buying apricot jam at the store, and I learned that the word I had been using for finish was the one Moroccans use for pay. So I had been dutifully informing my family I was all paid up in the bathroom.

Then there was my default word for OK, the one that automatically tripped off my tongue in agreement, to keep a conversation rolling. This was the Egyptian word *mashi*. It took me a week to realize that in Darija, *mashi* meant "nothing."

I also couldn't quite believe that the verb I used for to walk meant to go in Morocco. Not a terrible misstep, but in a taxi, I told my driver, as I always had in Cairo, "OK, this is good. I can walk from here." I gestured to the side of the road.

The driver turned abruptly into a side street and kept driving, his eyes catching mine in the rearview mirror, in affirmation of my impulsive wishes. I had basically said, while pointing imperiously, "Not a thing! Go from here!"

One afternoon I came home from class to see a lady in a trim white pantsuit and flower-print headscarf coming out the front door. I readied my GAOs for meeting strangers.

But it was no stranger; it was my host mom, Btissam. I had not recognized her because, in two and a half weeks, I had only ever seen her in ripped leggings and a shapeless T-shirt.

To be honest, I had been slightly taken aback by her slovenliness, as well as the rest of the family's. Yacine was always in sweatpants, except when he stripped down to a saggy white tank top and gym teacher's shorts. Should I be seeing this man's legs? I wondered.

But now, as I waved to sharp-dressed Btissam, complete with a patent-leather clutch under her arm, I realized how silly my reaction had been. Back in New York, I had my own set of baggy old house clothes. Any guests who stayed more than a few days got to see me in my bathrobe. So why had I expected Btissam and Yacine to pull themselves together for me, in their own home? Looking at it this way, I was touched that the family had welcomed me so quickly, so unconditionally.

My assumptions only highlighted how little time I had spent in people's homes, with families, in the Arab world. Aside from the couple of nights I had spent with Farah and Abdallah in Abu Dhabi (where, I now recalled, they had mostly worn pajamas), I had interacted with people on the street. So I had packed to make a good impression in public: a whole array of modest but stylish cotton pants and long-sleeve silk shirts, with long tank tops underneath, to avoid showing skin when I stretched or leaned.

Loungewear, however—that I had not packed. For a good two weeks I had been wearing my street clothes around the house. To my host family I must have looked ridiculous, perched awkwardly at the dinner table in the same pink linen blouse and khaki capris I'd worn to school. There was even something a bit unhygienic about it, now that I thought about it.

That night, I stripped off my blouse and wore my tank top to dinner. Everyone seemed to relax a little, now that the wide elastic of my sports bra was sticking out.

The next afternoon when I came home from school, I changed into my nightgown, a floor-length pink paisley thing. Bra or no bra?

I wavered, then committed to full home-casual. When I wafted into the dining room in a cloud of cheap rayon, I felt almost naked. No one batted an eye.

Yacine had changed his house wardrobe that day too. Instead of his usual undershirt, he had donned a frayed white tee that read, in a sort of eye-chart layout:

I

CAN'T

SAY WHAT I'M

THINKING RIGHT NOW

During the many lulls in conversation, I read and reread this message. Yacine had given me the motto of my entire Arabic-learning life.

God Is Beautiful

My mother arrived in Fes swaddled in flowing cottons and a bit teary-eyed. "Oh, honey, I feel like I'm home!" she exclaimed at the door of the hotel where I'd installed her. (Btissam and Yacine would probably have welcomed her at our house, but it seemed too confusing to mix host family and real family.) She was on her way south to meet friends; later, we would meet again up north, with my father. Her two days in Fes were a trial run of my tour-guide abilities and my Darija skills.

Theoretically, Beverly shouldn't have needed my help at all. She and my father, Patrick, had traipsed around Morocco more than forty years before, alone, with none of the comforts or resources modern travelers like myself took for granted—in many ways, a far braver trip than I had ever undertaken. Yet something had happened over the years: I became the independent, intrepid one, and my mother tagged along at my heels, saying, "Whatever you want to do, honey, it's fine with me."

I did at least have a working knowledge of the Fes medina, which was where Beverly and I walked first. Fassis call the medina Fes al-

Bali, literally "Old Fes." The root of the word *bali* implies decay and dilapidation, but the medina was a lively, functional city, with schools, shops, homes, and my mother's hotel inside its fortified walls. It even smelled alive: rosewater, freshly carved cedar, grassy dung from the donkeys that swayed through the lanes.

I loved the place because it conjured medieval Andalusian texts I had read in graduate school. It was easy to stumble into a quiet cul-de-sac where recent centuries had yet to intrude, with only the sound of murmured Arabic coming from a high window. There was also a direct connection between this city and the court of Córdoba. Fes, established in 789, became a refuge for intellectuals and aristocrats forced out of Islamic Spain at various points, especially when the Catholic kings took over.

These refugees brought many things that are now considered distinctly Moroccan: the ornate plaster and tile decoration that made my classroom such a confection, for instance, and rich court foods such as the pigeon pie called *bstilla*. The exiled Andalusians also brought a particular kind of Arabic that, way out here in the west, cut off from the center of the empire in Baghdad, had developed distinct patterns and preserved some old details. That was why Fassis pronounced the *qaf*, Si Taoufik had explained to us — it was a linguistic relic.

Sections of the medina were dedicated to traditional trades. In class we had learned these terms, and with each new word, Si Mohamed had asked, "Do you have this in America?" Not in quite the same way. To find an American weaver, you had to go to a craft show; to find a blacksmith, you went to a "living history" museum staffed with reenactors. In Fes, you went to the medina.

In the dyers' quarter, Beverly and I watched men wrestle skeins of brilliant indigo floss out of giant vats; in the coppersmiths' square, the ping of small hammers rang out. At the woodworkers' square, we happened across the tradesman's ethic applied to language. In a museum of carpentry, one case displayed small wooden planks that students traditionally used as rudimentary chalkboards, coated with a daub of clay and inscribed with the day's Quran lesson. The shaky, overlarge letters reminded me of my own attempts to control my pen in my first year of Arabic.

In an adjacent case was another set of planks, worn soft at the edges, patched with copper, and covered in elegant ribbons of calligraphy in that angular but looping Moroccan style. The heavily used planks were the students' diplomas. I would have liked to have received my master's degree in the same way, inscribed on the duct-taped cover of my Hans Wehr dictionary.

Late in the afternoon, I led Beverly to the perfumers' quarter. We turned into a shaded lane and stooped to enter a rough wooden door. The difference between outside and in was as striking as Btissam's transformation at the threshold of her own house. The narrow medina streets were often covered, so they felt like interior halls. Meanwhile, "inside" this building was completely open to the sky. The walls of the courtyard whirled and exploded with the finest Andalusian craftwork: mosaic tile patterns, wood carved so fine it resembled lace, plaster incised with vines and interlocking words.

A hadeeth, a saying of the prophet Muhammad, advises, "*Allahu jameel wa-yuhibb al-jamal*" — God is beautiful, and He loves beauty. Strictly speaking, this was the Prophet's answer to the question of whether it was a sin of pride to wear fancy clothes. But the principle, especially as it seemed to be practiced in highly decorated Fes, extended to all ornamentation: it was good as long as it was for God. So in this space, a Quran school built in the fourteenth century, the students had not toiled in austerity with nothing but their wooden slates. They had studied inside a physical reminder of one of God's many fine qualities.

Beverly and I rested there in silence for a while. I tried to trace the letters cut in the plaster, but my eyes skittered from pattern to pattern, texture to texture. Eventually I relaxed enough to focus on a single shape within the greater decoration: a star, say, then a hexagon. From each point radiated another, more complex pattern, transforming and expanding. This was a physical representation of how Arabic worked, another metaphor for the infinitely flexible root system. In the big picture, the ornament of it was overwhelming, something I could never grasp completely. But if I concentrated on what was in front of me — that I might master.

At the end of the day, Beverly flopped in her café seat at a bend in a busy lane. She looked pale and small in her chair, her cloud of silver hair disheveled — perhaps I had pulled her too far along with me. Fortunately, she revived as we dipped into our spiced lentils. "The women are all dressed like beautiful birds now," she marveled, watching the passing crowd.

In Morocco in the 1960s, Beverly said, clothes had all been gray and brown, a country of sparrows. Now women flitted by in robes of emerald green with yellow in the sleeves, cobalt blue with fuchsia trim, dove gray and pink, with a box gift-wrapped to match. God was beautiful, and He loved beauty.

For this trip, Beverly was playing hooky from her Spanish classes at home in New Mexico. That was fine with her, she said. She had hit a roadblock. "Whenever someone speaks directly to me, I freeze," she said, demonstrating her deer-in-the-headlights look, mouth agape. "My teacher calls it *quedarse en blanco* — to blank out. At least I learned that!"

I recognized this blankness, the panic brought on by the fear of an impending question. It had happened even in the relative comfort of my lessons with Manal in Dubai, and it happened all the time here in Morocco. No matter how well I performed in class for Si Mohamed and Si Taoufik, in the streets, I froze. I never had this problem in Spanish, or in Egyptian dialect — I could usually latch on to a few words in a question, then toss out some basic phrase to keep a conversation going in what I hoped was the right direction. Here, I heard little and spoke less in response. Perhaps my stumbling in Morocco was a defense mechanism, because if I were to speak Darija, then people might reply in Darija. In excruciatingly fast, vowel-free Darija. On the occasions I could muster an answer, I found myself doing so in Fusha. It bought me time, and it signaled, "I'm not from these parts. Be kind."

Though I sympathized with my mother, I couldn't help needling her a little. I was reminded of all the times she had called me in college. "Hey, you always told me just to wing it," I said. "Why don't you do that yourself?"

As I spoke the words, I heard an echo: Dr. Badawi's voice, telling me, "Just make something up!" It was the same idea, that you don't have to know absolutely everything before moving forward, yet I had never considered his and my mother's advice synonymous. In college, I had been so bent on distancing myself from home that I hadn't even admitted to myself that my interest in Arabic might be related to my parents' travels. I certainly hadn't mentioned it to Beverly, lest it validate her parenting style and all her hippie axioms. Only years later, when I felt fully independent — fully grown into the name my mother gave me — was I able to take Dr. Badawi's advice to heart.

A fine drizzle started. Barely breaking stride, the passing women pulled up the hoods of their djellabas; the points stuck up like cardinals' crests.

"One of my friends offered me some self-hypnosis tapes," Beverly said, ignoring my dig. "I think that might do the trick."

This was how my mother and I differed, and perhaps why I found it so hard to take her advice. I had been thinking the trick to better listening comprehension might be something more concrete, less woo-woo. I wanted to find videos or recordings with a transcription of the dialogue, so I could match the written syllables with how they sounded.

But my mother was probably right — much as it pained me to admit it — that good listening required some broader, more abstract skill. When I was able to listen well, it seemed to happen in some separate lobe of my brain, safe from my usual rule-checking, case-ending-verifying, dictionary-referencing self. I needed some way to access that quieter self, the one I had briefly felt in the madrasa in the medina while staring at a single point in the ornament. Comprehension was a rare bird. You had to be calm and let it alight, then stay still enough not to chase it off.

"When is your mother coming for tea?" Btissam asked me every time we crossed paths at home. I had been avoiding translating for my mother, out of nervousness, but I couldn't stall much longer. Fine, I said, this afternoon.

Walking to the house, Beverly and I ran into Btissam's housekeeper, Fatima. The first time I had met this wiry woman with flashing black eyes, she had told me she wasn't married, then launched into a story I didn't follow. From the intimate way she had greeted me ever since, I wondered if she might have confessed something very personal.

Here on the street, she grabbed my wrists with her strong hands and kissed me loudly, once on one cheek, twice on the other, *tak, tik-tik,* like the start of a song. Then she squeezed Beverly in her iron grip and kissed her too, as though she had always known her.

At the house, I told Btissam I'd seen Fatima. "Who?" Btissam replied.

"Fatima, the woman who works here," I said.

"Who?"

"FA-ti-ma. The *shaghghala,* the *khaddama,* the . . ." I couldn't remember the Darija word for housekeeper, so I threw out all the words that came to mind, as Ahmed the Word Lord of Cairo might have done. Btissam looked perplexed.

"Oh, Fa-TI-ma," she finally said, subtly shifting the emphasis to the second syllable. There was no good reason for this pronunciation; it went directly against how the name was spelled. Something tugged in my chest, not as hard as when Zaina in Beirut had spelled words "wrong," but enough to make me think my infatuation with Darija might have worn off.

Btissam bypassed the villa's grand salons—two adjacent rooms with a cutaway wall between, always kept dim and empty, awaiting a party of forty—and beckoned us into the small room where the family and I usually ate dinner and watched TV. Like the larger rooms, the small salon was edged in deep upholstered banquettes with heavy matching pillows, but this room was snug enough that everyone fit easily around the plastic-covered dining table. It was a low, round table on wheels, which Btissam would roll into position, just above my lap; it reminded me of being locked into a seat on a roller coaster. Sitting down with her and my mother, as a translator rather than a student and host daughter, was like boarding the tallest, scariest ride yet.

Btissam had put on a purple T-shirt and pulled her frizzy hair into a little ponytail. She served the sweet mint tea from the fancier teapot, then offered us bowl upon bowl of candied chickpeas, crumbly cookies, and other snacks I had never seen before in this house.

After my talk with Beverly about listening comprehension, this was my first opportunity to practice it. *Breathe, be quiet,* I told myself. *Just relax and listen.* Our conversation went fairly smoothly, though it helped that Btissam spoke slowly for my sake. I explained Beverly's past in Morocco, her current work as a teacher of herbal medicine, how many children she had—answering all the usual questions. It was small talk, the kind that, in a classroom setting, could so easily dull the brain. But now it gave me purpose—I felt useful rather than trivial. It was a far cry from simultaneous translation, but for fleeting moments I felt that other part of my brain, the one that was safe from my own perfectionist nitpicking, fully light up. Before I knew it, an hour and a half had passed, and Beverly looked sleepy enough that I knew it was time to take her back to her hotel.

In the taxi, I must have still looked like a relaxed and capable conversationalist, because the driver launched into a story, in somewhat halting Fusha, about his Scottish girlfriend and the problems they'd been having. She didn't want to move to Morocco to be with him;

he couldn't afford to move to Scotland. They could live together in Spain and both find work, but he wasn't sure she was committed, and besides, the Spanish treated him like a pariah. She was beautiful and strong, but maybe she drank too much.

He told me all this as he sped across the mile-long gap between the *ville nouvelle* and the medina. When we arrived near the medina gate, we sat a few minutes longer in the car as he wrapped up his tale. "Thank you," he finally said. "I feel better that I talked to someone about this."

"Wow, honey," Beverly told me as I walked with her through the lane to her hotel. "You speak so well! You're so expressive, so assured."

I had said only a few words to the driver: "Very hard!" "That is bad!" Before that, my translation between Beverly and Btissam had shrunk both women's eloquent comments to basic platitudes. My mother couldn't hear all my awkward changes in register—here Fusha, there Darija, there a desperate reach for Egyptian. All she saw was that the language had worked: I had communicated. Which was the important thing, and the thing I was always forgetting.

Most days before class, Btissam and I drank mint tea and ate toast, and she would ask, "Did you study?"

"Yes, I studied a lot," I would answer.

"Good. Studying is very good," she would reply.

It wasn't much of a Darija conversation, but at a quarter to eight in the morning, it was all I could handle.

Beverly's visit opened some communication channel. Perhaps it had given Btissam a better context for me, so I wasn't just some wrong-aged alien in inappropriate clothes, perched nervously in front of her TV. I was a real person, because I had a real mother.

The following day, as Btissam dunked her bread in her tea, she spoke at length. She had worked all her life as a seamstress. She had wanted to go to college, but she hadn't had the opportunity. After she married, Yacine had gone to work in Kenya and Nigeria, while she had focused on putting the kids through good schools. Her two older sons were out in the world, she said, employed and doing well. Amal, so much younger, wasn't taking school seriously, though. "I want her to study, because I wasn't able to," Btissam said. She looked tired.

Btissam's story, confessed in the same way many other strangers had shared with me, explained so much: her Coke-bottle glasses, from the close work of sewing, her halfhearted cooking, her frequent exasperation with her daughter, even her morning queries about my homework. Only later, in class, did I realize I had understood every word.

Speaking Mexican

IN THE AFTERNOONS, Amal and I usually sat in the salon, sort of doing our homework and sort of watching TV—I guess like sisters everywhere. We got along fine, at a basic level. When Amal learned that I spoke Egyptian Arabic, she said she did too. Or, well, she and her friends pretended to speak Egyptian when they wanted to be funny. Did I want to hear?

She took a deep breath and stared down at her hands, getting into character. Then she swung her thick, black hair up with a dramatic toss. "And you do this to me *why?!*" she squawked.

I had to laugh. Not only had she grasped that Ammiya quirk of putting the question word at the end, but she had used the distinctive lightbulb-turning gesture Egyptians use to demand explanation. She also confirmed my suspicion that, to non-Egyptian ears, this inverted sentence structure sounded as overwrought as it did in English. It was a habit I had not been able to break, neither in Lebanon nor here in Morocco.

At 4 p.m., we both stowed our books and concentrated on the screen, because it was time for Amal's favorite TV show. *Hareem as-*

Sultan (The Sultan's Harem), as it was called in Arabic, was a soap opera made in Turkey and set in the sixteenth-century Istanbul court of Suleiman the Magnificent. It was a hit in its native country and all over the Arab world.

At its peak under Suleiman, the Ottoman empire reached west to present-day Algeria—but, except for a few years at the end of the sixteenth century when the Turks had occupied Fes, no farther. Morocco, unlike most other countries in the Middle East, showed virtually no Turkish cultural influence: no hookahs, no borrowed Turkish titles or suffixes, not even common Turkish foods like chicken kebab. It helped explain why Morocco seemed so different from the rest of the Arab world—and it made for an especially transfixing and exotic TV show for teenage Amal. As for me, I would cheerfully watch any soap opera in Arabic. The language of melodrama was never complicated.

The first scene opened in the harem, populated with concubines in jewel-toned dresses. Amal loved the red-haired heroine. "She is very, very, very beautiful," she breathed.

Amal and I usually spoke English together. She spoke it the way I spoke Arabic. She sounded convincing enough with basic phrases. "Hel-lo! How are youuuu!" she sang out every time she saw me. After that, her vocabulary stalled.

"Oh, my teacher, he is very, very bad," Amal told me once. "He talks, talks, blah blah blah blah. He makes me very mad. He is very stupid. He does this." Here she puffed out her cheeks and crossed her big eyes.

"And we laugh, laugh." She shook her head wildly to convey the full force of her criticism.

But then, thinking better of it, she softened the blow. "But it is OK. He is good."

How many times had I made elaborate gestures like this? How many times had I repeated myself, for lack of more to add? How many times had I contradicted myself because I couldn't remember nuanced adjectives? And how often had I made my conversation partner grit her teeth and want to flee the room?

On TV, the scene switched from harem intrigue to a raucous battle, all thundering horses and flashing scimitars. I had pegged Amal as a princess-loving girly-girl—she did have that giant poster of Muslim Barbie over her (my) bed. But now she leaned forward, rapt. "This are my favorite part."

I preferred the harem scenes. I found Arabic much easier to understand in the domestic sphere, even when it was being whispered menacingly in a palace hallway. Out on a battlefield, words were distorted by being bellowed at top volume, and all those clashing swords and smashing skulls made it harder to hear.

This particular show was also a bit tricky to understand because it was dubbed in Syrian Arabic. It sounded lovely, as graceful as Lebanese, but slower, though I didn't recognize all the vocabulary. This dialect dubbing was a striking change from when I had last watched Arabic TV, back in the late 1990s in Cairo. Then, my roommates and I had been hooked on nightly episodes of the American primetime soap *Santa Barbara,* dubbed into country-neutral Fusha. "Thou hast betrayed me, she-devil!" a wronged wife, all shoulder pads and puffy hair, would lament; the mistress would retort, "No, my beloved, this is justice!"

It sounded absurd to me as a language learner, but Arab viewers loved it. Occasionally I would be out during the *Santa Barbara* hour and pass the corner coffeehouse, filled with men staring rapt at the TV in the corner of the room.

At that time, in the late 1990s, Fusha dubbing was still relatively progressive. For decades, virtually all foreign shows in the Arab world had been subtitled. Then in 1991 a Lebanese production company purchased the rights to a Mexican telenovela called *Tú o nadie* (You or No One) and dubbed it in Fusha. It was a massive hit. The dark-eyed beauties, weeping copious tears, were naturally adored by Arab audiences, and the characters' passion and big hair counterbalanced the formality of the words the producers put in their mouths. Over the next decade, the same company dubbed many more Mexican and Brazilian soaps, and the phrase "speaking Mexican" (*yitkallim mekseeki*) became a joking euphemism for speaking Fusha. My *Santa Barbara*, with its Spanish name, was caught up in the wave — it was all in "Mexican" too.

In the time since I had last watched Arabic television, the Mexican speakers disappeared, replaced by dubbing that reflected how Arabs actually spoke. The first soap dubbed in dialect, a Turkish production, was released in 2008, in Syrian. *Noor*, as it was called in Arabic, drew eighty-five million viewers and the condemnation of a Saudi cleric, who called it "replete with evil" — a sure sign of success. Some of that success was due to the star actor, who resembled Brad Pitt, but many also credited the language, which was refreshingly informal and accessible, even to non-Syrian viewers. Dubbing in dialect rapidly became the norm. Syrian, generally considered clear and light, was most often used for historical dramas. Comedy could be dubbed in wisecracking Egyptian, though Lebanese was used for some sitcoms. And here in Morocco, I had seen a couple of shows dubbed in Darija — or I had assumed that's what it was, as the words went by at triple speed.

Children's shows were the last bastion of Fusha dubbing, because they were considered educational. With anime, it sounded jarring, because the grand Arabic dialogue alternated with distinctly Japanese grunts and gasps of surprise. Nerdy SpongeBob SquarePants, however, sounded as though he had been born to speak Fusha.

Amal was past all that, at least today, as she was fully absorbed in the adult world of *Hareem as-Sultan*. The action had shifted back to women reclining on divans, nibbling sweets and scheming.

"Do you understand the Syrian well?" I asked Amal as the final credits rolled.

"Oh, yes," she replied with a toss of her thick black hair. "It sound very, very nice!" Would Amal, one day years in the future, quote Syrian phrases she had learned on this show, the way my high school friends and I still repeated the occasional Monty Python punchline? If Fusha did ever fade, perhaps this was how the western edge of the Arab world would stay connected to the eastern one.

One of Si Taoufik's main academic interests was Arabic dialects. After my last class, I asked to hear his theories, and we sat in the school's garden to discuss them. "Imagine taking a trip," he said. We were speaking in English, but out of teaching habit, he picked up a pantomime suitcase. "You set out walking, in Iraq," he said, swinging his arms a little. "And you walk west. As you walk, you would not notice any specific point where the language shifted. But when you reach here, in Morocco, you would be speaking a very different type of Arabic."

This range of Arabic he described made a wonderful image, and it illustrated how fruitless it was for me to try to speak each kind of Arabic precisely matched to wherever I was. There were a few natural barriers — rivers, mountains, patches of desert — that hindered the pure flow of language across the Arab world, but overall, Arabic was a spectrum, not discrete chunks with labels.

This didn't prevent Si Taoufik from, in the next breath, broadly stereotyping the dialects. "To me, Algerian sounds very aggressive, a little vulgar," he confided. I had never heard an Algerian speak, so I couldn't judge, but I wondered whether his perception was related to having a nearly million-square-mile neighbor with which the border was closed.

"Lebanese sounds ... womanish," he went on. "And Egyptian Ammiya — that sounds womanish too. But in a different way, you know?"

"Right," I said. "Like, Lebanese is all soft and glamorous, like some pretty girl." Though I had seen the complications of Beirut firsthand, they hadn't totally changed my impression. "But Ammiya — that sounds like a middle-aged woman telling jokes."

Si Taoufik was sipping his coffee, so he didn't immediately reply.

In the pause, I rewound what I had just said. Wait, *I* was a middle-aged woman telling jokes!

Here I'd been casting about for alternatives to my Egyptian dialect, imagining I could have had a different life in Arabic — more glamorous if I'd been in Beirut, more medieval and rich if I'd been here in Fes, more fluent if I had studied any spoken language sooner, in more depth. But the problem wasn't the dialect. It was me, of course.

I had been so young most of the time I'd studied in Egypt, and that soap-opera clip, with the woman shaking her shoulders and squawking, "You mean *what*, exactly?" — in my twenties, that had made me cringe. It stood for everything that was wrong with the Egyptian accent. Now, though, when my teenage host sister Amal had mocked that same melodramatic intonation, I had felt a certain pride — yes, that's just how I sounded.

A middle-aged woman telling jokes, indeed. I laughed out loud, and Si Taoufik cocked his head, questioning.

"I . . . it's because . . ." I gasped, slapping my thigh so hard I sloshed my mint tea out of its glass. "Ha! I mean, I just turned forty, and . . . I guess I've finally aged into my Arabic accent."

Let's Chat in Arabic

R ABAT, MOROCCO'S CAPITAL, had a great imperial history, defended by an impressive fort, but its modern reputation was one of dull bureaucracy. When I had told Yacine my travel plans, he flicked his eyebrows up and huffed, "Eh, Rabat."

I thought it was fantastic. I had three days in this new city, alone, before meeting my family in Tangier. It was a relief to have no role to play for anyone. Overnight, the last bit of enchantment that had made me Btissam and Yacine's daughter wore off, and I woke up a plain old boarder. I was free, in my traveling clothes, in a city that, after subdued, inward-looking Fes, felt as anonymous and cosmopolitan as Paris. In the lobby of my hotel, businessmen with gold watches huddled in negotiations, and intellectuals with sculpted hair pored over the day's French paper. I walked to the city tram, just to ride and admire the scenery.

I had intended to wander around the neighborhood at the end of the line, but when we arrived it was drizzling, the air was biting cold, and the streets looked dull and sterile. I ducked back into the warm tram, to go back the way I had come.

A minute later, a young woman sat down across from me. She stared pensively out the window, checked her phone, pulled her sheer leopard-print scarf tighter at her ears, checked her phone again. It was a natural extension of her fidgeting when she leaned over and asked me something in French.

I studiously told her I did not speak French, and she answered, "Oh, good, you speak Arabic." Then she let loose a torrent of Darija. As soon as I could get a word in, I explained my situation — the time in Egypt, the newness of Darija, the total failure in listening comprehension.

And when she answered me, I understood her perfectly. "OK, no problem," she said. "My cousin is from Port Said, so I learned to speak Ammiya. Now, *yalla ndardish.*"

She used the very phrase that had been the title of my first Egyptian-colloquial textbook, from my first visit to Cairo all the way back in 1992: *Let's Chat in Arabic.*

"*Yalla ndardish,*" I said. It was the first time I had used the phrase in a natural context. Yes, let's chat. The tram doors dinged, and the train eased into motion.

"Where are you from? Europe?" she asked.

When I told her I was from New York, her eyes lit up. "Oh! America! There are only two places in the world I want to go, Mecca and America." She clapped her hands together. "Forget Europe — *pfft.*"

She lived in Rabat, and she had been visiting her brother here on the edge of Salé. He was recently married and had a new baby, born not long after the wedding. "They did things a little backwards," she said with a conspiratorial laugh.

Her name was Houria — freedom. With her long face and big, dark eyes, she had looked serious when she sat down, but when she smiled now, she lit up and looked ready for anything. As the tram zipped along its route, Houria told me she worked at a fancy restaurant, but her mother didn't approve because the place served alcohol. "My mother would prefer that I just sit in the house until I get married," she said.

"But how are you supposed to get married if you don't leave the house? Just wait around?" I mimed looking bored, peering out the window.

"Right—wait around. For my *destiny!*" She did a fake swoon. I was thrilled to get her joke.

As we neared the main train station in Rabat, we swapped phone numbers. "Let's meet tomorrow," she said. "My day is *empty* every day after three."

Cairo had plenty of men-only spaces, but these social conventions had never chafed because I rarely wanted to be in their spit-and-sawdust coffeehouses. There was always somewhere nicer and more mixed to go. Morocco, though, was full of elegant old *salons de thé* and cheerful bargain restaurants where I could easily picture myself—until I saw the wall of men, smoking louchely and facing the street, as if to defend their territory. On my first day in Rabat, I felt a sudden surge of rage when I happened to walk past a chicken-and-rice restaurant. The men out front all seemed to be glaring. I glared right back.

Now, the next day, Houria was marching us right toward that same restaurant, elbowing in among the men and sitting us down at the sidewalk tables. She waved at the waiter, who smiled in recognition. Inside, two women were chatting and nibbling chicken lunches. Apparently I had not looked closely enough at the clientele.

"I love this place," Houria said, "but for a long time I came here every day after work, and I got so fat!"

Picking up where we'd left off on the tram, Houria told me that in high school she had run track, traveling with her team—Tunisia, Libya, all around Morocco. Her grades hadn't been great, so she didn't apply to college. Now, at age twenty-six, she was feeling stuck.

She didn't like her job at the restaurant, and she hadn't met any good men.

She showed me photos of her friends at her restaurant job — the hostesses in their tight-fitting, knee-length dresses, the bathroom attendant in her white smock, and Houria herself in black-and-white-check kitchen trousers and a white snap-front top. Morocco was filled with women in such uniforms, mopping hallways and pushing carts of cleaning supplies. I had been looking right past them, just as I had glossed over women in niqabs in the Gulf, not bothering to imagine them with any other life.

Houria asked if I had any children. I told her no, and I probably wouldn't.

"Oh, but you have to!" she said.

Families were different in America, I explained. We lived spread out across the country, without aunts and uncles and cousins and grandparents (I used all the words I'd learned in class) around to help raise the kids.

"I have the solution," she declared with her brilliant, up-for-anything smile. "I will come to New York and be the nanny. Now, tell me what the weather is like there, so I can prepare."

In that moment, in which I understood both Houria's joke and the personality behind it, I knew I had made a friend.

When we finished eating, Houria proposed we go to her grandmother's house — not far, and a nice place to kill time until her evening work shift. Walking to the corner, we passed two other cafés, and I noticed a handful of women at each one. At Houria's side, Morocco looked different.

"When we get to the house," she said as we climbed into a cab, "I'll give you a *beejama*, and we can take a little nap." New cognate vocabulary, and an afternoon snooze! This was turning into an excellent date.

Granny's place was in a middle-class subdivision, and pajamas turned out to be a yellow cotton nightie. Houria handed it to me, along with plastic sandals, as soon as we arrived, and gestured for me to change in the side salon. Having finally grasped the importance of loungewear with my host family in Fes, I wasn't going to resist. I wanted to make a good, properly relaxed impression with this new family. Still, it was awkward—there was Granny and the housekeeper, and no real wall between the salons, much less a door to close. Houria strode in and stripped down to her bra and underwear.

If it seemed intimate to change clothes with someone I'd just met, it also seemed a bit intimate to lie down and take a nap in the same room with her. But Moroccan salon sofas are firm and wide, ideal for napping, and even the arrival of Houria's two-year-old nephew didn't keep me from sleep.

When I woke up an hour later, Houria's grandmother, clad in a big stretchy housedress with a hole in the armpit, had laid out a tray of sweets and tea. Houria was already dressed in her street clothes. "Go ahead and eat while I pray," she told me as she arranged a prayer rug in the farthest sitting area.

Over tea, we talked—or rather, Houria and her grandmother talked, and occasionally Houria translated to Ammiya for me. Our one-on-one lunch conversation had taken a lot out of me, and post-nap, I was having a hard time tuning in. I slumped back on the pillows, watching a dubbed Bollywood movie on TV, a swirl of color and syllables I couldn't piece together.

"Oh, Lalla Zora, you're tired." Houria patted my knee affectionately. "And it's time for me to go to work. *Yalla, habibti.*"

I smiled up at her. One afternoon, and I was not just her friend, but her *habeeba,* her darling.

Sweet Sensation

AT WHAT POINT had I agreed to go home with Houria? I re-wound the day in my head, trying to find the turn in the conversation. We had met that morning, the day after napping at Gran's, and strolled around Rabat together, stopping to admire the silvery sea from the ramparts of the casbah. We had nibbled almond cookies in a café, sheltered from the rain. Just after that, in a garden crawling with cats, we had definitely discussed going to her house—but with inconclusive results, I had thought.

Then I had followed her across lanes of traffic, her arm firmly looped through mine, and into the front seat of one white Mercedes taxi, then another. And then we were walking down a poorly lit street in a part of the city that I could only identify as "uphill from the cemetery."

At the entrance to her apartment building, in a pool of dark where the streetlights didn't reach, Houria had fumbled with her keys in the lock, and I had suddenly seen my situation from outside and thought, Have I done something very stupid? The door had opened, into further pitch-black, and Houria grabbed my hand and pulled me in. *Perhaps.*

But I had not been jumped and robbed and knifed in a dark stairwell. Houria's mother, a Berber woman with skin so pale and papery she resembled a Walker Evans portrait, had greeted me at the apartment door, squeezed me, and kissed me, *tak, tik-tik.*

Now Houria and I were the picture of Moroccan domesticity, lounging on the banquettes in the central salon in our *beejama* (this time, mine was a floral-print nylon caftan with red-and-gold brocade trim). It was 9:30 p.m., and I was yawning.

"We don't usually go to sleep this early," my new friend said, her fair brow wrinkling. "Maybe we'll have a little snack, but we won't eat dinner until my dad gets home, about midnight. Then we can sleep."

Oh. Well. That was funny. I had been thinking her dad's arrival was imminent, and then he'd drive me back down the hill, to a part of Rabat I vaguely recognized, in his taxi. That was, however, only a story I'd made up in my head, Dr. Badawi style, after we had arrived at Houria's. I had taken a few language clues — father, taxi, dinner — and strung them together in a story. I couldn't possibly be spending the night here, could I? Somewhere else in the city, my hotel room sat empty.

Houria's mother was in the kitchen, rattling pots and pans, and her brother, a skinny sixteen-year-old who looked about twelve, was flopped on the floor, studiously ignoring us. On the Arabic version of *The Voice*, a coach clambered up on his red chair and applauded, crowing theatrically, *"Allahu akbar!"*

"Come to the roof with me, Zora," Houria said, standing up from the sofa. She could see I was about to doze off. "I have to put my laundry out to dry."

We ventured into the dark stairwell again, Houria lighting the way with her phone screen. The apartment building was new, still unfinished, and we climbed over broken bags of cement. From the roof,

I saw we were at the very edge of the city—to one side stood more housing blocks like this one, stretching down a hill toward a dense glow of light; to the other side was darkness.

Houria's family had moved here not long after she finished high school. She liked it; they had more room. Although they didn't have a room for her, precisely. To change into our caftans, we first had to shoo her brother out of his bedroom, decorated with posters of Tupac and Bob Marley. Houria had folded her street clothes in a neat stack, then brought them out and set them on a banquette in a side salon, instructing me to do the same.

When I had asked where she slept, she indicated the same banquette. Her parents hadn't built her a separate bedroom, she explained, because they had been sure she'd be married soon. Six years had passed, and she was lobbying her father to wall off the side salon. "It would be easy—it would hardly cost anything!" She bent to smooth the folds in her blouse.

Up on the roof, Houria pinned her work uniform to the laundry line. "Lalla Zora, come here," she said. "I need to tell you my problem." She pulled me past another pile of construction materials, into the shadows, and we squatted by the roof's perimeter wall. She was saying something about a man, a difficult situation, a test. My energy was flagging—my brain could no longer process euphemism, or perhaps Houria had lapsed out of Ammiya and back into Darija.

"I'm sorry, Houria, but I don't understand. What did you say?" I asked her. *Breathe, relax. Just listen.*

"I. Lost. My. Virginity," she said.

She had met a man at the restaurant where she worked, and they went on a few dates. He was older, and married, and a bit fat. But he was very nice to her, and one time he invited her to his apartment. "I felt a *hass hilu*"—sweet sensation—"with him," Houria said meaningfully. "But I paid a very high price."

There had been some blood. Afterward, she had gone to two doctors to confirm what she feared: there was not enough of her hymen left for her to bleed on her wedding night. This had happened months ago, but she couldn't stop thinking about it. She was saving up money to have an operation. For now, she tried to pray and keep busy, to keep her mind off it.

I muttered and stammered. Not, for once, because I couldn't find the Arabic words, but because I had no counsel, in any language. "Well, at least you enjoyed yourself?" I finally said, lamely.

"Oh, no, it wasn't that good." Houria pursed her lips. "But the man who was calling me today" — she had borrowed my phone a few times that afternoon, to talk to a second man she knew from the restaurant — "he has made me feel, you know . . . *'ishq* and *mut'a* and everything."

These were juicy words: *'ishq* was passion; *mut'a*, gratification. Far juicier than the *hass hilu*, the sweet sensation she had described with the fat man. She had already told me that the man she'd spoken with today was terrible, untrustworthy, also old and married. I was glad it was dark — she couldn't see me gaping at her revelations.

"What about with your boyfriend?" I asked. "In high school? How did he make you feel?"

She had told me about this boyfriend earlier that day, when she pointed out a dark-skinned tourist in the café. "See that black one? I had a boyfriend like that," she had said wistfully. He had been her first love. They had wanted to get married, but her father had said no; at sixteen, she was too young. After school had ended, the boyfriend went to work in Spain, where he met someone else. She still thought of him all the time, had even dreamed of him the night before: he had been wearing white and had taken her in his arms.

"That was different too," she explained. "With him, I felt *hubb* and *farha*" — love and joy. "We did things, but we had certain positions, you know, so I didn't have to worry about my virginity. But I didn't feel *mut'a*."

I admired Houria's ability to identify what she felt. At her age, I had hopelessly muddled love and passion. Arabic and its wealth of synonyms was helpful here — precision was encouraged. And Houria hadn't even touched on so many other possible words: *maram*, craving; *huyam*, love like thirst; *hawan*, love that feels like falling; *shahwa*, a greedy lust.

"Sex is like food and water," Houria went on, a little indignant. "It's something everyone needs." She only felt bad that she had taken it too far and ruined the evidence of her virginity, which created a problem for her whole family. "My parents would *kill* me if they found out," she said. I was pretty sure she didn't mean this literally — Morocco wasn't known for its judgmental religious fanatics.

But as if on cue, Houria pointed over the parapet, down to the street below. "Look, it's our neighbors, the Shoulds." She had used a funny adjective for their nickname, *multazimeen*, which I remembered from Egypt, where it meant dedicated. Its root suggested being morally obligated, but also a bit holier-than-thou. I peeked over the edge of the roof. The Shoulds dressed as they should, he in a beard and a just-above-the-ankles tunic and she in an all-encompassing black robe. The whole time I had been in Morocco, I hadn't seen anyone in this fundamentalist uniform.

Houria laughed. "They have the apartment there, across from ours. What they must think of my brother and his Tupac!" She didn't seem concerned with what they thought of her. Why should she? She prayed five times a day, and she believed that Islam was the best religion, the one true path — she had told me this earlier, during our stroll around Rabat. She dressed modestly, though not as conservatively as her mother would have liked. Unfortunately, the very thing her mother feared had already happened.

A cool breeze blew in the one small window in the salon. "Did the flies wake you?" Houria asked as I sat up, bleary and disoriented.

She was already dressed, her hair brushed back neatly. The flies had woken me earlier, but I had pulled my sheet over my head and dozed another hour.

"At first they annoyed me," she said as she checked her outfit in a mirror outside the bathroom, "but now I think of them as my alarm clock. They come at exactly the time I need to get up." She was like a fairy-tale princess before the magic happened, so utterly good.

Houria's mother emerged from the kitchen with a tray of breads and cheese and honey, a bowl of hearty beans, and thermoses of coffee and hot milk. As I ate and drank, I recalled brief flashes of the night before: a beef tagine with cardoons for dinner, a short exchange with Houria's tired father, then flopping down to sleep on a banquette as the family chatted next to me. The feeling had reminded me of nights as a kid, when colorful friends of my parents would show up at the house, mid–road trip or in between jobs. The grownups would stay up late telling stories, and I would listen as long as I could stay awake. Now I was both the overtired toddler and the exotic grownup guest, and not since I'd been a child had I given myself over to other people's whims for so long. My brain felt empty now, but the passivity I felt in Houria's home had helped me to stretch myself in Arabic, to really make a connection, as I had the previous night.

When Houria and I set out for the bus, I had a better look at her neighborhood. The city had chewed up the countryside here, but not yet digested it. Between four-story apartment blocks sat a vacant lot, studded with neat rows of onion greens. Next to a goat pen stood a cement mixer. As Houria and I rode into Rabat on the bus, the city seemed to knit together in front of us, growing more whole. In her smart khaki pants, tailored blouse with a bow at the neck, and sheer headscarf, Houria had looked out of place dodging construction debris en route to the bus. Now she blended in with the morning commuters.

At the central station, Houria kissed me goodbye, *tak, tik-tik*. The whole morning I had barely spoken — I was exhausted. "You'll meet a good man soon," I managed to say. "I know it." It didn't begin to convey all the good I wished for her.

"I hope you are right, Zora. I pray to God you are right."

She walked into the crowd, and I lost sight of her among the other young women.

Up in the Old Hotel

WHENEVER PEOPLE ASKED me what my parents were doing in Tangier before I was born, I would say, "Oh, you know. It was the sixties." I didn't know exactly what they had been doing, but the anecdotes I'd heard over the years added up to typical hippie-era bohemianism. It wasn't as if my parents had been *working*, or anything as tedious as that.

They would work in Los Angeles for a while, to save up money, then take off on months-long trips — Germany, Bulgaria, Turkey. At some point along the hippie travel trail, they heard Morocco was neat, so they went; they liked it and returned. And then, on one of the longer stays in Los Angeles, my parents had me, and we all moved to New Mexico. Forty years passed.

Now, in 2012, I was standing with my mother and my father, Beverly and Patrick, in Tangier. Up the hill behind, the city spread like a cubist painter's dream, a series of blocky buildings, all light and shadow, gray and ocher. The light glinted through fine sea haze from the Mediterranean behind us. In front of us was the Tangier hotel where they had stayed for several months in 1967.

The Ourida. My mother remembered the name, and how it had a front door facing the water and a back one opening into the medina. At that front door, a man named Hussein smiled with sugar-blackened teeth and beckoned us in.

The Ourida had been converted into a café, and Hussein, enjoying a break from polishing tea glasses, sprinted up and down the spiral staircase with keys, showing us all the rooms, then up to the roof to see the view across the Strait of Gibraltar, to Spain beyond.

The café patrons looked on, amused, as Beverly and Patrick pointed and conferred, peering out of windows to assess the view, pacing along where old walls may have stood. At least Tangier had a long history of Western oddballs washing up here, so surely this wasn't a rare occurrence: a tanned man with a gray ponytail, a woman in flowing layers and sensible sandals, both squinting to make the past pop into focus again.

"This is my mother, and this is my father," I explained to a young couple at a table on the second floor, using the phrases I had prepared my first day in Darija class, weeks before. "They lived here more than forty years ago. First time in Tangier since!"

There was a lot more to the story than that, and while my parents were occupied with reconstructing the Ourida of memory, I was tempted to tell these strangers everything, to pull up a chair at the couple's table. I would order tea from Hussein and pour out all the details, as so many people had poured out their stories to me. I imagined myself beginning: My parents divorced when I was very young, but my father stayed with us, moving into a bedroom in the guesthouse. My mother remarried; my brother was born. The year I was fourteen, we all moved to a new house, with a separate apartment for my father. He stayed on after my mother left her second husband, and moved out only after my brother graduated from high school.

But it was fine, it really was, I would rush to assure the couple in the café, my new imaginary friends—everybody got along pretty well, at least as far as I knew. So it was nice that we were all here now, really. The three of us had never traveled together as adults.

And, actually, it was hard to believe my parents had ever been married. My mother talked and talked; my father thought and thought. She believed everything was *interesting,* coincidental, part of some mystical system; he subscribed to *Scientific American.* And here was the sad part, I'd say, the real reason I'd felt the urge to tell these strangers the whole story: According to my mother, she and my father had split on something more basic. My mother had mistaken my father's lack of speech for lack of love.

My parents' story didn't involve death, doomed love, or accidental deflowering. Still, it had always pricked at me, this fundamental miscommunication. (If that's what it was. If I had asked my father, he might have had some more practical explanation, or just said "Hmmm.") My mother could see hidden magic in everything, but she hadn't been able to read my father's gestures of devotion. As I retold the story in my head in the simplest Arabic, in my fantasy conversation with the couple in the café, it lost its sting. These things happened to us all, I saw now. We all had to learn — we weren't born fluent in anything, not even love.

Hussein was waving to me from the bottom of the spiral staircase. Beverly and Patrick had gone down to the main level. I nodded goodbye to the café couple, my imaginary confessors. They were so young, they hadn't been alive when my parents had lived here.

Downstairs, Hussein walked to the main wall, painted with a three-dimensional woodland mural. He fumbled for a switch, and a rainbow of lights glowed and a fountain gurgled, sending a tiny stream through the middle of the forest.

"Wow, that's pretty neat," my father said. "*That* sure wasn't here before."

After the Ourida, we made our way to Café Central on the legendary Petit Socco. This was where the Beats had lounged, Bowles had scribbled, Burroughs had nodded. Many of my parents' more dubious stories had started here too—somewhere nearby was the place they referred to as the Dancing-Boy Café.

"Remember Flute in the Boot?" Patrick said to Beverly after our tea had arrived. "He sold drugs right there?" He pointed across the square.

"Why did you call him Flute in the Boot?" I asked. I had heard snippets of all these stories, never imagining I would one day hear them told in the place where they happened.

"He always kept a little flute tucked in his boot," Patrick answered. A tour group shuffled into the plaza, its leader holding up a paddle with a number on it; like the fountain at the ex-Ourida, cruise-ship day-trippers hadn't been here before either.

Flute in the Boot had picked a fight when the guy became convinced my dad was cutting in on his turf. "We got into a big yelling match," my father said. "Right there in the middle of the square. It was a very Arab fight, a big, loud scene. After that, he didn't bother me anymore."

A showy altercation was a remarkable thing for Patrick, who raised his voice only at his car—and once, just once, at my mother, years after the divorce.

"And just up that street to the right was where Betty Blowjob got her apartment, on our second trip," my mother said. I didn't bother asking how Betty got her name.

"She was in a big fight too," my mother continued. "Remember? The neighborhood prostitutes threatened her with a knife because she was turning tricks to pay her rent."

I smoothed down my ankle-length skirt and tried to imagine myself on the road with my parents back then. I loved their stories, but would I have enjoyed the trip? The thought of having an "Arab" fight with a drug dealer or traveling with a part-time hooker made me cringe with self-consciousness. Striving for fluency—both linguistic and cultural—called for being as inconspicuous as possible. In Morocco, no one had ever offered me hash, and though I wouldn't have minded some, I saw it as a point of pride, because it meant no one mistook me for a hippie tourist.

The tour group shuffled on. In its stead came a man pushing a baby carriage filled with a blaring speaker, powered by a car battery. The music reminded Beverly of a party—that one in someone's basement where they had drunk too much Chaud-Soleil, the Moroccan rosé they had liked, and a veiled woman had tried to kiss her.

"What were we thinking?" my mother mused, with four decades of hindsight. "We were in the medina. It really wasn't cool to drink wine in the medina."

My parents had traveled in Morocco barely aware of the guidelines for behavior, such as not drinking in the most traditional urban quarters. But they had also been free of the self-consciousness I carried. My mother had worn a pixie haircut and no bra. They spoke only English and some textbook Spanish, which helped in Tangier but not much farther south. Unlike me, with my sharpened pencils and my dictionary at the ready, they had winged it, just made it all up, and had a fine time.

Moroccans had been fine with them too—they didn't wilt at the sight of a few odd visitors in a beat-up VW Bug. Al-Maghrib, the place-where-the-sun-sets, shares a root with *ghareeb*, the word for strange, and Morocco and strangeness do seem to go together. Was that an albino kid stealing fruit in the market? Was that a donkey wearing pants? Was that a couple of stoned Americans with backpacks? People shrugged it off. *Nta fil-maghrib, fa-la tastaghrib*, the saying went. You're in Morocco, don't be surprised.

"So, what was Tangier like then?" I prodded them. "How does it compare to now? Has it changed a lot?"

Patrick was looking around the square again. The baby-carriage music vendor had been joined by another one, playing dueling music. Mopeds buzzed past, weaving between the pedestrians. "I'm surprised at how dirty it is," he said tentatively.

I had hoped coming to Morocco would revive good old memories for my parents, not show how the world had changed for the worse. Patrick looked tired; he had arrived only that morning from California. I probably shouldn't have dragged him out like this after such a long flight, but I was hungry for his stories.

Patrick had sucked his mint tea down to the syrupy bottom. "*Mizyan bzaf,* right?" he said to me. "That means very good? And *zweyna*—that's pretty. And the numbers: *wahad, zhuzh* . . ." Even after forty years away and twenty-four hours of air travel, he spoke better Darija than I did. I still never remembered to use that special word for two.

The waiter, a fleshy man with slightly crossed eyes, arrived. As he bent down to leave the bill, he murmured in my ear, "*Ana uhibb al-fatat al-ladheedha.*" He pursed his plump lips in a suggestive smile, then turned to the next table.

"What did he say to you?" Beverly asked, leaning forward.

I explained that our attentive waiter had advised me, in quite formal Arabic, that he loved the delicious ladies.

"Oh, really?" Patrick said, pulling a tiny spiral notebook from his shirt pocket. "What are the words exactly?" His pen was poised for dictation.

What Is the Name of This?

"OH, HONEY, it's amazing!" Beverly exclaimed, bounding up the street in Chefchaouen. The medina in this mountain town was built up a hillside and painted every shade of blue, from the doorsills to the parapets. It felt like an Escher drawing at the bottom of a swimming pool.

"Ooh," Patrick mused. "Hmm. Ahh." He stopped periodically to look down side alleys or glance back to appreciate the view.

Chaouen was the center of the Rif Mountains' pot-growing zone, which should have made it an obvious destination in my parents' earlier travels, but somehow they had never come here. Our apartment was a stack of rooms, one above another, up to a tippy-top roof terrace with cushions set around the edges. From here, we could see across the whole valley and up the mountains behind. The sun was just setting.

Patrick leaned back on the cushions and let out a long, satisfied sigh. He had dozed on the ride up and seemed to have recovered from his slump in Tangier. "Ahhhh," he said, smacking his lips with satisfaction. "No mopeds."

Here, in Chaouen's calm dusk, without the background buzz of engines, we could hear thin threads of melodious conversations winding up from the street below.

"Oh, it sounds like Tangier used to!" my mother said to Patrick. "Remember? It was lovely to lie in bed and listen to the sounds outside the window."

"Ahh, yes, just this soft *shush-shush-shush*," he said. "The sound of hundreds of feet walking."

"And the call to prayer—there were no microphones," Beverly added. This was harder for me to imagine than no mopeds. In comparison with the overwhelming *adhan* of Cairo, modern Tangier's soundscape, in which only a few muezzins competed, was positively serene. Still, I envied my parents' experience with the *adhan* in its original form, an invitation cast into the air through the power of the human voice alone.

I had heard something almost like it here in Chaouen, in fact, on a previous trip. My traveling companion and I were both lovesick, for different reasons, and I proposed a distracting hike up into the mountains. There we met a handsome young goatherd who happened to speak lovely Fusha. I played translator, which made me feel useful, and the goatherd offered to sing for us, a classical love song. Out came pure silken sound, a ribbon of notes that rose and rippled in the thin air between the mountains. I couldn't translate the words, but my friend and I felt their meaning. It was the first moment I understood how people could fall in love across cultures and languages, how communication encompassed so much more than the words we spoke.

Now, here in the medina with my parents, the light had faded from the landscape, and the day's last *adhan* rang out over the hills. One call came from a whitewashed tower like a pile of sugar cubes on a far hill, and another rang out closer, from somewhere below us in the medina. The calls fell in and out of sync, the far voice smooth and well modulated, the nearer one creaky and faltering. Perhaps that muezzin had sung his heart out back in the days before microphones.

After breakfast, I found Patrick frozen midstep on a landing, peering down the stairs. He had discovered an ancient baggie of hash in the kitchen, left behind by some previous guests, and smoked some.

"Phew," he said when he heard me. "I'm glad this house is so small. And all stacked up like it is. You only have to think in two dimensions."

We headed downhill to the weekly street market, where the sidewalks were lined with secondhand clothes, fresh eggs, live sheep. At a heap of brushy, gray-green weeds, Beverly stopped to rub their leaves. Her professional curiosity, as an herbalist, was piqued.

"What's the name of that?" I asked the tiny man attending them. I used my best beginner-Darija-class diction. For myself, with silly things like cotton candy, I couldn't be bothered to ask these questions. But for my mother I wanted to be helpful.

The little man peered up at me. "What? In *Arabic?*" he croaked, his eyebrows wrinkled in confusion.

It figured that when I finally worked up the nerve to use the little bit of Darija I had learned, I would be in a place where it wasn't commonly spoken. All around us, I noticed now, was the buzz of Berber.

The Berber people had been in North Africa long before the Arabs marched across, and their language gave Darija its distinct accent and complete lack of vowels — or that's the way it sounded to me. Whenever I overheard Berber spoken on the street, I felt I should understand its rush of sibilant *sh*'s, staccato *t*'s, and buzzy *r*'s. Then I was relieved to find it was not just the world's fastest Darija, but a language I genuinely did not know.

In Fes, with its deep Arab roots, I didn't hear much Berber spoken in the streets. Across the country, though, censuses showed that anywhere from a third to half the population used it daily. In 2011,

Tamazight (as Berber is more properly called) was declared an official language of Morocco, alongside Arabic; the spare, alien-cunei-
form alphabet could now be seen on government buildings as well as
in mobile-phone ads. This was a major reversal from the 1950s, when
Arab nationalists were so bent on spreading their message of linguistic unity that they had imported Syrians to teach Fusha in remote
Berber villages.

Still, the official acknowledgment of Berber culture was so recent
that Moroccan identity was in flux. At a lecture at my school in Fes,
I had witnessed its negotiation in real time. Midway through a professor's talk on modern Morocco, a college-age woman in a black
hijab had raised her hand and asked, "What is the need of this Berber
movement, Professor? What did they *do?* Who are the heroes?"

"You're not Amazigh, are you?" the professor had replied, using
the now-preferred terminology for the Berber people. As for the heroes, did she know Tariq ibn Ziyad, the general who led the Arabs
into Iberia in 711? Did she know, as every Arab student should, his famous speech, delivered after burning his own ships on the European
shore? "My men, where will you flee?" the general had thundered.
"The enemy is ahead, and the sea behind you!" And did she know
his seven thousand troops rousted Visigoth king Roderic's hundred
thousand, thus extending the Islamic empire across the Mediterranean and into Europe? Well, Tariq ibn Ziyad was Amazigh.

When the professor moved on to discuss the influence of the
Tamazight language, the student again objected. "They accept Islam," she said, "so they must accept Arabic!" The professor pointed
out that no one expected Chinese Muslims to speak Arabic; maybe
they read a bit of the Quran in Arabic, but they spoke Chinese, lived
their whole lives in Chinese. The exchange gave me uncomfortable
flashbacks to Lebanon and its identity issues. But when the woman
approached the professor after the lecture, it was not to continue the
argument but to thank him.

The town of Chaouen, in the Rif Mountains, was a majority

Amazigh town in the middle of a deeply Amazigh region. For nearly five years in the 1920s, the region had declared itself an independent republic. As my parents and I strolled through the market, Berber culture was still in evidence everywhere. Older Berber women, swaddled in woolen garments tied over one shoulder, bustled from vendor to vendor, pursing their lips critically at the goods. Some wore traditional red-and-white-striped blankets; others were wrapped in terry-cloth towels.

On the way back up the hill, we passed a cemetery. At the gates, women were selling bundles of some woody shrub. I decided to try again. "Excuse me, what's the name of this?" I asked one of the women. Her outermost layer was a thick white towel, covered in a pattern of large marijuana leaves.

"*Rihan*," she said to me, crushing one of the leaves for me to smell.

This at least was Arabic, not Tamazight — it meant fragrant. In my personal dictionary, compiled in Cairo, where I had said *Badawwar 'ala rihan* to every greengrocer, it meant basil.

My mother joined me. "Oh, that's myrtle, honey," she said. I thought of Si Taoufik's idea of walking across the Arab world, through the spectrum of dialects — at some point between the Nile and the Rif Mountains, *rihan* had transformed from one fragrant green to another.

One night, I took Beverly to the hammam, the public bathhouse. The word *hammam*, with a whispery *h* like the relaxed exhale it provokes, comes from the verb *hamma*, to heat. (With a different vowel, the verb becomes *humma*, to decree, by God — so, really, we were obligated to go, I told my mother.) *Hammam* also means bathroom, so context is important. Fortunately, the hammam bucket, an essential part of the bathing process, announced one's destination as if it had been said aloud. I had spent the afternoon collecting everything to carry in our bucket: towels, flip-flops, shampoo, gooey black olive-oil soap, and, for each of us, a *kees*, a little crêpe de Chine scrubbing mitt. On the way there, bucket in hand, I nodded in silent recognition to other such bucket carriers, women headed home with hair wrapped in a towel, *beejama* peeking out from under their djellabas, and blissed-out smiles.

I was taking my mother to the hammam because I wanted to share previous great public bathing moments. The first one had come under the steam-filled dome of a fifteenth-century bathhouse in Aleppo, where I was scrubbed furiously by a mountainous woman in nothing but a red nylon string bikini. As she scraped at my armpits, behind my ears, down the bridge of my nose, she chatted and laughed with her similarly unattired colleagues. It was like *Moby-Dick*, when Ishmael worked the spermaceti with his fellow sailors and was overcome with love for mankind. Except I was the great glob of whale wax, kneaded and prodded, all the lumps worked out.

I also wanted to go to the bath to be quiet. As I had learned in Aleppo, the hammam was a place where language was unnecessary, and I wanted the pleasure of a mute hour in the heat, with no translating responsibilities.

I didn't go into the Chaouen hammam expecting the soaring dome of that old Aleppo building, which had been redone for tourists, nor its turned-wood footstools, plush cushions, and brass tea trays. I was expecting something a bit closer to a Marrakech bath I'd visited years before, a graceful shell with a gritty concrete finish. Here in Morocco, where many medina homes could not accommodate private baths, the hammam was still a local institution, and function often took precedence over form. In Chaouen, the stairs dumped us into an even rougher place than I had anticipated, a fluorescent-lit changing area with all the ambiance of a YMCA locker room.

"Um, honey?" my mother said, peering around me. I gripped the bucket handle and gave her a determined smile.

A very small woman was waiting for us. Bundled in flannel pajamas, leg warmers, and a sweater, with a towel around her waist and one over a shoulder, she was dressed for work in a walk-in freezer, not a steam room. In a mishmash of high-pitched syllables — Darija? Berber? I couldn't tell — she directed Beverly and me to undress. She took our bucket, and we followed her down a white-tile-lined hall.

After several turns, past dark and joyless single bath stalls, she threw open a door to reveal a low-ceilinged, rough-walled room with tiled bench seats for twenty. It looked like the worst wing of a mental ward. "Huh," Beverly said politely.

The tiny attendant switched on the tap in a deep tub in the corner, then walked out, pulling the door tightly shut behind her.

"This isn't like . . . other . . . hammams I've been to," I conceded. "I guess we wait?" I wasn't able to deduce anything from the words the attendant had uttered before leaving.

We took our seats on the bench. The steam rose and my worries eased. So the setting wasn't splendid, but the climate still worked its magic. And I wouldn't have to speak for at least an hour.

"Well, we may as well start," I said as moisture beaded on my skin. We didn't need the attendant for the first step.

I unpacked our bucket and filled it with hot water, then directed Beverly to slather every visible patch of skin with the *saboon baldi*, the black olive-oil soap. *Baldi*, which means country-style or native, was a thoroughly positive adjective in Morocco, at least according to Si Mohamed, who had taught my class the word and its opposite, *roomi*, foreign (literally "Roman"). *Baldi* tomatoes were lumpy but superior; *baldi* clothes were sturdy and warm. *Roomi* products were big and shiny, often cheap, but reliably awful — as Si Mohamed had conveyed in a pantomime involving a plump but tragically bland chicken. So, *baldi* soap for us — we would not be fooled by its resemblance to axle grease. With the luxuriant goo rubbed to a light lather, we lay back against the tile and waited.

The roly-poly attendant reappeared. "*Kees?*" she asked, holding up the flat of her hand. We showed our crêpe de Chine mitts. The woman took Beverly's and went to work. As the attendant scrubbed, Beverly's skin emerged, inch by inch, a vivid pink, tender and thrumming.

The attendant gestured to Beverly's crotch. Washing there was not the attendant's job, but she watched over Beverly like a stern mother, making sure she did it. She scrubbed me, and marched out again, without a word.

We sat against the wall, all aglow, like snakes slithered out of old skin. I was briefly sad that we had been sequestered in this apparently private room. Half the pleasure of the hammam was the camaraderie of being naked with strangers — young and old, taut and sagging, brown, white, and wheat-colored, but all bent on a common task. At the hammam I had visited in Marrakech, a young woman had walked through, a virtually perfect specimen, all youthful curves and cascading curly hair. In clothed life, I probably would have felt a pang of envy. In the communal heat of the hammam, I felt proud that we humans could be so flawless, sometimes.

Meanwhile, my mother and I were flawed in all the usual aging-human ways: squishy in spots, scarred in others, dressed in baggy, sodden underpants. I directed Beverly to move on to hair-washing. I poured warm water over her silver hair until the suds were gone. Parents loom so large, but here she was small, each vertebra visible — so much smaller than I remembered her from when I was young, and smaller than I imagined her back in the day in Morocco, striding into adventures alongside my father.

When we were all rinsed and scrubbed down to our toes, we wrapped ourselves in towels and flip-flopped out to the dressing room, where we sat to cool. "Honey, that was wonderful," my mother said. "I can't stop touching my skin!"

Walking back up the hill to our apartment, I heard a voice call out in English, "So, you've been to the hammam, yes?" It was the owner of a shop we passed several times a day; he had spotted our bucket and our dazed smiles. "*Bsahha!*" he said as we passed.

That was a nice Darija expression, like *bon appétit* but with a broader application: good meals, good baths — enjoy them "in health," as it literally means. It was used so frequently that it was the one case for which I had managed to memorize the proper God for All Occasions response.

"*Allah ya'teek as-sahha!*" I sang back to him. May God give you health.

On our last day in Chaouen, Patrick and I went down the hill to buy a souvenir for Beverly's brother. The shop owner who had wished Beverly and me good health the night before whisked us into his place, deep inside a back room. I explained what we were looking for: a light summer djellaba for my *khal,* my maternal uncle. Soon we had Patrick shimmying in and out of various robes, testing for fit. The shop owner and I covered the usual small talk in slowed-down Darija: where was I from, did I like Morocco, and what was my name?

I told him the story I usually told: my mother and father lived in Morocco before I was born . . . But this time it had more color, because here was my father, in the flesh! And he had seen my mother just the night before, did he remember? She had chosen my Moroccan name, from a woman they knew in Tangier.

"Oh, Zora?" the shop owner said. "It's a Moroccan name, as you say. But you know, that's not the full name." He paused to adjust the shoulders on the sedate navy-blue robe Patrick was modeling.

"The name," he said, turning back to me, "is Fatima Zora. Or, as you would say in Fusha" — he dropped his voice and enunciated slowly, shifting the rhythm of the syllables — "FA-tima az-ZAH-ra'."

Fatima az-Zahra'! Fatima was the powerful daughter of the prophet Muhammad, and az-Zahra' was an epithet: the Most Resplendent. The Darija accent had given the vowel a little curve, smoothed over the light *h,* and erased the stutter from the end, but still, not too shabby a name. Plus, my inner grammarian noted, it was a feminine superlative adjective, a relatively rare morphological form.

I recalled a comment Si Taoufik had made in class, about how women didn't like to be called by their names in public. If he needed to get his wife's attention in the street, he would say "Meela" instead of her full name, Jameela. So mine was the public name, not the full private one.

And now that the shopkeeper had said the name slowly and clearly, I could picture it — فاطمة الزهراء — and I realized I had passed up my personalized-keychain opportunity. At the street fair in Fes where I'd eaten the cotton candy, there *had* been a keychain that said Fatima-something, but I had set it aside without reading it all. Oh, and maybe that was why Btissam's housekeeper, Fa-TI-ma, had always squeezed me so hard — we were name-sisters. One offhand comment from a stranger and I was starting to see where I fit in Morocco.

"I think Fred would like this one," Patrick said. He had put on an elegant cream-colored djellaba.

The salesman reached up to adjust the hood, pulling up its point and folding over the front edge, then stepped back to admire. "There," he said, his mustache puffed with pride. "Doesn't he look Moroccan now?"

I had grown up seeing Patrick in a djellaba. He didn't look Moroccan, he looked like my father.

Crossing the Bridge

"LET'S GO BACK to the Ourida," Beverly proposed. We were in Tangier again, on her last day in the city. "I want to see if I can remember the way." She was no longer as tentative as when she had first arrived. She had started taking satisfaction in navigating on her own, first through the Fes medina, then Chaouen's. Tangier was the final test.

I wanted to go too. Since our earlier visit to the Ourida, I had begun to imagine a scene in the alley that led from the hotel's back door. One of the houses there, my mother couldn't say which one, was where my namesake had lived. In the scene in my head, we were standing by the Ourida's back door, and Zora-the-laundry-woman would enter the lane, on the way back to the house where she still lived after all this time. She would immediately recognize my mother and grab her in a warm embrace, kissing her, *tak, tik-tik.* I would explain in flawless Arabic what my parents had been up to the past forty-odd years, and then I would modestly introduce myself. We would all go into Zora's house to drink mint tea and hear how her life as a single mother had turned out. Because it was my imagination, she would have a triumphant, positive story, free of the usual constraints and frustrations. Together we would celebrate our independent natures.

Beverly led us from the Petit Socco, bearing left, right, left, following her own memory lane. Patrick chimed in now and then, confirming a correct turn. "Here's where I came to wash the dishes," he said as we passed under an arch by a public water tap. A man in an undershirt was standing in front of it, brushing his teeth. ("*Bsahha!*" I told him, for lack of a better greeting. Enjoy your teeth in good health.) This place was embedded in a fable. The shops and decorated doors we passed flickered in my parents' memories, and flashed bright and new in mine.

"We made it!" Beverly crowed as we came around a curve and recognized the green back door of the ex-Ourida.

I took a picture of her there, looking triumphant. Irrational as it was, disappointment was creeping around the edges of the scene. My Zora was not here, of course. The lane was silent, all the doors shut. From an upper-story window, two girls waved shyly at us. There was not much more to do in this dead-end street.

A door creaked open.

"I think that was Zora's house," Beverly whispered. I had learned my magical thinking from her, so she had probably envisioned the same meeting.

An older woman peered around the door frame at us. Her long hair was braided and tucked under a flower-print scarf, and her mouth was sunken, as if around missing teeth.

I caught Beverly's eye. Would she recognize her friend after all these years? She gave a minute shrug.

I walked over to the woman in the doorway and told the story. My Arabic was smooth, assured, correct. "My parents lived in that hotel for a while, back in the old days," I said, pointing across the lane to the green door. "They were friends with a woman who lived on this street. Her name was Zora. Do you . . . know her?"

The woman looked up at me, the corners of her mouth curling in a modest half-smile, protecting her toothless gums.

"Zora, you said?" she wheezed. "Heh, no."

A trio of kids dashed out a nearby door, running down the lane in a mad game of tag.

"That's a very common name, you know," the woman continued over the children's clamor. She jutted her chin toward one of them, a girl with pigtails. "That one's called Zora. And so's her cousin, and her aunt."

As the woman was gesturing toward the girl, her friend called out, "Zoooorrraaa!"

My name story wasn't going to end with a wondrous coincidence or a heartwarming reunion. It was going to end with the realization that, even if I was technically the Most Resplendent, the daughter of the Prophet, I was also so common as to be the Moroccan version of Jenny.

I thanked the old woman, shaking my head at my own foolishness. This made her crack a big, genuine smile. "Peace be with you," she said, and shut the door.

"Mint tea at the Café Central," my father said through the steam of the glass delivered by the usual waiter, the one who loved the delicious ladies. He smacked his lips and let out his signature *ahhh* of pleasure. "I can die a happy man."

Beverly had left that morning; Patrick and I would go tomorrow. For now, he was looking through his trip notebook, practicing the new Arabic phrases he had learned. I was reviewing my notes from a conversation with an Arabic professor I had met earlier that day.

In our brief meeting, the professor, Mostafa Ouajjani, had gently defused all my crankier, more radical ideas about Arabic—the ones

I had come to suspect were wrong but couldn't quite discard. No, he had said, just as Dr. Badawi had at the start of my travels, it made no sense to study only a dialect. Fusha was the necessary foundation. There were no shortcuts. And no, Fusha wasn't on the brink of death, nor should it be hurried along. It was still a crucial lingua franca, connecting Moroccans to all the people along the Mediterranean and into the deserts beyond.

Here on the western edge of the Arab world, Si Mostafa was less conflicted about Arabic than most people I had met farther east. He adored the language, Fusha and dialect alike, and he was also grateful that his father had raised him to speak Berber. Perhaps location helped. Thousands of miles from the contested Holy Land and the Arabian Peninsula, whence both Arabic and Islam sprang, the language could be something lighter and more flexible, not so rigid or weighed down by history and heritage.

In Morocco, I had learned — relearned; I was always relearning — that Arabic didn't have to be a looming concept, a complicated choice between dialects and formal structures, a vessel of scripture or poetry, a reflection of my whole self-image. It could simply be a way of creating a connection. "Moroccans will always cross the bridge," Si Mostafa had said, characterizing the effort required to communicate in some form of Arabic or another. The delicious-ladies waiter had switched to Fusha to make sure I understood his interests. Houria had crossed a second bridge, into Egyptian dialect, for my sake.

Before he took his leave, Si Mostafa had told me the expression he'd taught his class that morning: *Man shabb 'ala shay', shab 'alayh* — Grow up with something, and you'll grow gray with it, too. Generally, that meant we were the same at age eighty as at eight, but, Si Mostafa said, it could also refer to our interests in life and our destiny. Whatever we were exposed to when we were young stuck with us into old age. Music, writing, anything that required practice — you stepped out on that path when you were young, though you might not see it until much later.

Here at the storied Café Central, with dusk settling over the medina, I marveled at this serendipitous tongue twister, a fine motto for the end of my travels—and not just because I had noticeably more gray hairs than when I had started out the year before. I had thought I was done with Arabic for good, yet I had returned to it after all.

I had restarted my Arabic studies thinking my relationship to the language would be different now that I was older. Twenty-five, in hindsight, may have been my golden youth, but it was probably the worst age to have lived abroad and strived for fluency. Arabic, or any language for that matter, isn't something you can learn on your own without some real awkwardness. But at that stage in my life, I had been too bent on establishing my independence to ask for help and to open myself up to uncertain situations. At age forty, I was more self-assured. I had freely chatted with strangers in parking lots and accepted invitations to picnic lunches and afternoon naps, and learned plenty in the process.

Yet some parts of my personality had proven annoyingly consistent. I would never, as truly gifted foreign-language speakers do, plunge into conversations as if into churning rapids, my paddle flying. I still often portaged safely along the bank, examining each and every word before speaking. I still had to remind myself to wing it (in my mother's words, if not Dr. Badawi's), or to ask, "You mean *what*, exactly?" instead of nodding and going with the flow.

And, it seemed, I would always be intrigued by Arabic vocabulary oddities, even to my detriment. The back of my notebook, where I should have been collecting God for All Occasions phrases, currently had a list of utter impracticalities such as *ateet*, the moaning bray of a camel, and *qalah*, yellowness (of teeth). But now I had made the acquaintance of Ahmed the Word Lord in Cairo, who was fine company for dictionary browsing. He had sent me emails with his newest bits of English wordplay as well as classical Arabic brain teasers.

I had not, as I had hoped at the outset, learned this language right, correcting my grad-school missteps. In fact, quite the opposite had happened. After all my country-hopping, my vocabulary was a jumble of dialects, and my precious Fusha grammar was close to broken. Nevertheless, I now felt accomplished in Arabic, in a way I never had before. I had talked my way through a minor car crash and the ensuing bureaucracy, for one thing. For another, I had gotten close enough to people in Arabic that a spark of connection had arced over the language barrier. I had the phone numbers and a standing lunch invitation from the Egyptian family I had met at the museum. Houria had already texted me, in a mix of Egyptian and Darija chat alphabet, asking if I was back in New York yet and had found her a husband.

I was also in touch with Medo, who was still making plans to leave Egypt. Chatting on Facebook, we mostly typed in English, because I knew he wanted to practice. The last time, though, I had thrown in a bit of Arabic: *Sallimni 3ala Mama!*—Say hi to your mom for me! After I hit send, I fretted. Was it the right preposition, the right chat-alphabet number? Then Medo replied: "*Mstnyeenek* ☺"—We're waiting for you to visit. I felt like a magician all over again, just as I had twenty years before, ordering strawberry juice on my first trip to Cairo. A few random letters, strung together, had *worked*.

"☺," I typed back.

At the same time, in my Year of Speaking Arabic Badly, the language had shed a bit of its magic too. At the outset, I had thought I needed to acquire more knowledge, and the perfect, fluent combination of vocabulary and grammar would work like an incantation: when I got everything just right, a whole world would spring open to me in a flash. But in so many of the situations I had thrown myself into, Arabic worked more like a crude tool, a lever to pry open a door an inch or two. After the door was open, it almost didn't matter what I said, and sometimes I didn't have to say anything at all. That time I had afternoon tea in Lebanon with Tony and his overbearing, bird-loving father, the important thing was simply that I was there, helping Tony look good.

Ultimately, what mattered most to the people I met was not what I had learned in class that day, but what I practiced least often with my teachers: I listened. And I was heartened to know that even if I was never able to tell pitch-perfect jokes, read poems without a dictionary, or write an essay with flawless spelling and appropriate vocabulary, I would always be able to communicate, just by lending a sympathetic ear. Empathy, imagination, listening and nodding, saying thank you from the heart — these were skills I could use every day.

Even so, how to continue when I was headed home, away from classrooms and people who expected me to speak Arabic all the time? I remembered Alain in Sidon. As he had advised, it would be good enough if I practiced a few weeks a year. Perhaps I would corner an Arab tourist on the street in New York City and invite him home to lunch. One day I hoped to come back and retrace my travels — stay with Medo's family in Cairo, as his mother insisted I must, or take a road trip with Farah outside Abu Dhabi. I hoped I might attend Houria's wedding, to a good man who treasured her spirit and charm.

In the meantime, I would think of them, and all the others I had met, when I read the newspaper. There would be dramatic and violent reversals in Egypt's revolution; a car bomb in Beirut, blocks from where I had lived; a flood of refugees from Syria's civil war — but I would remember the stories from this year, of people grappling with the common concerns of building a future, connecting with family, and finding love.

The delicious-ladies waiter appeared at our table. "You look very happy with your father," he said. "Do you want me to take your picture?" We raised our tea glasses for a toast.

"I feel like we're part of the scenery now," Patrick said. "A tour group will come through and look at us, and think we've always been here."

A moped buzzed across the square and exited stage left. When it was gone, there was a momentary lull in traffic. We sat and listened to the murmur of Arabic and the *shush-shush-shush* of hundreds of feet walking.

Afterword to the Paperback Edition

On the flight back from Morocco, words began to slip away. The spell of Arabic gradually wore off. Months later, I was no longer a student playing charades, no longer a host daughter in a pink-upholstered bedroom. I was a regular middle-aged American adult, a thoroughly unmagicked frog. Even the process of writing this book couldn't fully revive the spell. I wrote about Arabic, but I was no longer thinking in it.

Then, in 2015, I finished my manuscript and went on vacation. By geopolitical accident, I happened to follow a route through Turkey and Greece that Syrians were using to flee the war in their country. As I arrived on the Greek island of Lesvos in August, the number of boats coming ashore every day had doubled from the month before.

Before the war, I had traveled to Syria several times, and it remains one of my favorite places, in large part due to the kind people I met there. Seeing Syrians on the road that summer, I wanted to repay the generosity, but I wasn't sure how to help. The situation on Lesvos was disorganized, and my one tangible skill, Arabic, had pretty well slipped away. I was worried that I would be bumbling and unhelpful or, worse, cause a problem through mistranslation. A journalist friend nudged me to the car. Of course I'd be useful, she assured me. People would be happy just to hear Arabic—even the way I spoke it.

The transit "camp" was an abandoned parking lot. When we arrived, a group of Greek volunteers was cooking lunch. They assigned me to help manage the crowd; hundreds of people had gathered around. As the Greeks started dishing out pasta, two young Syrian men sidled up and tried to cajole me into slipping them portions on the side.

"Please, I can't serve you here," I told them. These were the first Arabic words I'd spoken in at least a year, and they didn't come easily. I spoke slowly, gently. "Please join the line. There's enough food for everyone."

I braced myself for argument, but they nodded politely and loped off to the back of the growing queue.

There under the baking Greek summer sun, with cicadas droning in the background, I was dazzled all over again by the simple magic of language. Just a few syllables, and presto, an anxious crowd straightens into a line.

Although I mention Syria only in passing in this book, the country was one of my main inspirations for writing. To most Americans, Syria is a black spot on the map, a rogue state with a brutal dictatorship that helms the "axis of terror." The Syria I saw as a visitor, by contrast, was lovely: green mountains, vibrant cities, bountiful food, gracious people. Nowhere else in my travels before or since have I seen such a difference between American perception and real daily life. By the time I went to work on this book, unfortunately, I could not add a Syria section because the civil war was already underway.

When I met Syrian refugees in Greece, I was struck again by the gap between image and reality. These Syrians are no different from anyone else in this book—and no different from you or me, for that matter. We share the same interests: school, work, relationships. But news stories and photos usually focus on present misery, with no sense of what life was like in Syria before the war, of what has been lost. This lack of context, I believe, is directly responsible for Americans' overall lack of concern for Syrian refugees.

In the 1980s moral philosopher Peter Singer popularized the idea of the "circle of concern," a term first introduced in the late nineteenth century to describe the people and things we care about, whose lives we value. The moral circle expands naturally as we grow, Singer suggests, to encompass our families, our neighbors, our country, and beyond. And I would say a major element in expanding the circle is cultural knowledge. Knowing what people eat and wear, what music they like, how and where they work—all this helps us see others as individuals, which is the first step to empathy.

I used to imagine that if Americans had known more about Syria and Syrians, it might have averted the war. Familiarity would have created concern; concern would have brought international pressure. Now I think that's expecting too much, and too late anyway. But any bit of cultural familiarity could have helped Syrian refugees—and perhaps it still could.

Imagine if most Americans recognized the Citadel of Aleppo as quickly as they do the Eiffel Tower, or if they cooked dainty meatballs in sour-cherry sauce, or picked up the habit of listening to the Lebanese singer Fairuz over their morning coffee. What if we adopted *tamam* as a more fun way to say OK, just as some people say *ciao*, even if they don't speak Italian?

If Syrian culture had been woven into American life at this level, more people might have drawn their circle of concern larger. People would have seen commonalities instead of insurmountable differences. But lacking any familiarity, most Americans saw the Syrian refugee crisis as just another grim headline—a tragedy, but far outside their circle.

One of the easiest ways to learn familiarity, I appreciate after my years of study, is through language. The very process of language learning is one of making the strange so commonplace you no longer think about it. Difficult sounds—the strangled 'ayn, the whispery *ha*—become ordinary with repetition. Background noise separates into distinct words. Loops and dots on a page settle into a writing system that, after a certain point, you can't help but read.

Likewise, using a language out in the world inevitably normalizes the people and culture you encounter. You remember vocabulary as part of specific conversations with specific people. *Gaaaamid*, that drawn-out expression of ice-cold cool, is, for me, the cool of weaving through Cairo traffic with Medo. Proper names you might have once skimmed past soon become distinct, and conjure people you know. When I read the name Hassan, I will always think of the first Hassan I met, round-faced and laughing his raspy laugh on his Cairo rooftop.

This learned familiarity is almost physical. My ear has been trained to hear Arabic better: no longer the songs that all ran together on my Arabic music cassette, but specific poignant lyrics with meaning. And now my eyes see better too. As a kid, I barely knew where or what the Arab world was. Through my studies and travels, I learned to differentiate. At first, this was on a cultural level: that punchline, so Egyptian; that strong coffee, so Lebanese. With more practice, I was able to see Arabs as they deserve, as everyone in the world deserves: as individual people.

In the camp on Lesvos, people were not as they were often described in the news, a faceless "flood of refugees" (I had used this phrase myself, in the last chapter of this book, uncritically repeating media English; there is always more to learn). They were individuals. Some had medical degrees; some had torture scars. Some had shy smiles; some had quick tempers. A Syrian college student knew, unlike many Americans, that New Mexico was a state between Arizona and Texas, because he'd watched every episode of *Breaking Bad*.

One afternoon, I sat in a canvas tent with a young mother and her two children. She began to tell me about her journey. The boat trip from Lebanon to Turkey was the first she'd been on in her life. She was terrified, and she and the children were overcome with nausea. I recognized *qay'*, my very-old-favorite word for vomiting, but after that, as she crossed Turkey, her story picked up speed. I was sleepy from the heat, in the amber light of the sun through canvas, and her words rushed past me. I didn't want to interrupt her, though, because her shoulders were loosening, her voice steadying. As she talked, the weight of the ordeal lifted.

Finally, as she was describing her arrival in the camp, she paused. "You're not following all this, are you?" she asked.

I had to admit I wasn't. "But don't worry," I added, thinking of Dr. Badawi, "I'm making up a really good story in my head."

She laughed at that, and the smile that spread across her face brought her down to earth, down from the realm of global tragedy and into the circle of utter familiarity. She could have been a neighbor.

The little bit of Arabic I used on Lesvos was barely a parlor trick, but it was enough to keep me involved, even back at home. For the past two years, I've used Arabic in ways that feel both magical and mundane. I've labeled maps, compiled phrase lists ("please join the line" = *fit-taboor, law samahtu*), vetted translations of legal information. One night at the height of the boat traffic to Lesvos, I even made a phone call to warn people away from the dangerously rocky beaches and toward the flat, safe ones. The urgency stripped away my lingering perfectionism; only after I hung up did I remember that the thought of a phone call in Arabic had once filled me with cold dread.

Still, that is nothing compared with how often I use my familiarity with Syrian culture, and many Arab cultures. Knowing something about the Middle East fills in the holes in the news stories and photos. It helps me explain the refugee situation to others who don't know much about it. I show people my photos from peacetime Syria. In turn, knowing something about Syrian refugees has helped me understand how people fleeing other countries must feel. I've now met refugees from Syria, Afghanistan, Iraq, Congo, and Cameroon, and I write about them in hopes of expanding others' circles of concern, just as mine has expanded, bit by bit, since my first day in Arabic 101.

Fortunately, studying Arabic isn't essential to building this familiarity, this concern—it's just the rather inefficient and awkward way I've done it. What everyone can learn is the attitude of a language student, which opens you to information and empathy better than anything else I know.

Look outward. Read widely, and learn something new from every source. Sing along to music before you know all the words.

Talk to strangers. Watch body language and make wild guesses.

Ask for help. Set your ego aside. Listen as much as you speak.

Know that you will forget, but you can and will learn again—and again and again.

When you read news stories or see photographs from somewhere else in the world, look closely. Pick out the faces of individuals, and take time to imagine their names. Make up a story about them in your head; Dr. Badawi would approve.

We are all so connected now. More and more, our lives resemble one another's. The only lingering barrier is language, and even that is a small one.

Acknowledgments

THANK YOU, FROM THE HEART:

First, to James Conlon, whose life in Arabic was a model of practicality and opening channels of understanding; his unexpected death in 2009 made me reconsider my own relationship with Arabic (as well as what I've learned about communication in general), and started the gears turning for this book. Another inspiration that is largely absent from this text: Syria and its lovely people. To Koko the tailor, the bike man of Aleppo, the tamarind seller, the man who shared his salad, the boy who gave me his mother's phone number in Deir az Zor, the man who asked me what *tirmis* are called in English, and so many other kind, interesting, and interested people — thank you, and I hope you're safe.

Elsewhere in my travels, many people provided invaluable help, perspective, and local insights: Mandy McClure, Amgad Naguib, Cynthia Kling, Phil Weiss, Maala Kabbar, Manal Alami, Holly Warah, Arva Ahmed, Agnes Koltay, Jonty Summers, Andrew Mills, Mariam Dahrouj, Sara Al-Khalfan, Shatha Farajallah, Suneela Sunbula, Andrea and Gary Urbiel Goldner, and David Amster. And to Joanna

Marsh and Jose Pelleyá: very sorry I had to write you out; you deserve a chapter of your own.

My professors and brilliant colleagues got me through school, and some coached on this book: Andras Hamori, Margaret Larkin, Kamal Abdelmalek, Sherman Jackson, Suzanne Stetkevych, Adrienne Fricke, Amélie Cherlin, Susan Peters, Jennifer Rawlings, Jeremy Rich, and Adriana Valencia. I wish Magda al-Nowaihi and El-Said Badawi were alive to read this.

For more Arabic facts, stories, and deep thoughts, I was lucky to consult with Chris Stone, Humphrey Davies, Neil Hewison, Ramy Habeeb, Tim Mackintosh-Smith, Ali El Sayed, Wissam El Cheikh Hassan, Ahmed Seddik, and Kristl Schelm (who inspired the link between geometric design and morphology). Khaled Al Hilli, Ziad Bentahar, Mohamed A. Elgohari, and Nouf Al-Qasimi (and her parents) helped check the final Arabic and saved me from my Fusha-centric self. All remaining mistakes are mine, all mine.

I could not have made it out of the thickets of early drafts without Margaret Knox, Dan Baum, Annia Ciezadlo, Amy Karafin, Margaret Greer, Ilca Moskos, Elizabeth Faust, Jim Greer, Antares Boyle, Rod Ben Zeev, Lucía Terra, and Carole Bennett. Also thanks to Catherine Harris, for last-minute editing and support, and Marisa Robertson-Textor, for praise when I needed it most.

For space to write, I am indebted to Laura Pratt, Lee Christie at Genesis Retreat, and Alexis Averbuck. Back at home, Marla Garfield and the *Us Weekly* copy pit provided sanity, and I worked better in my own space with the help of the Queens Writers Fellows: Heather Hughes, Alla Katsnelson, Jeff Orlick, Sara Markel-Gonzalez, Howard Blue, Brooke Donnelly, and Siobhan Dunne.

Thanks to Gillian MacKenzie, my excellent agent, and to my acquiring editor, Amanda Cook: your initial confidence carried me through the rough patches. Also thanks to my editor Jenna Johnson, without whom this would have been a very different book, and Pilar Garcia-Brown, who also provided great feedback. Larry Cooper was a model for all manuscript editors; thanks for the countless elegant improvements.

Finally, thanks to my parents, who set me on such a fine path in life and have given me nothing but encouragement. And to Peter, حبيبي, for enduring my time away, in other countries and inside my head. I couldn't have done this without you.

Notes

page

xii *(the news is, by definition, the abnormal):* For this simple but resonant
insight, I am indebted to Dutch journalist Joris Luyendijk, who was a
Middle East correspondent in the years leading up to the second Gulf
War. In two books, he details the gaps between Western perceptions
and Middle Eastern realities. Many of these inaccuracies, he argues,
are inherent in the process of reporting from countries run by dictators, whose power is based almost entirely on how well they control
information. One book has been translated into English, by Michele
Hutchinson; in the United States, it is titled *People Like Us: Misrep-
resenting the Middle East* (Soft Skull Press, 2009). The U.K. edition is
Hello Everybody! One Journalist's Search for Truth in the Middle East
(Profile Books, 2010).

xiii *dictionary originally meant sea:* I am taking slight poetic license in im-
plying a true connection between "sea" and "dictionary." The change
in meaning probably came about more mechanically. The most in-
fluential medieval Arabic dictionary, compiled by Fairuzabadi in
the fourteenth century and used as a definitive reference for centuries after, was titled (in typical medieval rhyming style) *al-Qamoos
al-Muheet wal-Qaboos al-Waseet, al-Jami'a lima Dhahaba min Kilam
al-'Arab Shamameet.* In the following centuries, it was shortened to

315

al-Qamoos al-Muheet, literally "the Circumscribed Sea," and eventually, *qamoos* came to mean any dictionary, and not sea. I do like to imagine, though, that Fairuzabadi chose the original title as a bit of a boast—that his project could have drowned him, but he mastered it.

xvi   *the more arcane grammar details:* D̲ is the symbol used in the Hans Wehr Arabic-English dictionary for the letter ذ (*dhal*), which is pronounced like the *th* in "this."

5   *lose something in the translation:* In Fusha, one asks "How are you?" by saying *Kayf al-hal?* Literally this means "How is the state?" At the same time, a *hal* clause is a grammatical construct that describes a state and always takes the accusative case. So, *Kayf al-hal* also means "How do you treat the *hal* clause?" And the right answer is "Accusative" (*mansoob*).

If you like that, here's another. As a bonus, it involves the eighth-century grammarian Sibawayhi.

A student arrives late at night at the house of Sibawayhi's teacher, who is known for keeping strict hours. "Please, tell him Ahmad is here," the student tells the servant who opens the door. "*Insarif!*" (Scram!) says the servant. "*Ana mamnoo' min as-sarf*," Ahmad protests.

What just happened? The name Ahmad is a diptote, a noun that can take only two case endings instead of the usual three. His punchline could translate to "I can't scram," but he's also saying "I'm a diptote." Hilarious, right?

12   *Your Lord is the most generous:* This is my translation, though in general I prefer M.A.S. Abdel Haleem's exceptionally readable version (Oxford University Press, 2004), which also has good footnotes and a parallel Arabic text.

15   *a table with rows numbered I to XV:* The use of Roman numerals here should give you an idea how incredibly musty Arabic instruction was in Europe and America for a long time. The first European linguists to analyze Arabic were classicists who used a Latin framework for everything from grammatical terminology to numbers. Nowadays, Arabic teachers in the West more commonly refer to verb types as Arab grammarians do: not by number, but according to their pattern, using the verb *fa'ala* (فعل), to do: *istaf'ala* (استفعل), for example, instead of Form X.

In their compulsive enumerating, the European linguists would have done better to use the standard 1, 2, 3, and so on, because these at least came from the Arabs, who had adopted them from India. This numeral set includes the useful non-number zero (*sifr* in Arabic, whence English "cipher"), which the Romans never had.

But the notation styles diverged at some point centuries ago, and today many Arabs use numbers that only loosely resemble what Europeans call "Arabic" numerals. They go like this (from left to right, unlike the rest of the writing system):

٠١٢٣٤٥٦٧٨٩

In Arabic, these "Eastern Arabic" numerals are called *arqam hindiya* — "Indian" numbers — and they're used primarily in Egypt and countries north and east. Most countries in North Africa use Western Arabic numerals.

17   *apostle began a friendly letter:* Much later, I learned that other Arabic scholars were fond of this game too. One of the people who took it exceptionally far was Ibn Jinni, who, in the tenth century, developed a trippy theory he called *ishtiqaq kabeer,* grand derivation. His deep etymology not only considered words that share the same root, but also analyzed common meanings in roots with shared letters, even if they were in a different order. By his way of thinking, the words *'abeer* (fragrance, from the root *'ayn-ba-ra*), *rab'* (a spring campsite, from *ra-ba-'ayn*), and *ba'r* (dung, *ba-'ayn-ra*) were related because they all represented the concept of transfer: scent transferred through the air, transfer from winter to summer, transfer of food to waste. This is summarized — along with a fascinating modern theory that suggests Ibn Jinni was on to something — in Kees Versteegh's *The Arabic Language* (Columbia University Press, 2001).

18   *a good verse has:* Some of the older Arabic-only lexicons are even more absorbing than Lane. The first, written in the eighth century, is *Kitab al-'Ayn,* organized according to where in the mouth a letter is pronounced. It begins with the constricted *'ayn,* which comes from deep in the throat, continues through *meem,* which hums from the front of the lips, and concludes with the "letters of the air," the three vowels and the *hamza,* the glottal stop.

21   *"chaos with respect to people . . .":* Advanced Arabic students will recognize this as a direct translation of the grammatical construct known as *tamyeez,* in which an indefinite noun in the accusative case carries the additional meaning "with respect to" or "regarding."

30   *it means open space:* I trust this is true, and that the name does not

come from the root *ra-ha-ba*, with a regular *h*, whence the word *irhab*, terrorism.

31 *once characterized as diglossic:* Other places identified as diglossic include northern (German-speaking) Switzerland and Greece. Switzerland is not such an extreme case, as the Swiss German dialect is not considered "low" in status. Greece, however, resolved its diglossia in an extreme way in 1976 when the government abolished the self-consciously classical written language called Katharevousa. This was the final blow to the recently ousted conservative junta, which had championed the artificial language. Since then, the more casual demotic Greek — Dhimotiki — has been standard in print.

32 *I couldn't very well give up:* There is also a theory in linguistics that Semitic languages are not quite as root-based as they appear. Most of the research has been done on Hebrew, however, which is a slight outlier because for almost two thousand years it was not a spoken language, which may affect how native speakers use it and think about it. See Joseph Shimron's *Language Processing and Acquisition in Languages of Semitic, Root-based Morphology* (John Benjamins Publishing, 2003).

38 *Nobel laureate Naguib Mahfouz:* The Mahfouz quote came to me via Niloofar Haeri's excellent book on sociolinguistics in Egypt, *Sacred Language, Ordinary People: Dilemmas of Culture and Politics in Egypt* (Palgrave Macmillan, 2003). Much of her research on Ammiya and Fusha usage, as well as Arabs' opinions of their Fusha schooling, confirms what I've heard anecdotally.

55 *slipped into Arabic relatively unchanged:* There was apparently an attempt to Arabicize "television," as Hans Wehr includes the noun *tilfaz* (under the verb *talfaza*, to televise), which roughly follows the "noun of instrument" pattern (مفعال). This includes words such as *miftah*, a key, from *fataha*, to open — that is, the thing-with-which-you-open; or *meezan*, scales, from *wazana*, to weigh. The process of Arabicization is not strictly a modern problem, however; it was also discussed intensely in the ninth century, when translators in Baghdad deliberated how to translate ancient Greek medical texts. For ailments, they settled on the pattern *fu'al* (فعال), an emphatic form that was also linked to certain sounds. These most successful of Arabicizations are still used today, in common words such as *suda'* (with a heavy *s* and an *'ayn*), for headache, from the verb *sada'a*, to crack or split; and *duwar*, vertigo, from *dara*, to turn.

65 *a noisy fart:* There is an Arabic word for a quiet fart as well, *fasya*,

derived from the verb *fasa,* to fart silently. During the African Cup, I heard announcers on Egyptian TV refer to Burkina Faso as "Burkina Fazzo," to avoid saying "Burkina They-Farted-Silently."

"the season of the flood": Before the dam was built at Aswan, the Nile traditionally flooded in late summer and marked the beginning of the growing season. Its opposite, the springtime ebb, was marked in Pharaonic times with the festival of Shemu. Copts carried this tradition forward along with the name. Egyptians now celebrate spring with picnics on the Monday after Coptic Easter, with the Arabicized name of Shamm an-Neseem, "smelling the breeze."

88   *gender polarity in the numbers:* Then my Saudi pub friend went on to tell me about his time as an exchange student in Arkansas. "When I smell bacon," he said dreamily, "I forget all about Islam."

89   *relationship between* fatteh *and* hummus: This relationship, a way of expressing possession, is called an *idafa.* In this case, the literal translation of the *idafa* phrase is "the *fatteh* of *hummus*"; similarly, *kitab ar-rajul* is "the book of the man." But the *idafa* construction is so common in Arabic that (I can say from experience) it's easy to overlook when translating, and so fail to flip it around to the smoother English phrase — "the man's book," in this example.

One literal translation of the *idafa* is well known in English, however: Saddam Hussein's declaration, in the first Gulf War, that an American attack on his country would lead to *umm al-ma'arik,* the mother of all battles. English has since absorbed the phrase "the mother of all . . ." and uses it so liberally, it's hard to believe it wasn't known before 1991.

as lazy city slickers did nowadays: Linguists theorize that the *dl* sound lasted long enough to be borrowed by other languages. For example, the Spanish word *alcalde,* which means mayor, comes from *al-qadi* (the judge), which at the time of borrowing was probably pronounced more like *al-qadli.*

Incidentally, *al-* is the definite article in Arabic. When spoken, it is sometimes elided with the following consonant for euphony—to *an-* or *ad-,* for instance. When other languages incorporated Arabic words, they often took the article as well, which is why so many Arabic borrowings start with *a-* or *al-.*

90   *itself, its opposite, and a camel:* I first read this quip in Tim Mackintosh-Smith's book *Yemen: The Unknown Arabia* (Overlook, 2001), the

opening pages of which are a dizzying introduction to the wonders to be found in the Arabic dictionary.

Certain arcane schools of Quranic interpretation take the idea of paradoxical words to its logical extreme, contending that every word of the holy text has a hidden import contrary to its surface meaning — though these so-called Batinites (*batin* means inner or secret) usually leave camels out of it.

94   *more settled tribes were 'arab*: Still more complicated: the term *i'rab* (إعراب), another word from the same *'ayn-ra-ba* root, originally meant the correct use of the Arabic language — the form of the word literally meant "Arabizing." Later, *i'rab* came to refer specifically to declension, the application of case endings.

  to settle an argument in favor of the payee: Kees Versteegh's *The Arabic Language* provides a lot of this history concisely, and I have relied on it for many of the details about the development of Arabic in this book.

95   *outside the city, living out of doors*: In many of the Gulf states, Bedouin are outside borders too. When the United Arab Emirates became a country in 1971, some Bedouin did not do the paperwork for citizenship. Now they are so-called Bedoun — a word that looks like Bedouin but is in fact unrelated. *Bedoun* (بدون) is a preposition that means without, as these people live without papers or national identity.

  the numbers-for-letters chat alphabet: The book, which is quite entertaining, is *The Chronicles of Dathra, a Dowdy Girl from Kuwait*, self-published in 2011 by the pseudonymous blogger Danderma (which means ice cream).

103   *"created every living thing from water"*: This passage is from sura 21 (The Prophets), verse 30.

115   *the verse continues, a revelation*: This translation is by M.A.S. Abdel Haleem.

  just as Muhammad had: For this insight, and much more on recitation, see Kristina Nelson, *The Art of Reciting the Qur'an* (American University in Cairo Press, 2001), which I found through an episode of the radio show *Afropop Worldwide* in which Nelson is interviewed. First aired in 2012, the show is part of the "Hip Deep" series, titled "Egypt 1: Cairo Soundscape" (http://bit.ly/cairosound). Part of what makes Egyptian recitation so good is that reciters use some of the same modes of expression as popular singers. In particular, some say their goal is to induce *tarab*, a sort of emotional swoon, a feeling of grief and joy that is essential to Arab musical traditions.

116   *"taught man what he did not know"*: This is sura 96, verses 3–5. The su-
ras (chapters) of the Quran are presented not in the order they were revealed, but roughly by length, starting with the longest. So it happens
that the rather brief first revelation Muhammad received falls near the
end of the Quran.

120   *Halt, let us weep:* This is my translation; for the full poem, along with
other essential Arabic poetry, see *Night and Horses and the Desert: An
Anthology of Classical Arabic Literature* (Anchor Books, 2002), edited by Robert Irwin, who also provides engaging commentary on the
works.

121   *Who you travel with is more important:* Or, in the contemporary idiom, "Bros before roads."

129   *as her tribe moves one direction:* My Egyptian friend Ali El Sayed, a
chef-philosopher in New York City, has a more practical take. "The
Arabs created poetry because they're just out there in the desert," he
explained to me one night. "It's just them in the Sahara with the moon.
They are bored motherfuckers. So they look at the moon and say, 'It's
like her face.' And they look at the gazelle and see its big black eyes.
They're describing the different parts of their lover and knitting it together. That's the Arabs. That's poetry." Ali used the word "knitting"
because the Arabic word for love poetry is *ghazal,* from a verb that
means to flirt and woo, as well as to spin or weave.

      cheatin' hearts and open roads: My essay dealt specifically with the Da-
vid Allan Coe song "You Never Even Called Me by My Name," written
by Steve Goodman and released in 1975. Midway through the song,
Coe takes a break to point out that this would be a perfect country song
except it hasn't mentioned Mama, trains, trucks, prison, and gettin'
drunk — then proceeds to sing a verse incorporating all of these terms.
Arab poets writing well after the Jahiliya often employed the same
gambit, self-consciously checking off all the usual terms — campsites,
storms, traveling companions — to establish their credibility. This
became so common that Abu Nuwas, a famously debauched poet of
eighth-century Baghdad, skewered the whole practice with a first line
that reads, roughly: "One miserable guy stopped off to contemplate an
abandoned campsite, while I stopped to contemplate the local bar."

138   *a rant by Muammar Qaddafi:* Spare a thought for Qaddafi's interpreter.
When Qaddafi addressed the United Nations in 2009, he spoke for an
hour and a half, in a diatribe full of conspiracy theories and accusa-
tions. At minute 75, his interpreter reportedly shouted, "I just can't

take it anymore!" and collapsed. A UN staff interpreter stepped in to finish the job.

139   *quoted in the newspaper:* Niloofar Haeri's *Sacred Language, Ordinary People* has a great chapter on how copyeditors at magazines and newspapers in Egypt adjust the natural spoken language for appearance in print, according to the role of the speaker in society. Presidential quotes were the most frequently and heavily rewritten, to conform with Fusha standards, while the least tweaked were words from popular comedians. That is, politicians are expected to be formal and well educated in print, even if they aren't fluent in Fusha in real life; essentially vernacular comedians can stay just as they are.

145   *used the standard Fusha word,* tabeeb: Allow me to add here that an Afro, in Khaleeji dialect, is called a *jaksan* — or at least it was back when Michael Jackson had one.

166   *notorious for a grinding battle:* The word for camp in Arabic is *mukhayyam,* related to the one for tent. On my first visit to Beirut, in 1999, I had driven through a refugee "camp" on the south side of Beirut and was surprised to see no tents in sight. It looked like the rest of the city, just a bit more jumbled. Decades before, canvas had given way to cinder blocks.

173   *"What side are you on?":* As it happened, not too much later in my trip, I found a book that addressed these issues, *Etiquette in the City: Beirut,* by Sonya Sabbah. From this I learned that it was inappropriate to ask about religion, village of origin, or political opinions. Even sports were out, as a favorite team could reveal certain allegiances. Unrelated to identity issues, the book also advised that it was inappropriate to take a gun or any other type of weapon to a nightclub.

194   *the Syrian troops rolled home:* The Lebanese called this popular uprising the *intifadat al-istiqlal,* the Independence Intifada. But apparently this made the U.S. State Department too jumpy, as *intifada* — a poetic word conveying the shiver before waking — was too evocative of the Palestinian cause. And so the movement was dubbed, in the American media at least, the Cedar Revolution.

215   *the Aramaic alphabet, via Nabataean:* Aramaic, in turn, came from Phoenician, the culture on the shores of the Mediterranean in what is now Lebanon. The Phoenician alphabet was also the basis for the Greek and Latin alphabets, so as foreign as Arabic looks, it is actually a cousin, if several times removed, of the alphabet we use for English.

217   *strapped a reed pen to his stump:* Ibn Muqla's colorful life is expanded

in Rafik Schami's novel *The Calligrapher's Secret,* translated from the German by Anthea Bell (Interlink Publishing, 2011). Schami suggests that Ibn Muqla was secretly developing new letters for the Arabic alphabet, considered heretical at the time. I think this is purely Schami's invention, but it's a great story.

219 *the general-use font she named Mirsaal:* Mirsaal is the font used to spell Lebanon on page 151. The full font is published in Rana's book *Cultural Connectives* (Mark Batty Publisher, 2011), also a good basic introduction to how the Arabic alphabet works.

they never became standard on Arabic keyboards: Some readers may have noticed in the Egypt section that Medo's mother's name, Neveen, incorporates a non-native sound, *v* (written ڤ, an adapted *fa,* ف). I marveled at this, but Medo didn't think it was remarkable. It is in fact a Turkish name—more evidence of Ottoman influence in Egypt.

228 *a bride's accessory, a belly dancer's frippery:* I suspect this failure of English leads to some confusion, as there is little consistency in how it is used in the media. I have read some stories in which "veil" refers to a headscarf; in others, to a full-face veil. Many times, even in stories about legal efforts to ban "the veil," it's unclear just what form of head covering is being discussed. Although hijab and niqab are both in most English dictionaries, they are not widely known. We would do well to use them more often, for clarity.

240 *The dual was a Fusha eccentricity:* My English friend Carole, a longtime student of Arabic, makes a good case for the dual, as a kind of shibboleth: "It lets them know that *you* really know what's what," she says. A couple of other nifty details about Darija, for the grammar-obsessed: Darija doesn't bother with feminine adjectives for nonhuman plurals; if the noun is masculine, so is the adjective. Darija also uses a more sensible conjugation for first-person verbs: *naktab* (normally the third-person plural form) is "I write," and *naktaboo* is "we write," which is more consistent with second- and third-person plural verbs—even if it does make you sound like you're using the royal "we."

264 *common Turkish foods like chicken kebab:* My teacher Si Taoufik exemplified the cultural gulf. "What is all that Lebanese food?" he said with a disgust I had never once heard applied to this cuisine. "I never ate this, what is it, *tahini,* until I went to Paris. Yecch!" That something so universally loved as Lebanese food could be disliked, and that something as common as sesame paste could not be found in Morocco—that boggled my mind. Sesame is essential all around the eastern Mediter-

ranean and beyond. Ali Baba even yelled, "*Iftah, ya simsim!*" (Open, sesame!) to cleave a mountain.

266 *Nerdy SpongeBob SquarePants:* Children's TV Fusha leaves a lasting impression. To Arabs of a certain era, the theme from the Japanese space saga *Grendizer* is as moving and uniting as any nationalist speech by Nasser. More practically, words absorbed at a tender age can pop out unexpectedly years later. An Egyptian-Canadian acquaintance was once in a tense altercation in Cairo, and when the fight threatened to turn violent, he found himself bellowing in Fusha, "Here are my powers! Let us compare powers!" Then he raised his arm menacingly, conjuring super-strength. "I will deal you a devastating blow!" It was all dialogue from *Power Rangers* episodes he had watched as a kid, enunciated with full case endings. His opponent was so startled, he could ask only, "Would you like some tea?"

285 *You're in Morocco, don't be surprised:* If you look up this phrase on YouTube in Arabic (it's also written ما دمت في المغرب فلا تستغرب and simply في المغرب لا تستغرب), you'll find a treasure trove of illustrative videos.

295 *a relatively rare morphological form:* Comparative and superlative adjectives actually have the same form, which at first sounds easy (none of this "easier" and "easiest," as in English). But then gender gets involved. So, for *kabeer* (كبير), which means big or great, the comparative-and-superlative form (grammar books often call this elative) is *akbar* (أكبر) in the masculine—as seen in the expression *Allahu akbar*, God is the greatest. *Kubra* (كبرى) is the feminine form. Then you have to decide whether to use the masculine or feminine, and of course it doesn't depend just on the gender of the noun you're modifying. Suffice to say, the rules almost always call for a masculine elative, and that's just the way it is. Why? *Allahu 'alam:* God is the most knowing.

302 *classical Arabic brain teasers:* Write the vowel marks on the following letters so they mean something: ان ان ان ان ان اوانه. It's a poem, and the first half of the line goes الم الم الم الم بدائه.